AMERICAN
HISTORICAL ASSOCIATION

INVESTIGATION OF THE
SOCIAL STUDIES IN THE SCHOOLS

•   •
•

STAFF

A. C. KREY
Chairman, Director of the Investigation

G. S. COUNTS
Research Director

W. G. KIMMEL
Executive Secretary

T. L. KELLEY
Psychologist, Advisor on Tests

COMMISSION ON DIRECTION

A HISTORY OF FREEDOM OF TEACHING
IN AMERICAN SCHOOLS

REPORT OF THE COMMISSION
ON THE SOCIAL STUDIES
PART XVI

A HISTORY OF FREEDOM OF
TEACHING IN AMERICAN
SCHOOLS

BY *ennedy*

HOWARD K. BEALE, *1899 -*
ⁱⁱⁱ

1966
OCTAGON BOOKS, INC.
New York

Reprinted 1966
by special arrangement with Charles Scribner's Sons

OCTAGON BOOKS, INC.
175 FIFTH AVENUE
NEW YORK, N. Y. 10010

LIBRARY OF CONGRESS CATALOG CARD NUMBER: 66-17503

Printed in U.S.A. by
NOBLE OFFSET PRINTERS, INC.
NEW YORK 3, N. Y.

PREFACE

When the Commission on Social Studies in the Schools asked the present author to make a study of freedom in teaching, he protested that he was not an educator. Professor George S. Counts explained that the Commission wanted not an educator but an historian, partly because it wished the study to be a history done by some one trained in the critical method of the historian, partly because the study could be made more objective by some one who was not himself an educator. Out of this conference with Professor Counts in the winter of 1931–1932 grew the conception of this book. The author brought to the work a knowledge of the social and cultural setting, in which the schools have functioned at various periods of our history, and a background of two years' work on a projected history of tolerance in America. He had to read industriously in books on the theory and history of education in order to orient himself for this particular phase of the history of tolerance. Neither Professor Counts nor the author dreamed in that first conference how stupendous a task, how all-enveloping a subject lay ahead. Indeed, the first plan was to include freedom of teaching in both schools and colleges. When the Commission decided it preferred to limit the scope to teachers' colleges and schools below college grade, the author feared these would not provide sufficient material for a book. Instead of a paucity of material, however, the author's difficulty has been to condense into one book substance enough for several. Finally the work became two books, a detailed study of the problem of freedom in teaching since the World War under the title *Are American Teachers Free?* and this present history of the development of freedom for teachers through the various phases that repression has assumed from Colonial times to the present.

Obviously, no history of freedom in teaching could be written from a mere collection of cases of dismissal of teachers. For the period before the World War records of these cases do not exist. If they did, such material would by no means tell the story even of the restrictions on freedom in teaching. More subtle repressions are of greater importance. His social environment, for instance, and the opinion of the community in which he lives restrict a teacher as effectively as any specific punishment meted out to him or his fellows. The problem varies from school to school, from community to community, from age to age. It assumes different forms with pupils of different ages. The physical limitations of the school, the social status of the teacher, and the teacher's intelligence and training all affect his freedom. It is important to understand the forces, political, social, and economic, that control the schools. Men's purposes in seeking education for their children vary from period to period of our history and always play a significant rôle in determining how much freedom a teacher will have. Bound up inextricably with the problem of freedom are the ideas men live by, the social objectives that matter enough that men will fight or die for them. These change from era to era.

American history falls naturally into periods with the perpetual problem of freedom for teachers taking first one form and then another as men's interests have changed. In Colonial days it was on religion that teachers were most restricted. In the early national period religion and political views dominated. Conservatives tried to repress freedom when it meant promulgation of "dangerous" French views and the spread of democratic notions that endangered the *status quo*. Jeffersonian liberals, however, inspired by the Revolutionary tradition of liberty, ultimately succeeded in establishing an era of comparative freedom in ideas that affected the school. During the period of supremacy of the slave power, religion and early manifestations of nationalist feeling in the form of anti-foreign and anti-Catholic movements assumed importance and affected teachers. Overshadowing everything else, however, was the slavery question so vitally important to men, North and South, that freedom to discuss it was vigorously suppressed. Successively, after the Civil War, reconstruction and political and sectional views, the problem of science and its conflict with authoritarian religion, the age-old problem of religious instruction, and new issues of moral teaching in the schools caused trouble. Then reform movements, as reformers sought to use the schools for propaganda purposes, and finally, just before the World War, problems created by the new industrialism arose, *seriatim,* to plague teachers. It was in the period following the World War, however, that life became so complex that the old battle of freedom for teachers raged about a great variety of vital questions all at once, with new impetus now given to the struggle because more and more teachers sought to express unconventional views, because teachers were becoming professionally conscious and were gaining great strength through newly created teacher organizations, and because emotionalism aroused during the War gave popular support to repression. Repressions of freedom, therefore, multiplied many-fold; but so did cases in which teachers insisted upon exercising freedom. These historic phases of the problem of educational freedom bear distinct relationship to other great cultural movements.

The significant fact is that the problem of freedom in teaching is essentially the same in all these diverse manifestations. The causes of difficulty and the principles out of which ultimate solution must grow are the same, whether it be evolution or communism, anti-Catholicism or dancing, that provokes the immediate trouble. Particularly provocative of sober thought are the striking parallels between the attitudes of slaveholders of yesteryear and big-business men of today toward the schools and toward teachers who question the virtues of the dominant economic systems of their respective periods. In the twentieth century Americans no longer deny men the right to criticize the slave system. Indeed, they would almost unanimously support teachers in freedom to analyze it critically and to point out its evils. They look upon the slavocracy's stifling free discussion of slavery as the narrowness of an outmoded age. Nevertheless, they criticize slaveholders not because they themselves believe in freedom, but because they do not have faith in chattel slavery and do not depend upon it for a livelihood and for maintenance of the political and social order to which they are accustomed. They fail to see the startling similarity between their attitude toward socialism and communism, which threaten to destroy their economic order, and the slaveholder's treatment of abolitionism, which threatened his.

Repression, then, takes on varied forms in different environments. It assumes sectional guises. Sometimes it wears a social, sometimes a moral, sometimes an economic, garb. Sir William Berkeley thanking God that "there are no free schools,"[1] J. D. B. De Bow pleading in his *Review* for schools, teachers, and texts that would not preach abolitionism,[2] and Samuel Insull and Bernard J. Mullaney organizing the Illinois Committee on Public Utility Information to prevent the teaching of socialistic doctrines in the schools[3] are all playing the same rôle. The costumes, the makeup, the language, the scenery are changed to fit the period of the play, but the motivation, the philosophy of life, and the educational theory embraced by each are identical. Much can be learned in attempting to solve the current problem of freedom in teaching by a survey of it in earlier manifestations.

The problem of freedom for the teacher has usually involved the teacher's choice of texts and methods by which he might teach, his expression of views inside or outside the classroom,

[1] *Infra*, 33, 34.
[2] *Infra*, 132–167.
[3] See H. K. Beale, *Are American Teachers Free?* 554–571.

his public activities as a citizen, the causes he may have supported or opposed in the community, his personal life and habits, and, finally, his inability to get appointed as a teacher at all if he belonged to any of a number of groups against whom popular prejudice was strong.[4] A definition of freedom for the teacher, the question whether freedom is desirable or possible and, if so, how much, and the means by which more freedom may be won are all left for treatment elsewhere.[5] A history of academic freedom in the colleges is yet to be written. The present work is limited to an historical account of the restrictions on freedom and the development of freedom for teachers in schools below college level, from period to period of American history. The study reveals that the gradual development of the American school system has tended to improve the quality of both school and teacher, and that, by freeing the teacher from the inadequacies of his physical equipment and of his own training, it has tended to increase the possibilities of enjoyment of real freedom. In recent years, however, highly organized school systems have developed a tendency to subject this now potentially free teacher to new restrictions of supervision, imposition of administrative will, and requirements of uniformity such as teachers in the poorer schools of earlier times never encountered. Organized religion and the religious purpose of the schools have been present throughout American history as restrictive forces but have tended to become relatively less important in recent years as many other issues have come to occupy places as important as religion in the American mind. The effects of democracy and evangelicism upon the American ways of thinking have exerted definitely restrictive, if subtler, pressure upon freedom in teaching. Throughout American history a tendency of teachers to reflect conventional community points of view has at once kept freedom a merely academic question for the aver-

[4] See *ibid.*, 9.
[5] See *ibid.*, 1–17, 659–778.

age teacher, who has felt no need of it, and made the problem a more difficult one for the exceptional teacher, who has needed it and found his fellow-teachers unsympathetic. Throughout American history, too, there has been a persistent purpose on the part of those supporting and controlling the schools to use the schools as a means of preserving the *status quo* and preventing unrest and "novile dispositions." The development of intelligent citizens capable of independent thinking is possible only in schools in which teachers and pupils alike are encouraged to think for themselves. Cultivation of conformity, on the other hand, is incompatible with freedom for either child or teacher. Use of the schools for preservation of the *status quo* implies a theory of education based on handing down to children the views, attitudes, prejudices, and ideals of the older generation to be accepted, learned, and lived by without questioning or analysis. The desire to use the schools to create support for the *status quo* has therefore created a permanent tendency to restrict freedom for teachers as destructive of this function. Finally, this study indicates that teachers are usually allowed freedom to impose conventional views upon their classes, that they are even expected so to impose orthodox views. It also makes clear that men usually object to the expression, without imposition, of unorthodox views or even to a type of teaching that causes children to question orthodox attitudes, even if the teacher does not himself express unconventional views. Men usually "tolerate" opposing views on subjects that they do not regard as important, and then rationalize "intolerance" into necessity when disagreement involves a matter vital to them. Thus the twentieth century looks upon religious intolerance of the seventeenth century as a relic of the Dark Ages largely because it has ceased to care seriously about religion, whereas it is ready to suppress attacks on its economic system or refusals to conform to the dictates of nationalism as vigorously as its ancestors punished religious heresy. It is not that one age is more tolerant or intolerant than the other, but merely that the seventeenth century cared tremendously about religion and was unconcerned about capitalist economics or nationalistic patriotism, while the twentieth century has lost its interest in theology and is vitally interested both emotionally and materially in capitalist economics and nationalistic patriotism. Evolution can usually be taught in the North and not in the rural South, not because the North believes more in freedom for teachers but because the North is generally indifferent to fundamentalist religion, which the evolutionary hypothesis endangers, whereas the rural South still devoutly believes in fundamentalist tenets. Northern critics of Tennessean "intolerance" suppress the teaching of socialism and communism in their own schools because the economic system that such theories endanger seems vitally important to Northern communities. Thus teachers in each century and locality have been allowed freedom to discuss subjects that did not seem to matter and denied freedom on issues about which men did seriously care.

Material on this subject has been extraordinarily difficult to get. In the period before the World War information bearing directly on the problem was almost non-existent. Local and state histories are concerned not at all with freedom of teaching or other problems of social and intellectual development. Furthermore, they are notoriously unreliable. The author went through literally hundreds of them hoping to find something but found them almost useless for this study. Histories of particular schools and of education in individual states proved almost equally barren. Historians of education have not been interested in the problem of freedom nor in other social problems. Furthermore, such similarity was there from volume to volume that one suspected that histories were taken largely one from another. One became fearful of accepting anything on the authority of such historians. A few works like those of Ellwood P. Cubberley of Stanford University and Edgar W. Knight of the University of North Carolina had the earmarks of careful work and contained material that was useful. Most of the material antedating the World War had, however, to be gleaned painstakingly from scattered sources, an item here, an item there, at the expense of an enormous amount of wasted time and effort in wading through the tedious and useless tomes that yielded perhaps one item each or nothing at all. Even then the paucity of records made it necessary to draw on the general aspects of history of thought and what one already knew of contemporary public attitudes in order to reproduce the story in the earlier periods of our history.

For the period since the World War there is an abundance of material.[6] It is, however, difficult to gather together. In a few places like the issues of *School and Society* and the files of the American Civil Liberties Union, one does find valuable collections of information. Nevertheless, most recent material, too, has to be gleaned from a variety of scattered sources, local newspaper files, clipping collections, even more from personal correspondence and interviews with teachers and other educators. The author resorted to extensive use of a rather exhaustive questionnaire.[7] In the absence of printed material, information about many of the cases involving freedom and many of the facts concerning the more subtle pressures on teachers could be obtained only by talking to men and women actually teaching in the schools.[8]

The author wishes to acknowledge with gratitude the assistance of hundreds of people over the country, professors, teachers, administrators, school board members, and other interested citizens, who have aided him in the preparation of this work. None of these people is responsible for the views here expressed. For these the author assumes all responsibility. Indeed, two or three people who have completely disagreed with the author's views, have, through their criticism, been especially

---

[6] See *ibid.*   [7] See *infra,* Appendix.
[8] For the difficulties involved in getting this information see H. K. Beale, *op. cit.,* iii–x.

helpful. To several a special debt of gratitude is due. Charles A. Beard, George S. Counts, and Jesse H. Newlon provided encouragement, understanding, and inspiration without which this book could never have been completed. Conyers Read, executive secretary of the American Historical Association, and his wife, Evelyn P. Read, have gone over the manuscript carefully and have conferred with the author on various occasions over particular passages. To them the author is deeply indebted for innumerable suggestions of great value. Their patience in the expenditure of their time has been equalled only by the wisdom of their counsel on difficult questions. To Laurence H. Eldredge, of Montgomery and McCracken in Philadelphia, the author is deeply obligated. The author is indebted to his colleagues, A. Ray Newsome and J. Carlyle Sitterson, of the University of North Carolina, and to his friend, B. I. Wiley, of the University of Mississippi, for critical suggestions on the analysis of lack of freedom in the South. The author is obligated to his friend, Paul Lewinson, for suggestions provided in many discussions of this subject both by his argumentative bent and by his penetrating comments upon his recent experience in education courses. Jean Spaulding, a teacher in English in Washington, D. C., and J. Kester Svendsen, instructor in English at the University of North Carolina, painstakingly read the manuscript and offered valuable stylistic criticism. Katharine Elizabeth Crane, assistant editor of the *Dictionary of American Biography,* gave the manuscript the incisive, sometimes savage, criticism that only editorial experience and true friendship can offer. Merle E. Curti, professor at Columbia University, contributed innumerable valuable suggestions and inspiration in the process of gathering material, and many criticisms and suggestions that resulted from his patient reading of the finished manuscript. The author's father, Frank A. Beale, and his mother, Nellie K. Beale, did a large share of the stupendous labor of compiling the results of the questionnaire and have given criticism throughout the writing of the book. The author's father gathered many examples from the various state session laws. Miriam Idleman Knapp of New York City gave intelligent help in using the immense collection of American Civil Liberties Union manuscripts. Two research assistants, Enid Frazier Gilluly and Jane Kline of Washington, D. C., did careful and intelligent research on special problems. Six successive secretaries, T. Eliot Weil of Quincy, Massachusetts, David Blumenstock of Chicago, Illinois, Jessie E. Lauscher, Anne King Behrens, and Lida Smith Mayo of Washington, D. C., and James B. McMillan of McDonald, North Carolina, have worked faithfully and with interest that has greatly facilitated the work. Mrs. Behrens has done most of the verifying of references. To the Library of Congress the author is deeply indebted for the use of a study and for excellent and unending service throughout the preparation of this book. To Martin J. Roberts, superintendent of the Reading Room, Robert C. Gooch, Willard Webb, and Harold O. Thomen, his assistants, V. Volta Parma, curator of the Rare Book Room, Olive M. Jack, assistant director of the Law Division, the Law Division staff, and the staff of the Periodical Division—the author is especially grateful for cheerful and efficient assistance. The Dartmouth College Library and Georgia Faison of the University of North Carolina Library have been very helpful. Acknowledgment of assistance and coöperation is due to many former students at Grinnell and Bowdoin colleges who have contribted to this work from their experience as teachers. For the painstaking aid in proofreading, the author is indebted to his former student, S. Branson Marley, of Raleigh, North Carolina, and to his assistant, T. Franklin Williams, of Landis, North Carolina.

HOWARD K. BEALE

Thetford, Vermont.

CONTENTS

xvii

A HISTORY OF FREEDOM OF TEACHING
IN AMERICAN SCHOOLS

CHAPTER I

FREEDOM IN COLONIAL AMERICA, 1607-1776

In Colonial America there were few schools. Those few were simple institutions that left scant record of their activities. Besides, men who did describe them were not interested in freedom for teachers. A problem difficult to study in contemporary America, where printing presses, educational associations, and research students annually turn out an appalling volume of material, becomes almost inscrutable in the shadowy beginnings of American education. The very inadequacy of Colonial schools directly influenced the teacher's freedom. Certain general tendencies of American Colonial thinking vitally affected teachers. Colonial schools and thought, then, must be analyzed before the early teacher's position can be understood.

The first colonists brought from England a tradition of education. Among Protestants everywhere, Lutherans in Germany, Calvinists in Holland, Presbyterians in Scotland, but especially among English dissenters, the Reformation had given a religious stimulus to education, since Protestant emphasis upon the individual necessitated teaching him to read and understand religious books. Besides, the England left behind by these first colonists offered elementary schooling to many of her people. In the seventeenth century education was, moreover, beginning to be an aid to "getting on" in the world; it combined religious and economic advantages. So the first Americans were keenly eager for schools. Not only New Englanders whose educational laws are well known, but Southerners and Middle-Colony settlers brought a tradition of elementary education. Furthermore, the home governments encouraged schools. James I, for instance, in 1616 ordered the

Bishop of London to collect funds for a college in Virginia. Governor Yeardley in 1618 received instructions for "the planting of a university."[1] In 1621 Sir Francis Wyatt brought orders to see that each town "teach some children fit for the college, intended to be built."[2] In 1629 the Dutch West India Company instructed its patroons and colonists to "endeavor to devise some means whereby they will be able to support . . . a Schoolmaster."[3]

The colonists needed little urging. Harvard College was founded in 1636; by 1639 Connecticut was planning elementary and secondary schools, and a college; New Haven provided for a "free schoole" in 1641.[4] The Massachusetts General Court in 1642 required all towns to see that parents and masters taught their children to read; in 1647 it ordered towns of fifty families to appoint teachers of reading and writing and towns of one hundred families to set up grammar schools.[5] Connecticut enacted an identical law in 1650.[6] Plymouth in 1673 provided funds for a "free schoole"; in 1677 it required all towns to provide elementary teachers and towns of fifty families to maintain grammar schools; in 1684 it ordered all select-

[1] Edwin G. Dexter, *A History of Education in the United States*, 2.

[2] William W. Hening, *Statutes at Large of Virginia*, I, 114.

[3] "Draft of Freedoms and Exemptions for New Netherland," *Documents Relative to the Colonial History of the State of New York* (Edmund B. O'Callaghan, ed.), I, 405.

[4] *Records of the Colony and Plantation of New Haven*, I (1638–1649), 62, 210.

[5] *Records of the Governor and Company of the Massachusetts Bay in New England* (Nathaniel B. Shurtleff, ed.), II, 6, 8–9; *ibid.*, II, 203. This law was re-enacted in 1671 with the penalty increased to ten pounds (*General Laws and Liberties of the Massachusetts Colony . . . 1672*, sec. 1, p. 136), again in 1692 with the ten-pound penalty (*Acts and Laws of His Majesty's Province of the Massachusetts-Bay in New-England* [1742], chap. X, p. 18), and again in 1701 with the penalty raised to twenty pounds (*ibid.*, chap. XIX, p. 149).

[6] "Schooles," *Code of 1650, Being a Compilation of the Earliest Laws and Orders of the General Court of Connecticut.* . . . In 1672, each town of "Fifty Householders" (*Book of the General Laws for the People within the Jurisdiction of Connecticut; . . . Lately Revised. . . . 1672* [1673], 62–63); in 1678, each town of "thirty familys" (*Public Records of the Colony of Connecticut*, III [1678–1689], 9); and in 1702, each town of "seventy Householders" (*Acts and Laws of His Majesty's Colony of Connecticut in New-England. . . . 1702* [revised and reprinted in 1715], p. 110) was required to maintain a school.

men to "have a vigilant eye" to seeing that parents and masters taught their children "so much learning as through the Blessing of God they may attain"; and in 1685 it decreed that every town should maintain a Latin school, for whose aid Plymouth offered public money.[7] New Netherlands colonists petitioned for a school in 1649.[8] The Friends in Philadelphia established one as early as 1689; William Penn aspired to universal education; the Legislature in 1683 ordered parents and masters to provide instruction for the children.[9] Maryland failed to get a school in 1671 only because of religious differences; she did establish King William's School in 1696; legislation of 1723 required a school in each county.[10] Virginia voted land for a school in 1661-1662 and in 1699 required reports of every county upon the qualifications of teachers.[11] According to Channing, "The early Virginia settlers, who were drawn from the same social strata as the New Englanders, were equally solicitous about education."[12]

Nevertheless, neither the colonists' desire for instruction nor even their legislative provision for it could establish and maintain school buildings and supply trained teachers. Even the Massachusetts law that has often been hailed as the beginning of general free public education fell far short of that description.[13] Education was by no means general, except in theory,

[7] *Book of General Laws of the Inhabitants of the Jurisdiction of New-Plimouth,* . . . *1685,* chap. V, p. 12; *Compact, Charter and Laws of the Colony of New Plymouth, 1836,* part III, chap. XV, p. 300.

[8] E. G. Dexter, *op. cit.,* 16.

[9] Louise G. and Matthew J. Walsh, *History and Organization of Education in Pennsylvania,* 1-11; *Charter to William Penn and Laws of the Province of Pennsylvania* (1879), 142—"Abrogated by William and Mary, King and Queen, in the Year 1693."

[10] *Proceedings and Acts of the General Assembly of Maryland, 1666-1676,* I (*Maryland Archives,* II), 262-264; Thomas Bacon, *Laws of Maryland at Large* (1765 ed.), 1696, chap. XVII, sec. 2; *ibid.,* 1723, chap. XIX, sec. 2.

[11] October, 1660, W. W. Hening, *op. cit.,* II, 25; Philip A. Bruce, *Institutional History of Virginia,* I, 338.

[12] Edward Channing, *A History of the United States,* I, 432.

[13] James Truslow Adams goes so far as to declare that "the old picture of every village with its free school and a population athirst for learning is a pure figment of the imagination." *Provincial Society, 1690-1763,* 132-133.

and school attendance was nowhere compulsory. Schools were not free except to "charity pupils." They were "free" only in that social status excluded no one possessed of the necessary fees. Education was primarily religious rather than public, except in so far as church and state were one.[14] To call Colonial schooling "education" is an exaggeration, since it did little more than provide moral precepts, ability to read the Bible, and enough writing and figuring to avoid becoming a public charge. By no means all towns fulfilled the requirements of the law. Even Massachusetts Puritans disliked being taxed to provide schools for the community's children. In fact in 1715 the General Court, in raising the penalty on towns that did not provide schools, plaintively declared, ". . . notwithstanding the many good and wholesome Laws of this Province for the encouraging of Schools, and the Penalty first of ten Pounds, and afterwards increased to twenty Pounds, of such Towns as are obliged to have a Grammar School-Master, and neglect the same: Yet by sad Experience it is found that many Towns . . . chuse rather to incur and pay the Fine or Penalty than maintain a Grammar School."[15] Yet on the whole, considering the difficulties of a frontier community, in comparison with those of other colonies one can call Massachusetts and Connecticut schools both numerous and good. New Hampshire and Rhode Island had only a few. The District of Maine had none until 1701.[16]

After the first generation of colonists educated in England passed from the scene, there was a notable decline in education even in Massachusetts and Connecticut. "The intellectual streams," Wertenbaker explains, "were in large measure dried up in the arid wastes of theological disputation."[17] As towns grew in size, quarrels arose about the location of schools and the incidence of taxation for their support. New England's

---

[14] Charles A. and Mary R. Beard, *Rise of American Civilization*, I, 178–180.
[15] *Acts and Laws of His Majesty's Province of the Massachusetts-Bay in New-England* (1742), chap. IX, p. 216.   [16] J. T. Adams, *op. cit.*, 132–133.
[17] Thomas J. Wertenbaker, *The First Americans, 1607–1690*, 237.

Indian and Colonial wars brought losses and poverty in their train. In the newer frontier communities life was hard; mere subsistence was difficult enough without worrying about the luxury of a school.[18] Through all the Colonies the less prosperous depended upon the labor of children of school age for help in gaining a livelihood. Letters, wills, and records of men of the second and third generations reveal a marked decline in ability to write, spell, and construct sentences. Eggleston believes that the decline in education was not only universal but inevitable.[19]

Education outside of New England, while it was better and more widespread than has until recently been believed, was far from general. In New York there were few schools. Men objected to public expenditure for instruction.[20] Pennsylvania soon abandoned Penn's effort to make education a function of the state.[21] There, too, all pleas for public schools were opposed by those who would have had to pay the bill. Furthermore, in a day when religion was a chief motive for instruction, sectarian diversity in the Middle Colonies precluded any agreement on a public school system.[22]

Farther south the plantation system through its scattering of population made schooling almost impossible to those who could not afford the luxury of a private tutor. Children could scarcely ever be found close enough together to obtain support for a community teacher.[23] Then, too, Church of England settlers in the South lacked the religious enthusiasm that in New England provided the major motive for schools. The local Anglican clergy took comparatively slight interest in education. Furthermore, even at this early date a Southern tendency to individualism made Southerners less eager for schools

---

18 J. T. Adams, *op. cit.*, 133–134.

19 Edward Eggleston, *The Transit of Civilization from England to America in the Seventeenth Century*, 233.   20 J. T. Adams, *op. cit.*, 131–132.

21 *Ibid.*, 131.   22 E. Channing, *op. cit.*, II, 465–466.

23 T. J. Wertenbaker, *op. cit.*, 250–251; Virginius Dabney, *Liberalism in the South*, 42–43.

than were New Englanders living under community-controlled thought.[24] New England historians have often exaggerated the backwardness of the South.[25] Southern historians have sought to idealize from a few schools and a small number of unusually cultivated families a much more general education than existed. More recent studies have painted a truer picture than either.[26] Most Southern colonies at a very early date did have a few schools, chiefly private institutions like the endowed Symmes Free School founded in Virginia in 1634, or "old field schools" where several families divided the expense. By the middle of the eighteenth century the South possessed a number of such schools.[27] But the general situation must not be judged by these few well-known institutions. In 1662 "R. G." described an "almost general want of Schooles" in Virginia which is "most of all bewailed of Parents there."[28] As late as 1736 Governor Johnston rebuked the North Carolina Assembly for never having taken the least care to erect a school or educate the colony's children.[29] Full consideration, then, of Colonial educational facilities shows that the great mass of the population in the middle and southern colonies and more people than tradition has led us to believe in New England had no schools.[30]

[24] Loc. cit.

[25] Even McMaster (History of the People of the United States, I, 26–27) seems to have been guilty of this. See Edward McCrady's reply to McMaster in his Education in South Carolina Prior to and During the Revolution.

[26] Cf. Channing's acceptance (op. cit., I, 432) of Governor Berkeley's report that there were no free schools in Virginia in 1660 with Philip A. Bruce's discovery of contradictory evidence (op. cit., I, 354) and then with T. J. Wertenbaker's more recent statement about early Virginia schools (op. cit., 252).

[27] See, e.g., T. J. Wertenbaker, op. cit., 252; J. T. Adams, op. cit., 136–137; E. Channing, op. cit., II, 465–466; Alice M. Earle, Child Life in Colonial Days, 65–66; V. Dabney, op. cit., 144–145; P. A. Bruce, op. cit., I, 331–361; Cornelius J. Heatwole, A History of Education in Virginia, 60–61; Guy F. Wells, Parish Education in Colonial Virginia, 30–57; James Ramage, Local Government and Free Schools in South Carolina, 29–35.

[28] R. G. [Roger Green(?)], Virginia's Cure, 6.

[29] Herbert L. Osgood, The American Colonies in the Eighteenth Century, III, 116.

[30] E. Channing, op. cit., II, 465–466; Charles M. Andrews, Colonial Folk-

What is more important for this study than the paucity of schools is the character of those that did exist. Often instruction was given in the minister's home, in the kitchen of some elderly woman, or in the church or meeting-house. Where there was a separate school building, it was rude, uncomfortable, usually overcrowded, often badly ventilated, and probably cold. New Amsterdam's schoolroom of 1656 could not be warmed.[31] Textbooks were often completely lacking; at best they were scarce. The teacher had to use whatever was available. Paper, blackboards, slates, crayons, and other modern necessities were wanting. Lessons were usually learned by rote and then recited individually to the teacher. Schools were almost always ungraded, one-teacher institutions, where children of all ages met together. The terms were short. Weather conditions, need of child labor at home or in the fields, and other conditions of primitive life made attendance irregular. Under these physical handicaps little opportunity existed for the exercise of either freedom or restraint.

Furthermore, instruction was generally of the most elementary sort. Reading, writing, spelling, and simple calculations leave little room for the expression of ideas. The method was as primitive as the school equipment. Children learned, without understanding. Recitation took the place of practical application and had decided limitations. In the higher schools, moreover, Greek, Latin, rhetoric, logic, morals, and ethics were taught as subjects to be "learned," not to be discussed, questioned, or understood. The teacher's function was to hear recitations and correct errors until the child could repeat his lesson letter-perfect.

An even more serious limitation on freedom was the inadequacy of the teachers themselves. Often the schoolmaster was a minister who augmented his clerical salary by instruction of the community children. In early Colonial days these

ways, 136; J. T. Adams, _op. cit._, 131–137; Ulrich B. Phillips, _Life and Labor in the Old South_, 33; V. Dabney, _op. cit._, 41–43; Charles L. Smith, _History of Education in North Carolina_, 13–23.   [31] E. Channing, _op. cit._, I, 467.

ministers had been trained in England and were usually well educated.[32] As the second and third generation replaced the first colonists, most New England ministers were locally trained. By an act of 1701 Massachusetts was, moreover, deprived altogether of her ministerial supply of teachers. That act declared that "no minister of any town shall be deemed, held, or accepted to be the school-master of such town within the intent of the law."[33] The purpose of this restriction was not to deprive ministers of control over schools, which they still exercised, but to improve the schools in a period when many towns were evading the school law by having their ministers do a little teaching on the side. This act purposed forcing all towns to provide a real school with a full-time teacher in charge. Actually, it deprived the towns of their best-educated teachers. In the South, where many of the Church of England clergy were still exported from England, constant complaint arose because, as Governor Berkeley put it, as with all other commodities, so with ministers, only "the worst are sent us."[34] Education as well as religion suffered from laziness and dissolute habits of the ministerial portion of Southern teachers. Toward the end of the Colonial period, Scotch Presbyterian missionaries, not infrequently Princeton graduates, did begin to work their way up the western valleys into Virginia and North Carolina as schoolmaster-clergymen who were better educated than most teachers.

Elementary education was frequently conducted by women, often elderly housewives or ministers' daughters, who kept "dame schools." Occasionally these women were unusual persons and excellent teachers. Frequently, however, they were

---

[32] This was true in the South as well as in New England. P. A. Bruce, *op. cit.*, I, 332–333.

[33] *Acts and Resolves of the Province of the Massachusetts Bay* (1869 ed.), I (1692–1714), 470. In the school law of 1789 this prohibition against ministers' serving as teachers was reaffirmed. *Massachusetts Session Laws*, 1788–1789, 418.

[34] W. H. Hening, *op. cit.*, II, 517–518. Inquiries propounded in 1670; answered in 1671.

completely incompetent. In a day when women received only the rudiments of knowledge, they had usually gone little farther than the elementals that they were themselves teaching to others. Teachers of any kind were hard to procure. New communities could offer little in salaries. There was no future in the profession; indeed, it was scarcely a profession at all. Teaching was usually a temporary or secondary occupation. Men who migrated to the discomforts and hardships of America, even though they came for freedom to practice their religion in their own way, usually were interested in material advancement if they had any ability or ambition. All about the school were opportunities for economic gain and independence for him who would work. The same factors, then, that made servants or efficient hired laborers difficult to procure without buying them rendered the problem of finding teachers a serious one. After all, Harvard in the seventeenth century, or Harvard, William and Mary, and Yale in the eighteenth, could not have trained enough good teachers for the Colonies had they tried, and they were primarily concerned with educating clergymen. "Grammar schools" were proportionately almost as scarce as colleges and were chiefly concerned with preparing future ministers for college.

Colonial records abound in regrets that no suitable teachers could be obtained. New Amsterdam's first schoolmaster, Adam Roelantsen, quarreled constantly with his neighbors and was several times in court. Finally he so far overstepped the proprieties of Dutch life that he was sentenced to be flogged and banished.[35] In 1649 a "memorandum" from leaders of the New Netherlands to the Dutch West India Company complained that "the school is kept very irregularly, one and another keeping it according to his pleasure and as long as he thinks proper."[36] Repeated royal instructions in the South to see that

[35] The sentence was not executed. Emma Van Vechten, *Early Schools and Schoolmasters of New Amsterdam*, 322–327.
[36] "In What Manner New Netherland Should Be Redressed," New York Historical Society, *Collections*, 2 series, II, 319.

teachers were licensed indicate difficulty in requiring licenses. Governor Howard's instructions in 1688 commanded him to forbid any man to teach without a license from the Bishop of London or, if he had not come from England, then from the Governor himself.[37] He had in 1686 already summoned all schoolmasters in the colony of Virginia to present evidence of competence or be deprived of their schools. There is no evidence that the teachers all came. In fact, the House of Burgesses begged him to allow certification in the local communities since "several knowing and skillful schoolmasters . . . had left off their employments" as a result of his demand that they come to Jamestown. Governor Nicholson in 1698 was likewise instructed to insist upon strict licensing of teachers.[38] In 1699 each county court was ordered to report to the Council in Jamestown any unlicensed instructors. This time the county court was empowered to examine the teacher's qualifications; so scarce were suitable persons that any competent teacher who satisfied the county court was to be certified without charge. Governors' instructions and colonial enactments were more honored in the breach than in the fulfilment and must not be taken too seriously. Communities had to take whom they could get for teachers, and Colonial schoolmasters were often incompetent and careless in behavior if not actually ignorant.[39] Franklin appealed to this need for better teachers in 1750 when, in seeking support for an academy in Philadelphia, he listed among its values the fact that it would educate the poor to become schoolmasters.[40]

Often the colonists had to obtain their teachers by purchasing indentured servants who had a little learning.[41] Indentured

---

[37] *Virginia Magazine of History and Biography,* XIX (October, 1911), 342.

[38] "Instructions for Francis Nicholson, Sept. 13, 1698," Library of Congress Transcript from Public Record Office, Colonial Office, class 5, vol. 1359, p. 282.

[39] See, e.g., Thomas E. Barksdale, "Progress of Education in the County of Halifax from Its Formation," *Virginia School Report,* 1885, 87.

[40] L. G. and M. J. Walsh, *op. cit.,* 70.

[41] C. A. and M. R. Beard, *op. cit.,* I, 181; A. M. Earle, *op. cit.,* 72; E. Eggleston, *op. cit.,* 224; Elmer E. Brown, *The Making of Our Middle Schools,* 119;

teachers were used not only in the South but in the Middle Colonies. About 1725 the Reverend George Ross of New Castle, Delaware, testified that the private schools of his district were "very often put into the hands of those who are brought into the country and sold for servants." "When a ship arrives in the river," he wrote, "it is a common expression with those who stand in need of an instructor for their children, *let us go and buy a school master.*"[42] As late as 1773 Jonathan Boucher could write in Maryland, "Not a ship arrives either with redemptioners or convicts, in which schoolmasters are not as regularly advertised for sale, as weavers, tailors, or any other trade; with little other difference, that I can hear of, excepting perhaps that the former do not usually fetch so good a price as the latter."[43] He testified that ". . . at least two thirds of the little education we receive are derived from instructors, who are either INDENTED SERVANTS, OR TRANSPORTED FELONS."[44] Advertisers in the *Pennsylvania Gazette* often sought to buy teachers: for example, "a Servant . . . who is a Scholar, and can teach children Reading, Writing, and Arithmetick"; "a single Person, well qualified for a school-master"; "a sober person that is capable of teaching a School."[45] Or the servant sought a master: in 1735 one advertised for a "Township or Neighbourhood" to buy him;[46] in 1762 a Bristol servant sought to sell himself as a schoolmaster for a period not to exceed seven years.[47] Sometimes the ship captain who imported white servants advertised that the men he had for sale knew Latin, or

Cheesman A. Herrick, *White Servitude in Pennsylvania,* 271–272; Eugene I. McCormac, *White Servitude in Maryland, 1734–1820,* 41, 76.

[42] E. G. Dexter, *op. cit.,* 58.

[43] Jonathan Boucher, *A View of the Causes and Consequences of the American Revolution: in Thirteen Discourses, Preached in North America between the Years 1763 and 1775,* 184.   [44] *Ibid.,* 183–184, 189.

[45] *Pennsylvania Gazette,* Jan. 28, Feb. 4, 1735, quoted in R. F. Seybolt, *The Private School,* 83; *Pennsylvania Gazette,* Aug. 18, 1755, quoted in Karl F. Geiser, *Redemptioners and Indentured Servants in the Colony and Commonwealth of Pennsylvania,* 107–108; *Pennsylvania Gazette,* Dec. 11, 1755.

[46] *Pennsylvania Gazette,* Jan. 2, 1735.

[47] *Ibid.,* May 6, 1762, quoted in C. A. Herrick, *op. cit.,* 271.

sometimes French, or that they wrote good hands, or could teach reading and accounts. Newspaper notices now and then gave warning of schoolmasters who had run away or forged passes.[48] Though Geiser found no evidence that convicts were bought as teachers in Pennsylvania, he concluded: ". . . the servant formed no small proportion of the teaching force of the community. Scarcely a vessel arrived in which there were not schoolmasters regularly advertised for sale." [49] In Antrim, New Hampshire, Deacon Aiken contracted with a stranger who appeared at his door during a freshet to give the man his board in return for service, and we are told that since the man proved a good reader he "resided in the family some years, and made himself useful by laboring on the farm and teaching the children."[50] Just about the time the Declaration of Independence declared all men "born free and equal," a Colonial newspaper editorial commented that the *Maryland Journal* had advertised for sale "various Irish commodities, among which are school masters, beef, pork and potatoes," imported in the ship *Paca* arrived in Baltimore from Belfast and Cork.[51]

Sometimes these were the best teachers of all—men of really good education who, through misfortune or persecution at home, had been driven to bind themselves out to service for a term of years in order to earn a fresh start in the New World. Occasionally an English university man thus sold himself into temporary serfdom. In 1736 a lawyer and political offender named Henry Justice was sold into servitude in Virginia for stealing a Bible, a prayer book, and a book on horsemanship from the Library of Trinity College, Cambridge.[52] Several Virginia Prestons and Breckenridges were educated by a servant named Palfrenan, bought in Williamsburg in 1776, who

[48] C. A. Herrick, *op. cit.*, 272.   [49] K. F. Geiser, *op. cit.*, 108.
[50] Walter H. Small, *Early New England Schools,* 109.
[51] "Requirements Affecting Appointment, Retention, and Promotion of Teachers," National Education Association, *Research Bulletin,* VI (September, 1928), 213.
[52] Alfred M. Heston, *Story of the Slave, Slavery and Servitude in New Jersey,* 28.

was "a poet and scholar" and was reputed to be a friend of Samuel Johnson.[53] In Virginia the indentured teachers "included many cultivated Scotchmen who had thus sought to escape the unwholesome conditions at home."[54]

Too often, however, indentured teachers were convicts shipped from English prisons to America. Whatever their origin, they were likely not to be of the best character. Advertisements frequently specified sobriety in prospective teachers. One master advertising for a runaway servant described him as a "Schoolmaster, much given to drinking and gambling."[55] "The truth is," wrote the Reverend Mr. Ross of Delaware about 1725, "the office and character of such a person is [sic] generally very mean and contemptible here, and it cannot be other ways 'til the public takes the Education of Children into their mature consideration."[56] Geiser in a study of indenture in Pennsylvania found these servant-teachers often lacking in sobriety, "dissolute" in their habits, guilty of low moral standards, and "extremely crude" in their methods and discipline.[57] One James Murphy, sought as a runaway teacher, was described by his master as "somewhat long visag'd, sharp nose, much pitted with the small-pox, . . . sometimes ties his hair behind with a string, a very proud fellow, loves drink and when drunk is very impudent and talkative, pretends much, and knows little, was sometime in the French service and can talk French."[58]

A teacher who has only the mere rudiments of an education has no time for anything but keeping ahead of his classes, particularly where he is further handicapped by lack of equipment. His chief concern is to pass on to his pupils the elementary tools he himself possesses. He has probably never progressed beyond the stage of acquiring facts and tools to the

[53] *Loc. cit.*   [54] Edgar W. Knight, *Public Education in the South,* 41.
[55] *Maryland Gazette,* quoted in A. M. Earle, *op. cit.,* 72.
[56] E. G. Dexter, *op. cit.,* 58.   [57] K. F. Geiser, *op. cit.,* 108.
[58] "Extracts from American Newspapers, Relating to New Jersey," *Archives of the State of New Jersey,* 1 series, XIX (1751–1755), 369–370.

point of thinking. He does not realize that he is not free because it is more his own internal limitations than external restrictions that imprison him. That fire that makes man desire freedom to think and to discuss and to experiment has not been kindled in him. If he did have the desire for freedom or borrowed from some one else a new idea, he would not have the intellectual training nor the factual backing to indulge in "novile dispositions," especially where the defenders of orthodoxy—the Colonial ministers—were the best-educated members of society. The incompetence and lack of education of Colonial teachers in most cases makes it fantastic to talk of freedom. To appreciate *how* fantastic, the citizen of twentieth-century America, particularly the teacher of educational theory, must visit rural one-teacher schools in the more backward parts of the country, especially in the South. There he will discover conditions such as most Colonial teachers faced. There he will come to see the relation of physical equipment, lack of schools, and inadequate training to the problem of freedom. Yet in any community it is not the average man, whose own limitations are his spirit's prison, but the unusual person with a capacity for freedom for whom freedom becomes a pressing problem. This exceptional teacher was painfully limited by the Colonial environment in which he lived.

All teachers were subjected to various controls in addition to their own incompetence and lack of training. They lived in small settlements under pressure that neighborhood opinion always exerts in small places. Teachers of "dame schools" and "old field schools" were watched by both community and fee-paying parents. In privately endowed schools a board of some sort supervised teachers. In "free public schools" there was official supervision, which in seventeenth-century New England meant a combined church-state control. Ministers and parish lay-readers who conducted schools taught under the restriction not only of community opinion but of their own strict sectarian tenets as well. In New England, where teachers were generally better trained and therefore more capable of exercising freedom, town organization, more effective religious control, a stricter code of conduct, and a better supply of teachers all combined to make the teacher less free than in the South and Middle Colonies.

The South was not more liberal in theory, but scattered settlements made control difficult. The Church of England clergy lacked the religious enthusiasm and the strict code of conduct of New England Puritans and therefore interfered less. The difficulty of getting a schoolmaster at all forced Southerners to accept almost anything in a man qualified and willing to teach their children.

Teachers who were indentured servants were, of course, virtually slaves for a period of years. It is interesting to speculate upon the effect of this servitude upon their freedom as teachers. Often the terms of indenture provided safeguards. John Carter's will, for instance, provided that a servant should be purchased for the *exclusive* purpose of teaching his son, Robert, English and Latin; Thomas Hellier in Westover Parish obtained in his contract a promise that his master would not put him to work in the fields except during seasons of an extraordinary demand for labor on the crops, and then only for a "short spurt."[59] John Warden refused to enter the service of one Virginia family without guarantees that the planter and his family would treat him "as a gentleman."[60] Besides, in a family or community of uneducated parents, economically prosperous enough to provide schooling for their children, a well-educated teaching servant might conceivably have occupied a position of respect. In a frontier community, however, physical prowess and qualities that would help conquer the wilderness were more respected than book learning. Since artisans or manual laborers usually brought higher prices than teachers in Colonial sales, superior education probably did not procure the teaching servant much favor. The indentured

[59] P. A. Bruce, *op. cit.*, I, 328–329.   [60] C. M. Andrews, *op. cit.*, 128

teacher was often treated as a servant. After all, the master did have legal power over him. He could be taken from teaching and set at difficult or disagreeable tasks. At best, unless especially protected in his indenture, he had to spend part of his time at manual labor. He could be corporally punished. He was frequently sold to another master perhaps to worse conditions, and this even where he had given satisfaction. John Hammond of Annapolis, for instance, advertised a schoolmaster for sale in 1774 with two years more to serve. "He is sold," the advertisement said, "for no fault, any more than we are done with him."[61] Another master advertised for sale "A Likely Servant Mans Time for 4 years who is very well qualified for a Clerk or to teach a School, he Reads, Writes, understands Arithmetick and Accompts very well."[62] The indentured teacher could be let out to others as a schoolmaster or laborer for profit to the master. If he found better employment and arranged for a substitute to finish out his term of indenture, and the new teacher proved unsatisfactory, he could be forced back into servitude or advertised as a runaway.[63] Many of these indentured teachers, like other servants, did run away and were then advertised as escaped slaves.[64] This class of teachers, then, could hardly be called free. Yet one wonders, after a study of conditions in recent years, if the indentured servant was actually any more a slave to the whims of his master than is the twentieth-century small-town teacher. The eighteenth-century schoolmaster was bound by his indenture; the modern rural teacher is bound by low wages, insecurity of tenure, and the impossibility of getting another position if he incurs the enmity of his superiors in the present one. One wonders, too, if the personal restriction and extra-curricular duties imposed upon the

[61] Bernard C. Steiner, *History of Education in Maryland,* 34.

[62] Ellwood P. Cubberley, *Public Education in the United States,* 34.

[63] C. A. Herrick, *op. cit.,* 272.

[64] See, e.g., in the *Pennsylvania Gazette,* April 27, 1738 (quoted in C. A. Herrick, *op. cit.,* 272), an advertisement for a servant schoolmaster owned by a number of families in Freehold, New Jersey, and one in the *Maryland Journal* quoted in A. M. Earle, *op. cit.,* 72. See also *supra,* 13.

indentured servant were, in a day when every one performed manual labor, any more onerous than those imposed by public opinion and tradition and the necessity of catering to important local personalities in the average small American community of today.

One other class of teachers must be considered, namely, the private tutors in the homes of the wealthy. If a Southerner could afford it he procured a tutor for his children who was not a servant but a free man living in the family and working for wages. Some of the best-educated colonials were taught by tutors trained in an American college or an English university. In one respect the tutor had a freedom that most Colonial schoolmasters and many rural teachers today could not enjoy. He had, on the larger plantations, a good library for his own reading and for use by his tutees, a library more varied in interest than New England theological collections. Furthermore, the free tutor was usually regarded as a member of the family, had some leisure time, and led a pleasant social life.

In 1774 one of these tutors, Philip V. Fithian, resident of New Jersey and graduate of Princeton, wrote to John Peck, his successor as tutor, a letter of advice on life in the Carter family in Westmoreland County, Virginia, that throws interesting light on the degree of freedom a tutor under the happiest circumstances enjoyed.[65] Concerning relations with the family, Fithian advises:

. . . place yourself, according to your most acute Calculation, at a perfect equidistance between the father & the eldest Son. Or let the same distance be observed in every article of behaviour between you & the eldest Son, as there ought to be, by the latest & most approved precepts of Moral-Philosophy, between the eldest Son & his next youngest Brother. . . . I commonly attend church; and often, at the request of Gentlemen, after Service according to the custom, dine abroad on Sunday—I seldom fail, when invited by M^r & Mrs *Carter* of going out with them; but I make it a point, however strongly solicited to the contrary, to return with them too

[65] Philip V. Fithian to John Peck, Nomini Hall, Aug. 12, 1774, P. V. Fithian, *Journal and Letters, 1767–1774,* 283–298.

—Except in one of these cases, I seldom go out, but with a valuable variety of books I live according to Horace's direction. & love "Secretum Iter et fallentis Semita Vitae." Close retirement and a life by Stealth. . . .

In regard to social life away from the Carter plantation he also gives counsel:

You will, in the first place, be often solicited probably oftner than you would wish, to ride abroad; this, however, if you do it moderately, & in seasonable time, & go to proper company, I recommend as conducive to health to one in your sedentary manner of living. But if you go much into company, you will find it extremely difficult to break away with any manner of credit till very late at night or in most cases for several days, & if you are wanting to your School, you do manifest injury to your Imployer. In this case, I advise you to copy Mr Carter. Whenever he invites you, ride. You may stay, and talk, & drink, & ride to as great excess as he; & may with safety associate yourself with those whom you find to be his intimates. In all other Cases, except when you ride to Church, at least till you are very intimate in the Colony, you had better ride to a certain Stump, or to some noted plantation, or pretty landscape; you will have in this every advantage of exercise, the additional advantage of undisturbed Meditation, & you will be under no Jealous apprehension in point of behaviour, nor any restraint as to the time of your return. . . . I solemnly injoin it upon you, that you never suffer the Spirit of a Pedagogue to attend you without the walls of your little Seminary. In all promiscuous Company be as silent & attentive as Decency will allow you, for you have nothing to communicate, which such company will hear with pleasure, but you may learn many things which, in after life, will do you singular service. . . .

About friends Fithian gives warning, too:

One considerable advantage which you promise yourself by coming to this Colony is to extend the Limits of your acquaintance; this is laudable, & if you have enough of prudence & firmness, it will be a singular advantage—Yet attempt slowly & with the most Jealous Circumspection—If you fix your familiarity wrong in a single instance, you are in danger of total, if not immediate ruin— . . . The last direction I shall venture to mention on this head, is, that you abstain totally from Women.

Certain obstacles the boys themselves placed in the way of their tutor's teaching as he chose. One of these was petitions for holidays. "You must have a good deal of steadiness," Fithian warns, "if you are able to evade cleverly this practice which has grown so habitual to your little charge from a false method in their early education that they absolutely claim it as a necessary right." Another difficulty "consists in knowing when, & in what measure to give the Boys Liberty to go from Home. The two younger Boys are wholly under your inspection; so that not only the progress they make in learning, but their moral Conduct (for both of these are critically observed & examined) either justifies or condemns your management to the World. If you keep them much at home, & close to business, they themselves will call you unfeeling and cruel; & refuse to be industrious; if you suffer them to go much abroad they are certainly out of the way of improvement by Study . . ."

Colonial life and the religious nature of the teaching profession imposed upon teachers certain characteristic duties that persist today only in small communities or special types of school. Specific times for religious instruction were often laid down in rules of the school. For instance, the Hopkins Grammar School at New Haven in 1684 prescribed that the teacher should examine the boys on Monday mornings upon the Sunday sermons and that Saturday afternoons were to "be improved by ye M^r in Catechizing of his Schollars y^t are Capeable."[66] In 1649 the master at Hampton, New Hampshire, bound himself by formal agreement to instruct his children "once in a week or more in some orthodox catechism."[67] In

---

[66] E. E. Brown, *op. cit.*, 137. The Dorchester town meeting laid down similar rules for its school in 1645 (William A. Mowry, "Historical Address," *Dorchester Celebration, 250th Anniversary of the Establishment of the First Public School in Dorchester, June 22, 1889*, 28–29) and the trustees of the grammar school at New Haven in 1684 (W. H. Small, *op. cit.*, 26). These are merely examples of a general practice. Adrian A. Holtz, *A Study of the Moral and Religious Elements in American Secondary Education up to 1800*, 51–52.

[67] W. H. Small, *op. cit.*, 299. John Prudden at Roxbury in 1668 and Mr. Norcros at Watertown in 1676 made similar contractual promises. W. H. Small, *op. cit.*, 115–116; A. A. Holtz, *op. cit.*, 28.

1679 Richard Norcros contracted "to teach both Latin & inglith Schollurs . . . & once a week to teach them thear catticise."[68] Toward the end of the seventeenth century Johannes von Eckhelen and the town of Flatbush, Long Island, made formal agreement that "when school begins, one of the children shall read the morning prayer as it stands in the catechism, and close with prayer before dinner; and in the afternoon, the same"; that "the evening school shall begin with the Lord's Prayer and close by singing a psalm"; and that the teacher "shall instruct the children in the common prayers, and in the questions and answers of the catechism on Wednesdays and Saturdays, to enable them to say them better on Sunday in the church."[69] The Society for the Propagation of the Gospel instructed its teachers "to take especial care of their [children's] manners, in and out of School; warning them seriously of those Vices to which children are most liable; teaching them to abhor Lying and Falsehood and to avoid all sorts of evil speaking; to love Truth and Honesty; to be modest, just and affable and courteous to all their companions, . . . to bring them in their tender years that Sense of Religion which may render it the constant Principle of their Lives and Actions."[70] Often teachers were required against their wills to accept poor children of the community into their schools.[71] Sometimes a

---

[68] *Watertown Records,* I and II, sec. 204, p. 137.

[69] Lyman Powell, *The History of Education in Delaware,* 26; B. F. Thompson, *History of Long Island,* I, 285, 286. In 1661 Evert Pietersen had been commanded by the burgomaster to teach "the Christian Prayers, commandments, baptism, Lord's supper, and the questions with answers of the catechism," and to "let the pupils sing some verses and a psalm" each day. Thomas E. Finegan, "Colonial Schools and Colleges in New York," New York State Historical Association, *Proceedings,* XVI (1917), 173.

[70] Frederick Dalcho, *An Historical Account of the Protestant Episcopal Church in South Carolina,* 50–51.

[71] For example, Maryland enacted a law in 1728 which declared "That the Master of every Public School within this Province, shall, and is hereby required to teach as many poor Children *gratis,* as the Visitors, or the Major Part of them, of the respective Schools shall order, or be immediately discharged and removed from his Trust in the said School, and a new Master be put in." T. Bacon, *Laws of Maryland* (1765 ed.), 1728, chap. VIII, sec. III.

teacher had to play an organ,[72] or conduct singing, or provide discipline and supervise his charges after school hours, particularly in private schools that had boarding pupils. One student of Colonial social life describes some of the schoolmaster's extra-curricular duties. He rang "the church bell on Sunday, read the Bible at service in church, and led in the singing; sometimes he read the sermon. He provided water for baptisms, bread and wine for communion, and in fact performed all the duties now done by a sexton, including sweeping out the church. He delivered invitations to funerals and carried messages. Sometimes he dug the graves, and often he visited and comforted the sick."[73]

Teachers were also restricted by certain Colonial attitudes that affected thought and expression generally. Religious freedom in its present sense was unknown. Even religious toleration was yet to be won. Rhode Island most nearly approached freedom, but even in Rhode Island atheists and, after 1719, Catholics were excluded from toleration. Pennsylvania tolerated all but Catholics, Jews, and persons who did not believe in God. Maryland's Catholic founders had sought toleration of Christian sects in order to insure freedom to members of their own church, but, under Church of England control, Maryland abandoned her early attitude and became as intolerant as other Southern colonies. Many of the colonists had come to America seeking freedom to worship God in their own sectarian way, but few of them had any notion of allowing this to men who differed from them. It was not for religious freedom, but for the sake of a unified religious community of saints, from which all error was excluded, that the Puritans had braved New England winters. Religious heresy would spoil their happiness. It might also corrupt their youth or bring God's punishment upon them for not extirpating it. Furthermore, once to tolerate error might mean ultimate con-

[72] William F. Dannehower, "The Sunneytown Academy," *Perkioman Region*, III (1925), no. 4, 62.   [73] A. M. Earle, *op. cit.*, 75.

trol of their new states by heretics, who in the end might again persecute true religion as it had been persecuted in England. Dutch, Scotch Presbyterians, and German Lutherans believed as firmly in uniformity of religion as did New England Puritans. Where religious diversity *was* tolerated in the Middle Colonies, the reason was that several sects, each too strong to be exterminated, found it necessary to live together. The reason for toleration there was not that any one sect was less convinced of its own infallibility than the Puritans, or less eager for enforced uniformity had that been feasible. In the South, Anglicans did not display the religious enthusiasm evinced elsewhere by dissenting sects, but there clerical prerogatives and loyalty to the Crown replaced religious fervor in demanding uniformity and allegiance to the established church. It was a day when most Americans were deeply concerned with religion, and when most religious men were unshakably convinced of the authority and infallibility of their own sectarian view of truth and their God-given duty to stamp out error. Strict religious orthodoxy, then, was expected of teachers as of every one else.

Teachers, moreover, were subjected to even stricter religious supervision than other members of the community because the motivating force behind education in Colonial America was primarily religious.[74] It was the fervor of sectarian come-outers that demanded schooling here. Had the physical difficulties of the wilderness proved less overwhelming, this religious purpose would have established schools more speedily and more widely. New England had other advantages in establishing schools, but undoubtedly an important element in her greater educational advancement was her greater religious fervor and uniformity. In Rhode Island, where diverse opinions were in-

---

[74] See, e.g., A. A. Holtz, *op. cit.*, 1, 6, 10, 13, 15, 17–18, 46; C. A. and M. R. Beard, *op. cit.*, I, 176–178; and Marcus W. Jernegan, "Factors Influencing the Development of American Education before the Revolution," Mississippi Valley Historical Association, *Proceedings*, V (1911–1912), 194–195. See also *supra*, 1–2.

termingled, united action in establishing schools with a sectarian purpose was impossible, and that colony was slower in developing schools than her more intolerant neighbors.

Early records throughout the colonies show this religious motive for public education. Massachusetts prefaced her famous school law of 1647 with the following preamble: "It being one chiefe piect of y^t ould deluder, Satan, to keepe men from the knowledge of ye Scriptures, as in form^r times by keeping y^m in an unknowne tongue, so in these latt^r times by pswading from ye use of tongues, y^t so at least ye true sence & meaning of ye originall might be clouded by false glosses of saint seeming deceivers, y^t learning may not be buried in ye grave of o^r fath^rs in ye church & commonwealth, the Lord assisting o^r endeavo^rs—It is therefore ord^red," etc.[75] Connecticut used this identical wording for its school law.[76] New Haven sought to give her children and apprentices enough schooling that they might "through Gods blessing, attain at least so much, as to be able duly to read the Scriptures, and other good and profitable printed Books in the English tongue, being their native language, and in some competent measure, to understand the main grounds and principles of Christian Religion necessary to Salvation."[77] Plymouth in passing her educational law of 1684 desired children and servants to have enough "learning" "at least to be able duely to read the Scriptures, and other profitable Books Printed in the English tongue, and the knowledge of the Capital Laws; and in some competent measure the main Grounds and Principles of Christian Religion, necessary to Salvation; by causing them to learn some orthodox catechism without book."[78]

[75] *Records of the Governor and Company of the Massachusetts Bay in New England* (N. B. Shurtleff, ed.), II, 203.

[76] "Schooles," *Code of 1650, Being a Compilation of the Earliest Laws and Orders of the General Court of Connecticut.*

[77] *Records of the Colony or Jurisdiction of New Haven, 1653–1665* (C. J. Hoadley, ed.), 583.

[78] *Book of General Laws of the Inhabitants of the Jurisdiction of New-Plimouth, . . . 1685,* chap. V, p. 12.

In the Dutch West India Company's "charter of exemptions" of 1629 the "Patroons and colonists" were enjoined "to find out ways and means whereby they may support a minister and schoolmaster, that thus the service of God and zeal for religion may not grow cool, and be neglected among them . . ."[79] In the famous "remonstrance" of 1649 the colonists asked "at least two good masters, so that first of all, in so wild a country, where there are many loose people, the youth be well taught and brought up, not only in reading and writing, but also in the knowledge and fear of the Lord."[80] Governor Francis Bernard's instructions for the Government of New Jersey in 1758 declared, "It is Our further *Will and Pleasure* that you recommend to the Assembly to enter upon proper Methods for the erecting and maintaining of Schools, in Order to the training up of Youth to Reading and to a necessary Knowledge of the principles of Religion, . . ."[81]

When in 1694 schools were established in Maryland, it was for the expressed purpose of "instructing our youth in the orthodox religion, preserving them from the infection of heterodox tenets and fitting them for the service of the church and state."[82] When Virginia's Assembly granted land for a free school in 1661-1662, it did so "for the advancement of learning, education of youth, supply of the ministry, and promotion of piety."[83] Terms of apprenticeship reveal this same purpose. In apprenticing a boy in the 1680's, the Rappahannock County Court required the master to give bond that he would put the "Apprentice to Schoole and learne him to Reade a Chapter in the Bible."[84] The Elizabeth County Court in 1694 bound out

[79] Edward B. O'Callaghan, *History of New Netherland*, I, 119.
[80] John R. Brodhead, *History of the State of New York*, I, 506.
[81] *Documents Relating to the Colonial History of the State of New Jersey* (*New Jersey Archives*, 1 series, IX), IX, 69.
[82] The Governor, the Secretary in behalf of the Council, and the Speaker of the House to the Right Reverend Father in God, Henry, Lord Bishop of London, Oct. 18, 1694, quoted in B. C. Steiner, *op. cit.*, 19-20.
[83] G. W. Dyer, *Democracy in the South before the Civil War*, 34.
[84] M. W. Jernegan, *Laboring and Dependent Classes in Colonial America, 1607-1783*, 163.

a boy on condition that the master "Teach him to Read a chapter in the Bible the Lords Prayer and Ten Commandments."[85] When North Carolina finally established a school in "Newbern" in 1766 it was established in order that "the rising generation may be brought up and instructed in the principles of the christian religion, and fitted for the several offices and purposes of life."[86]

Much of Colonial education was directly sponsored by religious groups. In New England, where originally church and state were one, state schools were church schools. In the South the Society for the Propagation of the Gospel in Foreign Parts did a great deal to aid the colonial governments in setting up schools. In the Middle Colonies, where religious diversity made public schools with a religious purpose difficult, public education languished, but the Society for the Propagation of the Gospel, the Friends, the Dutch, the German Lutherans, the Scotch Presbyterians founded parochial schools. Whatever the origin of schools, the purpose was religious, which meant sectarian.

The curricula and materials of Colonial schools were also largely religious. Memorizing the Lord's Prayer and the "twelve articles of the Christian faith," catechising in the principles of religion, and learning passages from the *Psalter,* the *Book of Common Prayer,* the Bible, and writings of religious leaders formed a large part of ordinary schooling. The *New England Primer* and contemporary spellers were highly flavored with religion. The Bible itself was often used as both speller and reader.[87]

Furthermore, the clergy, particularly in the well-organized

85 *Ibid.,* 162.
86 *Collection of Private Acts of the General Assembly of North Carolina,* 1794, chap. XIX, p. 49.
87 In the Mather School in Boston, for instance, there were three grades, a "Psalter class," a "Testament class," and a "Bible class." Those in the "Bible class" were required to read two chapters at the close of school and to spell the words in them. No other books were used until 1765. W. M. Mowry, *op. cit.,* 50–51.

New England towns, were often delegated to examine and license the teacher before he was appointed and then to visit and inspect the schools while he taught in them.[88] Often the pupils themselves were examined by the minister, sometimes publicly, to see if the teacher had done satisfactory work.[89] The purpose of examining prospective teachers was to determine their academic training, their moral fitness, and their religious orthodoxy. The minister was the member of the community best suited to pass on all three and most interested in maintaining educational standards. Hence in New England he was the natural judge of the teacher's qualifications.

Besides, specific religious tests were often imposed by law. The citizenship law of 1631 in Massachusetts had provided that "for time to come noe man shal be admitted to the freedome of this body polliticke, but such as are members of some of the churches, within the lymitts of the same."[90] The law of 1664 required for admission to citizenship "a Certificate under the hands of the Ministers or Minister of the place where they dwell, that they are Orthodox in Religion, and not vicious in their lives."[91] A law of 1692, re-enacted in 1701–1702, demanded such a ministerial certificate for all grammar-school teachers.[92] This practice grew until, in a Massachusetts law of 1789, min-

[88] T. J. Wertenbaker, *op. cit.*, 245; A. M. Earle, *op. cit.*, 67; E. P. Cubberley, *op. cit.*, 171–172; W. H. Small, *op. cit.*, 92, 334; Alden H. Abbott, "The New England Town School," *Education*, XXXII (November, 1911), 159; Henry Suzzallo, *The Rise of Local School Supervision in Massachusetts*, 51–53; Henry F. Jenks, *Catalogue of the Boston Public Latin School . . . with an Historical Sketch*, 32–33.

[89] In the New Netherlands the ministerial catechising was sometimes done in church. The schoolmasters in the South and Middle Colonies sent out by the Society for the Propagation of the Gospel recommended themselves to the Society in their reports by telling how pleased the older people were at their children's knowledge in public catechising. A. A. Holtz, *op. cit.*, 52.

[90] *Records of the Governor and Company of the Massachusetts Bay in New England* (N. B. Shurtleff, ed.), I, 87.

[91] *The General Laws and Liberties of the Massachusetts Colony . . . 1672*, 56.

[92] *Acts and Laws of His Majesty's Province of the Massachusetts-Bay in New-England* (1742), chap. XIX, p. 150; *Acts and Resolves of the Province of Massachusetts Bay* (1869 ed.), I (1701–1702), chap. X, sec. 2, p. 470.

isters were given official place on all school committees.[93] Boston in 1709 voted to "Appoint a Certain Number of Gentlemen, of Liberal Education, Together with Some of ye Rev'd Ministers of the Town, to be Inspectors of th S^d Schoole, . . . To visit ye schoole from time to time . . . to inform themselves of the methods used in teaching of ye Schollars and to inquire of their Proficiency."[94] In 1685 Plymouth required each master of a Latin school to be "judged by the Major part of the Ministers of the County, a Person capable to bring up Youth fit for the College."[95] During Dutch rule in the New Netherlands every teacher was required to have a license from civil and ecclesiastical authorities.[96] Later English law required a similar certificate from the Archbishop of Canterbury or the Bishop of London.[97] Wherever, indeed, as in all Southern colonies, the Church of England was the established church of a colony, this license from the Bishop of London was required for all teachers, except when, through necessity of obtaining any teacher at all, the local assembly set the rule aside and issued a certificate of its own on consultation with local clergy.

The purpose of licensing was, of course, to test the sectarian soundness of the teacher's religious tenets. The General Court of Massachusetts in 1654 commended it to "the serious Consideration and special care of our Overseers of the Colledg and

---

[93] *Laws of the Commonwealth of Massachusetts, 1788–1789,* II, chap. XIX, p. 20.

[94] "Boston Records," 1700–1728, sec. 308, *A Report of the Record Commissioner of the City of Boston, 1882,* doc. 137, p. 65.

[95] *Compact with the Charter and Laws of the Colony of New Plymouth, 1685* (Wm. Brigham, ed.), sec. 1, p. 300.

[96] E. G. Dexter, *op. cit.,* 15; Thomas E. Finegan, "Colonial Schools and Colleges in New York," New York State Historical Association, *Proceedings,* XVI (1917), 168.

[97] Instructions to Gov. Thomas Dongan, May 29, 1686, *Documents Relative to the Colonial History of the State of New York* (E. B. O'Callaghan, ed.), III, 372; to Governor Henry Slaughter, Jan. 31, 1689, *ibid.,* III, 688; to Governor Benjamin Fletcher, March 7, 1691/2, *ibid.,* III, 821; to the Earl of Belmont, Aug. 31, 1697, *ibid.,* IV, 288; to Governor Robert Hunter, Dec. 27, 1709, *ibid.,* V, 135. The 1686 instructions named both bishops; the others, only the Bishop of London. See also Katherine M. Cook, *State Laws and Regulations Governing Teachers' Certificates,* 9.

the Select men in the several townes, not to admit or suffer any
such to be continued in the Office or place of teaching, educating or instructing youth or children, in the Colledg or Schools,
that have manifested themselves unsound in the faith, or scan-
dalous in their lives and have not given satisfaction according
to the Rules of Christ."[98] During the heated religious controversies between the New Lights and Old Lights, the Connecticut Legislature in 1742, under Old Light domination, forbade
any one to conduct a school, other than those already legally
established, without legislative permission.[99] This measure
purposed the barring of any New Light teacher not only from
the public schools but even from a private school such as the
one the New Lights had recently established in New London.
Here, then, membership in the established church was not
enough; a teacher had to belong to the majority faction of the
established sect.

In the New Netherlands schoolmasters had to be members
of the Dutch Reformed Church. When New York became a
royal province, governor's instructions,[100] the activities of the
Society for the Propagation of the Gospel, and specific colonial
legislation requiring the Bishop of London's approval of a
teacher[101] combined to require all teachers to show orthodox
Church of England tenets. New Jersey used a similar test.[102]
Maryland established one in 1723.[103] Virginia tried to maintain the requirement but finally had to make exceptions for
both Friends and Presbyterians. The extension of the Schism
Act to North Carolina under the instructions of Governor Bur-
rington in 1730 and Governor Dobbs in 1754 excluded non-

---

98 "Scholes," *Book of the General Lavves and Libertyes Concerning the Inhabitants of Massachusets . . .* (1660), 71.

99 *Public Records of the Colony of Connecticut* (C. J. Hoadley, ed.), VIII
(1735-1743), 500-501.

100 See *supra,* 27, note 97.

101 *Colonial Laws of New York,* I (1664-1719), 517.

102 *New Jersey Archives,* 1 series, IX (1758), p. 68; *ibid.,* XX (1760), p.
498.

103 T. Bacon, *Laws of Maryland* (1765 ed.), 1723, chap. XIX, sec. 8.

conformist teachers.[104] When the state finally established a free school in 1766 at New Bern, the teacher was required by law to be an Anglican.[105] As late as 1769 Governor Tryon vetoed a bill establishing a school because it did not demand religious orthodoxy of the schoolmaster.[106] This was in a colony where a majority of the inhabitants were dissenters. In each of the crown colonies, the royal instructions to governors, the local government, and the established church all sought to force this test of Church of England orthodoxy upon teachers. Probably the law was not strictly enforced. Often, as in the Piedmont and the valleys of North Carolina and Virginia, a dissenting sect had its own schools and enforced tests of sectarian dissent in appointing teachers as rigidly as did the established church in the communities it controlled.

Americans of the seventeenth century, like their descendants of the twentieth, talked of education in terms of "good citizenship." To them this meant belief in the sectarian religious tenets of the community, ability to support oneself and avoid becoming a public charge, and, finally, knowledge of and obedience to the civil and criminal laws. The effect of the religious desideratum on teachers has been considered.

The importance of vocational training in Colonial education has usually been overlooked. Yet this was a motive of only slightly less importance than the religious one. New communities could not afford to carry useless members. Older settlements, as they accumulated taxable wealth, perceived that it not only increased the general prosperity but actually cost less to train each child to provide for his own needs than to carry him later in life as a public charge. This purpose of insuring society against the burden of pauperism accounted for the ap-

[104] *Colonial Records of North Carolina,* III (1728-1734), 111; *ibid.,* V (1752-1759), 1137.
[105] *Ibid.,* IV (1734-1752), 977; Charles L. Smith, "Schools and Education in Colonial Times," *North Carolina Booklet,* VIII (April, 1909), 320.
[106] *Colonial Records of North Carolina,* VIII (1769-1771), 6; *ibid.,* V (1752-1759), xviii, xxv.

prenticeship provisions of the great Elizabethan Poor Law of 1601. It underlay the apprenticeship rules of Colonial America and played no small part in the demand for schools. Moreover all middle- and upper-class citizens were ambitious to see their sons "make good" socially and economically. After the disappearance of the frontier stage of life, this involved knowing the rudiments of reading, writing, and figuring, as aids to the vocational training provided at home or under apprenticeship.

In 1642, therefore, the Massachusetts General Court, "taking into consideration the great neglect in many parents & masters in training up their children in learning, & labo^r, & other imployments wch may bee profitable to the common wealth," required officials of the various towns to "redresse this evill" and, as means thereto, to demand an accounting of parents and masters of the education given their children. The General Court empowered officials to take children and apprentices from those who were delinquent in providing proper training.[107] Connecticut required "that all parents and masters doe breed and bring up theire children and apprentices in some honest lawfull calling, labour or imployment, either in husbandry or some other trade proffitable for themselves and the commonwealth." Again, the selectmen might take children and apprentices away from delinquent parents or masters and bind them out to others.[108] Plymouth commanded its selectmen to make certain "that all Parents and Masters do breed and bring up their children and apprentices in some honest lawful Calling and employment, that may be profitable for themselves and the Country."[109] In 1711 the parents of Boston drew up a memorial protesting against the time spent studying Greek and

107 *Records of the Governor and Company of the Massachusetts Bay in New England* (N. B. Shurtleff, ed.), II, 8–9.
108 "Children," *Code of 1650 Being a Compilation of the Earliest Laws and Orders of the General Court of Connecticut.*
109 *Book of General Laws of the Inhabitants of the Jurisdiction of New-Plimouth . . . 1685*, chap. V, p. 12.

Latin which "hath proved of very Little, or no benefit as to their after Accomplishment." They urged "more easie and delightful methodes" for children not "designed for Schollars." At one time Boston established a "spinning school" for poor children.[110] An early eighteenth-century school in New York advertised the teaching of "all branches of mathematics . . . geography, navigation, and merchants' bookkeeping." The free school of Charleston, South Carolina, founded in 1712, taught ". . . merchants' accounts, and also the art of navigation and surveying and other useful and practical parts of mathematics."[111] Penn wished public schools partly because "the prosperity and welfare of any people depend in great measure, upon the good education of youth . . . qualifying them to serve their country and themselves, by breeding them in . . . useful arts and sciences."[112] A law of 1683 required that children "be taught some useful trade or skill, that the poor may work to live, and the rich if they become poor may not want."[113] Courts often required in apprentice bonds a provision protecting the community against later pauperism, as in the New York indenture of 1724 that compelled the master to teach the boy to "read write and Cypher so far as will be Sufficient to Manage his Trade."[114] In Bristol County, Virginia, in 1757 a petition to the General Assembly urged a "free school" in order that "poor Children should be brought up in a Religious, Virtuous and Industrious Course of Life so as to become useful members of the Community."[115] Probably, in fact, the solicitude of the state for education of apprenticed children was based more on a desire to prevent vagrancy and

---

110 E. Channing, *op. cit.*, II, 464–465.

111 C. A. and M. R. Beard, *op. cit.*, I, 176.

112 Thomas Woody, *Quaker Education in the Colony and State of New Jersey*, 10.

113 *Charter to William Penn and Laws of the Province of Pennsylvania* (1879 ed.), 142.

114 Robert F. Seybolt, *The Evening Schools of Colonial New York City*, 634.

115 A. A. Holtz, *op. cit.*, 22–23.

protect society against pauperism than it was on concern over the apprentice's soul.[116]

Back of this effort to train skilled workers and give every man a calling was more than a desire to avoid taxes for support of the poor. It was early learned that unskilled laborers were more likely to be idle, and that idleness and vagrancy bred discontent and "restlessness," which endangered the smooth working of established society. All through Colonial records runs a desire to maintain the *status quo* in both church and state. But the ordinary man in Colonial times left no records. He had no voice in government. In the royal colonies the officials of the Crown and the local landed aristocracy controlled the situation. In New England likewise, a dominant class in church and state ruled a larger nonprivileged group. The Puritan settlers brought servants and dependents to whom church membership and citizenship were denied. Because the one class left scant and the other fuller records, because nationalism has demanded a happy and romantic past, and because citizens of a democracy seek recompense in tracing their origins to aristocratic gentlemen in the South, to well-to-do town dwellers or landed gentry in the Middle Colonies, and to high-minded church fathers living in fine old Colonial mansions in New England, historians have tended to ignore the lower classes of Colonial society. On the frontier where classes had not developed, the vast number of failures, who, miserable and despairing, were destroyed by the struggle, have been romanticized out of the picture, and only the sturdier, successful pioneers have been painted for posterity. But the men who made laws and established schools and gave of their prosperity for the education of the poor were well aware of the presence of great numbers of ordinary men, even if the historian until recently has not been. By elementary education,

[116] See, e.g., W. A. Maddox, *The Free School Idea in Virginia before the Civil War*, 9–10; M. W. Jernegan, *Laboring and Dependent Classes in Colonial America, 1607–1783*, 88.

they hoped to make poor men obedient, law-abiding, and interested in the maintenance of the Colonial *status quo*—or, more euphemistically, they wished to "banish Idleness, advance Husbandrye," and put down all "evill discontent."

Obedience to the laws and regulations put upon poor men by those who ruled Colonial society necessitated reading the laws and becoming familiar with them. This was the other major purpose of education. Therefore, along with the requirement that enough learning be provided for the practice of religion and the pursuit of a trade goes the admonition to teach "so much learning, as may inable them perfectly to read the English tongue, and knowledge of the Capitall laws . . ."[117] William Smith of the College at Philadelphia averred in 1753, "Liberty is the most dangerous of all weapons, in the hands of those who know not the use and value of it. Those who are in most cases free to speak and act as they please, had need be well instructed how to speak and act; and it is well said by Montesquieu, that wherever there is most freedom, there the whole power of education is requisite to good government." But, he explained, reading, writing, figures, and "religious and civil truths and duties" are all that are necessary for the people. He urged fees for all other subjects "to prevent the vulgar from spending more than is necessary."[118]

By the end of the Colonial period, in spite of all that the schools could do toward providing proper understanding of religion and knowledge of the laws, this underprivileged class of men had won enough power—and schooling—to be able successfully to rise against the established order in both church and state and eventually to overthrow its rule. An important factor in the American Revolution was the effort of men whom Colonial society had denied social, economic, and political privileges, to obtain them. An important result of the Revolution was a gradual winning of political rights by the unprivi-

[117] "Children," *Code of 1650 Being a Compilation of the Earliest Laws and Orders of the General Court of Connecticut. . . .*
[118] James P. Wickersham, *A History of Education in Pennsylvania,* 66–67.

leged, and the expulsion from the country of many of the best educated leading citizens along with confiscation of their property by their less fortunate neighbors. One cause of the Revolution was fear of the tightening of Church of England control through the sending of a bishop to America. One result was the gradual overthrow of church establishments. It may, then, be that Governor Berkeley was wiser than the advocates of education when he declared, "I thank God, *there are no free schools* ... and I hope we shall not have, these hundred years, for *learning* has brought disobedience, and heresy, and sects into the world."[119]

Whichever view best served the end, there is abundant evidence that Colonial America believed obedience, orthodoxy, and strict enforcement of the laws would accompany literacy, particularly if ideas and books were properly censored so that literacy would be used to read only sound doctrine about church and society.[120]

Strict censorship was maintained in the Colonies. Berkeley thanked God, too, that there was no printing, since printing has "divulged" "disobedience, heresy, and sects" and "libels against the best Government."[121] In 1682 John Buckner was called before Governor Culpeper and his Council for printing the laws of 1680 without a license, and he and his printer were forced to give bond of £100 "not to print anything thereafter, until his majesty's pleasure should be known."[122] In New England control of ideas was so rigid that official censorship would hardly have seemed necessary. Yet it did exist.[123] During most of the seventeenth century the clergy exercised it. After their overthrow and the secularization of government

---

[119] " 'Enquiries to the Governor of Virginia' Submitted by the Lords Commissioners of Foreign Plantations, with the Governor's Answers to Each Distinct Head," W. W. Hening, *op. cit.*, II, 517–518.

[120] See, e.g., Merle E. Curti, *The Social Ideas of American Educators,* chap. I.   [121] W. W. Hening, *op. cit.*, II, 517–518.   [122] *Loc. cit.*

[123] T. J. Wertenbaker, *op. cit.*, 238–240; J. T. Adams, *The Founding of New England,* 370–371; Clyde A. Duniway, *The Development of Freedom of the Press in Massachusetts,* 22–103.

under Andros, the power passed to the civil authorities and thereafter enforcement slacked. Indeed, in all colonies, freedom of expression generally increased during the eighteenth century.

To understand the Colonial teacher's position, one must realize the popular attitude toward intellectual matters and religious beliefs. Each of the various sects was convinced of the infallibility of its views. Men were willing to remove into a wilderness or suffer martyrdom for their convictions. Science and an age of skepticism had not yet shaken men's certainty that right and wrong, good and evil, truth and error were distinct entities that could be delineated clearly. Several American colonies originated as attempts to establish ideal commonwealths. Men felt that error must not be allowed to destroy these attempts. Ideas changed. Each generation modified or cast aside its fathers' views. Yet men discarded old beliefs, not because people doubted man's ability to know beyond question what the truth was, but because the new generation had set new truths in the place of the old or had reinterpreted the old. Authoritarianism reigned supreme. And whenever men believe in infallibility, truth and the public welfare demand that error be extirpated. At the beginning of the period John Cotton, the spiritual leader of Massachusetts, proclaimed: "For an erroneous and blind conscience, (even in fundamentall and weighty points) it is not lawfull to persecute any, untill after admonition once or twice, . . . In fundamentall and principall points of Doctrine, or Worship, the Word of God is so clear, that he cannot but be convinced in conscience of the dangerous error of his way, after once and twice admonition wisely and faithfully dispensed. And then if any one persist it is not out of conscience, but against his conscience, . . . he is subverted and sinneth, being condemned of himselfe, *viz.* of his own conscience."[124] At the end of the period President Clap

124 John Cotton, *The Controversie Concerning Liberty of Conscience in Matters of Religion* . . . , 7–8.

of Yale declared: "Tho' every Man has a Right to examine and judge for *himself,* according to Truth; yet no Man has a *Right,* in the Sight of God, to judge *wrong;* . . . And if every particular Person has a Right to judge for *himself;* then surely *publick Bodies and Communities of Men* have a Right to judge *for themselves,* concerning their own publick State and Constitution, the Qualifications of their own Ministers and Instructors; and what Doctrines they would have preach'd to themselves and to their *Posterity:* . . ."[125]

This religious authoritarianism flowed over into secular realms and affected the whole intellectual life of the Colonies. A man who evidenced a "novile disposition" was dangerous. Massachusetts forbade the import of dangerous, heretical, and seditious writings. She banished Roger Williams and Anne Hutchinson. At carts' tails she whipped women stripped to the waist through the frozen winter streets of town after town. She hanged some of the Quakers. She exiled others. She burned their writings. Extreme cases, however, are unimportant in comparison with the attitude toward life that these exaggerated phenomena symbolized. Far more significant are the hundreds who voluntarily moved on to new communities to escape restraints and the thousands who stayed at home and silenced doubts and opinions and new ideas for fear of punishment or public disapproval.

An occasional record remains to testify to the revolt of some unconventional teacher against Colonial restrictions. One New York teacher was ousted during Leisler's rebellion for his radicalism. In Connecticut another lost his school because he ventured to teach girls.[126] But generally Colonial teachers conformed.

Scarcity of schools, then, the poor quality of most of those the Colonials did have, and the inadequate training of the

[125] Thomas Clap, *A Brief History and Vindications of the Doctrines Received and Established in the Churches of New England,* 23-24.
[126] Merle E. Curti, *op. cit.,* chap. I.

teachers themselves prevented exercise of freedom by the teacher, since a poorly-trained teacher handicapped by scant equipment is incapable of being truly free even if all external control be removed. In method, the teacher had no choice in a day when a narrowly confined curriculum was specified for him, when texts, materials for writing, and other physical equipment were so scarce that he had to make the best of whatever happened to be available, and when a traditional method of teaching by memorizing, and the necessity of seeing that certain religious formulæ were mastered for a ministerial examination of the children, left slight opportunity for originality. The teacher's conduct was hedged about not only by all the petty social taboos of a small community and by his rôle as an example and moral guardian of youth but also by the restrictions that the minister-schoolmaster's religious calling, the tutor's intimacy in the family, and the indentured teacher's servile status imposed upon large classes of teachers. An extraordinary array of outside duties further limited the teacher's activities. The religious purpose of education, churchly supervision of life in general but particularly of teaching, and specific religious tests imposed additional restrictions. Finally an authoritarian attitude toward thought in any realm, an inbred habit of conformity, the desire of supporters of schools to create docile, orderly individuals who obeyed laws but never questioned them, the fear among the ruling class of restlessness that might dispossess them of their privileges, combined to leave the teacher little freedom of ideas. Besides, dread of popular disapproval and the certainty of having to move on if they did not conform made many either voluntarily go west or silence their own heresies.

Balancing these restrictive tendencies were the scarcity of teachers, which made many communities tolerate much in order to get any sort of instruction, the general ignorance of Colonials, which raised the educated teacher above the possibility of strict supervision by most of the people, and a general tendency to accept learning as learning and not inquire further into it once the teacher had been passed upon as adequate. Furthermore, one must not forget that most Colonial teachers themselves regarded their task as mere supervision of acquisition of tools like reading and writing or the hearing of memorized recitations of authoritative truth. One must remember, too, that most teachers were primarily concerned with earning a livelihood or with training children in community orthodoxies. Few teachers had ever thought of differing from conventional views. Many regarded themselves as guardians of correct thinking. The limitations, then, upon a teacher's freedom were manifold; but many of them were the restrictions of the life and thought of the Colonial community, which probably did not bear too heavily upon teachers, since most of them shared in that life and thought and helped to perpetuate it.

CHAPTER II

FREEDOM IN JEFFERSONIAN AMERICA, 1776–1830

By the time of the Revolution, a decidedly good education could be obtained in America from primary grade through college. In fact, a comparison of the leaders of that day with those of the 1930's makes one wonder about the quality of the *modern* education. But in 1776 this opportunity of learning was available to relatively few Americans. Most of it had to be acquired under tutors or in private schools beyond the general reach. Usually education still stopped with primary schools. If one happened to be poor, he could in most communities obtain an education only as pauper relief. Even as charity, it was often not available to the poor man's child. Indeed, in spite of the spread of educational facilities and the growth in the number of schools as a whole, many regions, especially in the South and West, still offered no schooling whatsoever.

Under the impetus of Revolutionary thought a demand was made for free public education for all who wished it. There is no need to trace the movement in detail. The leaders of Revolutionary liberalism provided the ideal; the years following brought minor victories here and there; and the period from 1776 to 1830 saw a great increase in the number of communities that contributed to the education of those too poor to pay fees. It took, however, the dangers of ignorance under universal manhood suffrage and the rise of a well-organized labor party in the 'twenties and 'thirties to persuade reluctant taxpayers to establish general systems of public education.

During the first years under the new federal Constitution a reaction against Revolutionary equalitarianism and idealism actually brought a halt in the spread of schools. The educational law of 1789 in Massachusetts,[1] for instance, required only towns with two hundred "Housholders" to support a grammar school; whereas the law of 1647 had required it of all towns of one hundred "Housholders."[2] This removed from the obligation of a grammar school some one hundred twenty out of the two hundred thirty towns of the state.[3] Jefferson's Virginia rejected his educational program. Later it did carry out the portion of his plan that proposed a university, but not the part providing lower schools, which democratized the whole scheme. Virginia went only so far as to empower three aldermen in each county to establish tax-supported schools— "if it shall seem expedient to the said aldermen in any year."[4] The schooling—or lack of schooling—of Abraham Lincoln was typical of that of ordinary men's children during this period in both South and West. To win educational disestablishment of the privileged classes took the same long years of agitation required for religious, political, and economic disestablishment. By 1830 New England and New York had accepted the principle of the state's paying for primary education of those who could not otherwise afford it, and a few public high schools had been established. In 1827 Massachusetts required a tax-supported high school in every town of five hundred families. Through private religious schools Pennsylvania was providing fairly general education, but this very fact retarded the movement for free public schools in that state. In the South illiteracy was general among the poorer whites. The growth of public schools was retarded by the slavery system and by the habit of

[1] *Massachusetts Session Laws*, 1788–1789, 416.

[2] *Book of the General Lavves and Libertyes Concerning the Inhabitants of the Massachusets Collected out of the Records of the General Court . . . 1647* (1648), 47.

[3] George H. Martin, *The Evolution of the Massachusetts Public School System*, 85.

[4] *Acts Passed at a General Assembly of the Commonwealth of Virginia Begun and Held at the Capitol in the City of Richmond, on Tuesday, the Eighth Day of November, One Thousand Seven Hundred and Ninety-Six*, 1–2.

making public contribution to private schools.[5] In the Western frontier states poverty often precluded even an elementary education. Yet throughout this period the ideal of state-supported primary education gained in popularity, though in this period grants of land that were often squandered, laws, and constitutional provisions requiring certain standards in education must not be taken too seriously. None the less they did provide the basis for future school systems.

School equipment had improved only slightly since Colonial times. Textbooks were now more numerous, and new ones appeared. Most of the other equipment of the modern school was still lacking. Quill pens dipped in home-made ink were used to write in copybooks homemade of folded foolscap. The paper was blotted by throwing sand on the writing. A teacher generally had to use whatever text each individual child could obtain, and this was frequently a different one for each child.

"Dame-schools" still persisted. Through the South the most prevalent school was the "old-field school," held in a log house with a chimney that smoked at one end, a door that gave entrance to light only when open, a window that let in as much cold air as light, and a long table about which children of all ages crowded with copybooks while the teacher went from one to another hearing recitations.[6]

The catechetical method was still in vogue. The pupil memorized question and answer in other subjects just as he did the lists of words in spelling. Then he recited to the teacher, who asked the proper question to which he parroted the response. It did not occur to either teacher or pupil that some questions might have more than one possible reply, or perhaps an unknown answer. There was no explanation, no discussion, no raising of problems to which the authoritative answers were

[5] Virginius Dabney, *Liberalism in the South*, 56–57; Edgar W. Knight, *Public Education in the South*, 264.

[6] "The States' Duties in Regard to Education," *De Bow's Review*, XXV (October, 1858), 419.

not known. It was not necessary to *understand* what was "learned." One lad, in recalling that his Latin text always had the English translation in a parallel column, relates how the youngsters were always advised to put their hands over the English in studying the Latin, but how instead they memorized the English and recited the translation from memory while carefully covering the English with their fingers during this "recitation." Pike's *Arithmetic* contained 360 rules without a word of explanation.[7] In many cases the teacher was not able to *explain* the things he required to be "learned," even had he seen any necessity for so doing. Discipline was rigid. If the pupil was slow, the rod freely used was the customary stimulus to better work. The arbitrariness of pedagogical method and dictatorial power of the teacher over his pupils were not conducive to freedom of thought for either pupil or teacher.

The extra-curricular duties of Colonial days[8] remained to plague teachers. Occasionally, however, teachers now felt themselves strong enough to object to these infringements upon their freedom outside the school. Frequent complaints are recorded, for instance, that teachers in Friendly communities rebelled against having to take their pupils to meeting and keep order among them during the service.[9]

Teachers were still wretchedly untrained. Some turned to teaching after they had failed at other trades. Others found it less arduous to teach school than to split rails. Many of the best schoolmasters were college students teaching only temporarily to earn the next year's fees. Constant complaints were heard of the incompetence of teachers. John H. Rice complained in 1822 that "most of the tolerably reputable and decent schools [in Virginia] are conducted by young men, whose only object in teaching is to procure money to enable them to study

[7] Arthur Train, *Puritan's Progress*, 87.   [8] See *supra*, 19–21.
[9] Louise G. and Matthew J. Walsh, *History and Organization of Education in Pennsylvania*, 30.

a more respected . . . profession."[10] The Washington-Henry Academy in Hanover County, Virginia, had to adopt a by-law that no teacher should be at the same time a farmer.[11] In Wythe County some of the "old-field" teachers were "invalids, some were slaves to drunkenness, some were too lazy to work, most of them entirely ignorant of the art of teaching, and a terror to their pupils."[12] A report on primary schools declared in 1825 that "there have been but few instances, in Virginia, of men, well-qualified for teachers of English schools, devoting their lives to that occupation; and the reason was, the salaries of English teachers were insufficient and precarious. Almost every man who possessed the qualifications necessary for a good English teacher could in some other more agreeable occupation obtain a more competent and independent livelihood."[13] A Southerner educated in this period tells that though his teacher was supposed to be skilled in Latin "he would never consent to use any other copies of the classics but those of Clark, which contained the text and an English translation in parallel columns."[14]

When in 1829 the Philadelphia workingmen investigated the schools, their committee reported that "the elementary schools were irresponsible institutions, owned by individuals, sometimes destitute of all moral character, often grossly ignorant, and always carried on solely with a view to private gain." The teacher was sometimes "ignorant, brutal, and immoral."[15] In his annual message of 1826 DeWitt Clinton declared, "With the full admission of the merits of several who now officiate in that capacity, still it must be conceded that the information

[10] Alfred J. Morrison, *The Beginnings of Public Education in Virginia, 1776–1860*, 42.   [11] *Ibid.*, 109.

[12] W. G. Repass, "Brief History of Education in Wythe County," *Virginia School Report*, 1885, 288–289.

[13] "Primary Schools," *Literary and Evangelical Magazine*, VIII (1825), 371.

[14] "The States' Duties in Regard to Education," *De Bow's Review*, XXV (October, 1858), 420.

[15] John B. McMaster, *A History of the People of the United States*, V, 361–362.

of many of the instructors of the common schools does not extend beyond rudimental education."[16] In an appeal for normal training schools in 1827, he averred, "Too many [teachers] are destitute of the requisite qualifications and perhaps no inconsiderable number are unable to teach beyond rudimental instruction."[17] After the death in 1827 of Headmaster Parker, the Kingston Academy suffered under a series of "young men fresh from New England colleges" who "merely sojourned in the village of Kingston long enough to obtain a refurnishing of the purse that they might resume studies for some professional life. . . . [They] succeeded in reducing the influence and reputation of the noted academy to a low ebb."[18] A committee appointed by the Friends of Education investigated New Jersey schools and reported:

> As to the morals and qualifications of the teachers, the committee should perhaps be silent. But the importance of the matter, and the call for information, demand of them an answer without reserve. Some of the township committees are not so particular on these points as it was wished they should be; . . . many of those holding themselves forth as teachers, are incompetent to teach, or too loose in morality to deserve employment. The teachers of some schools are of transient stay; others inconstant in their attendance; —others incompetent to teach when employed, others immoral; and some intemperate. But the committee are glad to say, that some of the teachers are stated to be what they should be, and are regarded by their employers as competent, and of good moral character.[19]

Even New England schools suffered from poor teachers. In a speech at Yale in 1816, Denison Olmsted declared: "The great defect in our school education . . . is the ignorance and incompetency of schoolmasters. Now it is a notorious fact that a great part of our public school money is expended on . . .

---

[16] Edward A. Fitzpatrick, *The Educational Views and Influence of DeWitt Clinton*, 50.   [17] *Ibid.*, 51.

[18] "The Kingston Academy," *Olde Ulster*, IX (November, 1913), 323.

[19] *The Report of the Committee Appointed at a Public Meeting of the Friends of Education, Held at the State House, Trenton, Nov. 11, 1828*, 7–8.

teachers whose geography scarcely transcends the mountains that bound their horizon; whose science is the multiplication table; and whose language, history and belle[s]-lettres are all comprised in the 'American Preceptor' and Webster's spelling book."[20] James G. Carter wrote of Massachusetts schools:

The men teachers may be divided into three classes: (1) Those who think teaching is easier and possibly a little more remunerative than common labor. (2) Those who are acquiring, or have acquired, a good education, and who take up teaching as a temporary employment, either to earn money for pressing necessities or to give themselves time to choose deliberately a regular profession. (3) Those who, conscious of weakness, despair of distinction or even the means of subsistence by other means. . . . The teachers of the primary summer schools have rarely had any education beyond what they have acquired in the very schools where they begin to teach. Their attainments, therefore, to say the least, are usually *very moderate*. But this is not the worst of it. They are often very young, they are constantly changing their employment, and consequently can have but little experience; and, what is worse than all, they never have had any direct preparation for their profession. . . . No standard of attainments is fixed, at which they must arrive before they assume the business of instruction; so that any one *keeps school,* which is a very different thing from *teaching school,* who wishes to do it, and can persuade, by herself or her friends, a small district to employ her. And this is not a very difficult matter, especially when the remuneration for the employment is so very trifling. The farce of an examination and a certificate from the minister of the town . . . amounts to no efficient check upon the obtrusions of ignorance and inexperience. . . . If a young man be moral enough to keep out of State prison, he will find no difficulty in getting approbation for a schoolmaster.[21]

With the new century, women were more frequently becoming teachers. But there was still little provision for educating women beyond the elementary school. They were necessarily, then, limited in their training. Though the great feminine

[20] Walter H. Small, *Early New England Schools,* 93.
[21] James G. Carter, *The Schools of Massachusetts in 1824* (*Old South Leaflets,* no. 135), 21, 15, 16, and 19. See also his *Letters to the Hon. William Prescott, LL.D., on the Free Schools of New England, with Remarks upon the Principles of Instruction.*

influx into the teaching profession did not come until a period when better facilities existed for women's education, still their instructing at all, in a day when higher education, if not secondary schooling, was closed to them, augmented the supply of untrained teachers.

It was during this period that the Lancastrian schools became popular. Here the older pupils taught the younger ones the rudiments of education, which they themselves had just recently acquired from the teachers. The plan had the merit of making possible elementary mass education in regions where teachers of any sort were scarce; but it also contributed to the schools a new supply of teachers who were untrained and therefore not capable of exercising real freedom.

Yet, in spite of all the handicaps of poor equipment and poor training, perhaps even because of these, the schoolmaster was free from certain restrictions that irk modern teachers. Schools were informally run. A teacher's personal activity was frightfully hedged about by the fact that he had to live in the place provided for him, indeed, often had to "board around." But, on the other hand, if the teacher could overcome the physical handicaps, he often enjoyed a freedom from interference with his actual teaching for which no modern teacher can hope. One Southerner says of the "old-field school" where he was educated:

It was a wealthy neighborhood; two of the trustees, if trustees they might be called, were worth a hundred Negroes apiece; and they had sons who were here receiving the elements, on which a liberal education was to be afterwards engrafted. They had confidence in the master, and they left everything to his discretion. They had done their part when they employed him and gave him a place to teach in. There may be exceptions to this lax method of proceeding—cases in which a real supervision is exercised, but they are only exceptions, and not the rule. The voluntary system, for the most part, terminates the care and responsibilities of the neighborhood in the settlement of the teacher.[22]

[22] "The States' Duties in Regard to Education," *De Bow's Review*, XXV (October, 1858), 421.

There were no school boards, superintendents, supervisors, or principals to dictate methods or curricula or to introduce jealousies and politics into a school system in which one teacher was the whole staff. There were no reports or records to keep. There were no schools of education to impose favorite theories upon teachers. Under these circumstances the teacher really capable of exercising freedom generally had a free field within his own classroom. As Professor Channing put it: "Given a born teacher, one can hardly conceive of a more fruitful field for the display of pedagogical talents. Undoubtedly in many a town and district there was such a teacher and the young people who came under his or her influence must have been mentally stimulated and educated in the truest sense of the word,—far beyond what they can gain in the excellent graded schools and with the admirable text-books of our own time."[23]

During the decades following the Revolution, a remarkable group of Americans were writing treatises attempting to apply the theories of eighteenth-century European liberalism to education in America. Among them were Thomas Jefferson, Noah Webster, Benjamin Rush, Du Pont de Nemours, and others less known today but equally interesting for their educational theories.[24] These men expressed views so novel and so far ahead of their times that they anticipated almost every "new" theory of the nineteenth century. In analyzing the actual school system they pointed out the poor quality of teachers and the need of better equipment. They urged universal education even for women. They advocated free schooling supported by taxes and extending through the university. In this first burst of national enthusiasm they sought a national educational system and a national university. They described pedagogical methods that sound modern indeed. Most important, however, were the concepts that underlay their educational philosophy.

---

[23] Edward Channing, *A History of the United States*, V, 243.
[24] For an illuminating study of these men see Allen O. Hansen, *Liberalism and American Education in the Eighteenth Century*.

Their theories were based upon the eighteenth century's idea of the perfectibility of man and its belief in progress. Progress and the perfecting of man required flexibility, experimentation, and an evolving society. They attacked the old concepts of fixed truth, dogma, and changelessness of established institutions. Institutions were, indeed, to be valued only for their present utility to mankind. Education must be stripped of fear and prejudice. If progress was to be attained, all customs and dogmas, however sacred, must be analyzed and cast aside when found wanting. These theories taught an ideal of service to mankind in which the schools were to have an important function. The equal right of all men to liberty and progress was stressed. Society must furnish all people with the means of subsistence and a chance for happiness. This could become possible only if the government guaranteed to every child training in both the arts and sciences. "Education," declared Robert Coram, "should not be left to the caprice, or negligence of parents, to chance, or confined to the children of wealthy citizens: it is a shame, a scandal to civilized society, that part only of the citizens should be sent to colleges and universities to learn to cheat the rest of their liberties."[25] In place of the old passing on of carefully censored authoritative pronouncements, education was to consist in analysis and research into the causes of societal evils. It was to be based on unlimited freedom of discussion. Unfortunately for those interested in intelligent functioning of democracy and freedom in teaching, the liberal idealism of these leaders of educational thought did not permeate down to the practice of the schools. Instead, as so often happens, the proposals of the theorists were smashed upon the practical difficulties of indifference of the people and of opposition from the privileged groups, who would have lost their privileges had these theorists succeeded in improving society.

More general influences of eighteenth-century liberalism did,

[25] Robert Coram, *Political Inquiries: to Which Is Added, A Plan for the General Establishment of Schools Throughout the United States* (1791), 57.

however, affect the schools. Liberal political theory reached large classes of Americans. The democratic ideals of Jefferson's Declaration of Independence became a rallying point for many who could not understand or had never heard of his plan for education in Virginia. Long political debate, criticisms of government in the years preceding the Revolution, and the destruction of many of the "loyalists" who had dictated the ideas, beliefs, and conduct of Colonial America all tended to break the power of those controlling the schools. People in general became accustomed to freer discussion and disagreement on subjects concerning which somebody's authority would once have been accepted without question. Had a well-organized school system existed in 1776, either the theories of eighteenth-century liberalism and Revolutionary America would have spread through the schools, increasing the freedom of teachers and educating a new generation, which would have prevented the Federalist reaction; or else, perhaps more probably, the ruling classes would have possessed in the schoolmasters an instrument through which they could have created an obedience to the existing order that would have saved their own privileges and prevented the Revolution itself. But with the schools disorganized as they were, the liberalism of the day could not directly affect them, though the changed general attitudes of the people did indirectly break many of the old restraints and increase the freedom of teachers.

One result of the Revolution, the breaking of the power of church establishments, did directly increase the teacher's freedom. The origins of the process of secularizing the schools reached far back into Colonial history. The Massachusetts charter of 1691 divided church and state. This secularized the schools in the eyes of the law, even though extralegally the church still controlled the teachers. The gradual dissolution of the union between church and state during the post-Revolutionary period removed a number of the official sectarian controls under which teachers had worked. Licensing by the

Bishop of London had disappeared in the Revolution itself. Many of the sectarian tests disappeared in the new constitutions. Later laws disestablished the official church—not until 1833 in Massachusetts. With these laws fell legislative sectarian tests for teachers. Even in Massachusetts ministers were deprived of their official control of schools in the laws of 1826 and 1827 which took from them the licensing power and the duty of inspecting the schools. They were now left only the obligation to "exercise their influence, and use their best endeavours" toward the educating of all children.[26] Too much importance, however, must not be attached to the removal of these legal restraints.

However much leaders like Jefferson and Adams might wish it, the concept of religious freedom was not in the mind of the ordinary citizen nor of the legislator who voted for disestablishment. This generation desired merely religious toleration. Religious restrictions on teachers as on other citizens had not been so much loosened as broadened—broadened to include in legal recognition not one sect, but all evangelical Protestant Christians. Atheists, Jews, deists, Unitarians, even Catholic Christians were still excluded from teaching and other privileges. Indeed, toleration of other evangelical sects had not come because any one sect had adopted a theory of tolerance. Each still firmly believed in its own infallibility; each would still have liked to gain sufficient power to require conformity of all heretics. But in America sects were so numerous and, after the Episcopal church fell into disrepute for disloyalty, so evenly balanced, that no one could hope to control all the others. Besides, each had suffered by the efforts of another to maintain control over it. Hence not a change in theory, but the necessities of living together amicably and the discovery that simultaneous existence without injury was actually possible brought a compromise among sects, whereby they

[26] Henry Suzzallo, *The Rise of Local School Supervision in Massachusetts*, 58–59.

agreed to let one another alone for the sake of combining to preserve religion in the state. Sectarianism remained extra-legally—in fact, with the Great Awakening at the turn of the century, was revived with new intensity. But, so far as the law went, toleration of all evangelical Christians was established, partly because certain liberal leaders wished toleration or even religious liberty, but largely because the necessities of proximity and heterogeneity of sects forced denominations, still intolerant in theory, to "tolerate" each other in practice. This was the heritage eighteenth-century liberalism left American teachers.

All this applied only to "legal" restrictions on teachers. They were still subject to all the innumerable disabilities and restraints a religiously controlled school could place upon them in practice. In the early part of this period, teachers still had to catechise children in dogma.[27] Even at the end of the period schools were still largely dominated by religious and moral purposes. New Hampshire enacted a law in 1808 requiring towns to appoint school committees to insure the "progress of literature, morality, and religion" in the schools.[28] In pleading for state funds for education in North Carolina in 1816, A. D. Murphey argued that the state must take charge of "thousands of unfortunate children [who] are growing up in perfect

[27] In 1789, for instance, a rule was adopted by the town of Boston requiring that "the several Schoolmasters instruct the children under their care, or cause them to be instructed, in the Assemblie's Catechism, every Saturday, unless the Parents request that they may be taught any particular catechism of the religious Society to which they belong." Henry F. Jenks, *Catalogue of the Boston Public Latin School . . . with an Historical Sketch*, 290. In 1803 Madison, New Jersey, adopted a regulation requiring its teachers to "catechise the children at least once a week." Fred B. Bardon, *A Historical Recapitulation, the Public Schools of Madison, N. J.*, 11. In 1810 Dorchester, Massachusetts, adopted a ruling that "a part of Saturdays shall be spent in the recitation of the Catechism; and the master shall hear the Children in that Catechism which they shall severally bring with a written request from the Parents." William A. Mowry, "Historical Address," *Dorchester Celebration, 250th Anniversary of the Establishment of the First Public School in Dorchester, June 22, 1889*, 48.

[28] *The Public Laws of the State of New-Hampshire Passed at a Session of the General Court, Begun and Holden at Concord, on the Twenty-Third Day of November, 1808*, 34.

ignorance of their moral and religious duties."[29]   Although
sectarian dogma ceased to find a place in public-school curricula,[30] and, in fact, many states now passed laws forbidding
the teaching of "any religious tenets peculiar to any Christian
sect,"[31] still non-sectarian religion continued to bulk large in
public school programs. In 1789 the town of Boston "Voted,
That it be the indispensable duty of the several School-Masters,
daily to commence the duties of their office by prayer and reading a portion of the sacred Scriptures, at the hour assigned for
opening the School in the morning; and close the same in the
evening with prayer."[32]   Most schools expected this of their
teachers, though they did not all draw up formal rules.[33]   In
private religious schools the creedal training, too, remained.
Even in public schools teachers still faced the sectarian tests
and obligations that popular opinion can impose.

Control of education always had been and remained local.
Many of the restraints of Colonial days had been inherent in
the community life without any necessity of legal aid in en-
forcing them. These remained. An Episcopal teacher stood
little chance of employment in a Congregational community
in New England or a Presbyterian settlement in the Southern

[29] Charles L. Coon, *The Beginnings of Public Education in North Carolina,*
I, 108.

[30] For instance, the prospectus of Livingston County High School declares:
"The moral obligations which Nature and Revelation impose, are clear and
unanswerable, and ought to be inculcated by every instructor, who has any
regard to the character and welfare of his pupils. . . . As instructors, appointed
to the office of training up . . . young men, from families who have adopted
the creeds of various religious sects . . . we conceive it would be straying far,
far, beyond the limits our duty prescribes, to exert the influence which our situation gives us, in changing or affecting anyway the religious creeds of our
pupils." *View of the Livingston County High School: of Temple-Hill: Gene-
seo . . .,* 11–12.

[31] *Ohio Session Laws, 1814–1815,* 136; Edward A. Miller, "The History of
Educational Legislation in Ohio from 1803 to 1850," *Ohio Archæological and
Historical Quarterly,* XXVII (January, 1918), 103; Ellwood P. Cubberley, *Edu-
cation in the United States,* 175.   [32] H. F. Jenks, *op. cit.,* 289.

[33] See, e.g., the "Rules and Regulations to be Observed by the Teachers of
the Public Schools in Dorchester, 1810," William A. Mowry, "Historical Address," *Dorchester Celebration,* 48; "Rules for the Regulation of the School"
at Madison, New Jersey, F. B. Bardon, *op. cit.,* 11.

mountains; nor could a Presbyterian or Congregationalist hope to teach in a stronghold of old Anglicanism. Interferences of civil officials with teachers in a community of dissenters from the established religion were now removed. In certain regions, particularly cities, where sects were intermingled, public schools now escaped sectarian tests for teachers. In fact, in some such places where the multiplicity of sects brought at once a demand for desectarianizing of schools and an unwillingness completely to secularize them, a solution was found in the establishment of a "school society" essentially religious and Protestant, to which control of the schools was given. This practice, followed in Connecticut and New York City, left the schools neither free nor public, but religious though non-sectarian. For the average teacher, however, in a community that was religiously homogeneous, religious toleration probably meant little if he happened not to belong to the dominant sect. It took decades more of struggle before religious control of schools was finally broken, and, as will appear later,[34] it still persists to restrict teachers in large parts of America. But the change wrought in this period was none the less one major step toward religious freedom for the schools.

Another development of post-Revolutionary decades, the founding of numerous "academies," increased the freedom of teachers. Later the academies developed restrictions peculiar unto themselves. Even in the beginning they were subject to many of the general restraints of their environment. Some of them, established to perpetuate religious control in a day when public schools were becoming secularized, were closely controlled in the interest of one sect. But more often academies were founded to supply a local desire for schooling that was neither ecclesiastical nor sectarian. A growing and prosperous middle class demanded education for sons not intending to enter the professions. These men were ready to finance their

[34] See H. K. Beale, *Are American Teachers Free?* 208–224, 225–238, 245–248, 424–435, 447, 590; *infra,* 202–205, 207–218, 241–242.

own children's education but were as yet unwilling to pay for free public schools for poor men's children. The solution was the academy. These institutions were usually established by the benevolence of a wealthy man like John Phillips or through the enterprise of some individual teacher who saw an opportunity to earn a livelihood. In either case, academies were likely to be free from sectarian and ecclesiastical control.[35] The general purpose still included religious and moral training, but this did not overbalance all other desiderata. Besides, these schools began to humanize religion into moral philosophy, ethical conduct, and Christian character. The Bible was still read; religious exercises were still held. In fact, most prospectuses of academies right down through the nineteenth century included an assurance that the religious needs of pupils would be properly looked after with religious instruction, required prayers, and attendance at church on the Sabbath. Thus the Round Hill School of Northampton announced in 1823: "As the fear of God is the most sacred principle of action, there is none which should be developed with more care. Each day will begin and end with devotional exercises. The Lord's day must be sacredly observed, and the exercises of public worship constantly attended."[36] This was, however, more a duty of the academy *in loco parentis* in an era of daily family devotions than a primary purpose of schooling. The chief function of colleges, and therefore of schools preparatory for college, was still training for the ministry. By catering to a group who probably would not enter college, the new academies were freed from the curricular restrictions imposed by college entrance requirements and, therefore, much earlier than the colleges themselves, broke away from strictly classical or eccle-

[35] In a study of educational legislation in Ohio, for instance, Edward A. Miller found that of 171 secondary schools chartered between 1803 and 1850, only 21 were "more or less denominational in control or in sympathy, as indicated by the act of incorporation or the name." E. A. Miller, *op. cit.*, 95–96, 102.

[36] Joseph H. Coit, *Memorials of St. Paul's School*, 13–14.

siastical training and broadened their curricula to secular subjects, even to history.

When Phillips Academy at Andover was established in 1778 the only religious restrictions were a general statement that its *first* and *principal* object was the "promotion of true PIETY and VIRTUE,"[37] and a summary of correct Protestant Christian doctrine that instructors should use as a guide in their teaching.[38] In the constitution of Phillips Exeter Academy drawn up in 1782 the only religious requirements were that the principal should be "a member of a Church of Christ, in compleat standing," professing "sentiments" similar to those of the founder expressed in the constitution, and that trustees and teachers must all be Protestant Christians.[39] These were religious but not sectarian restraints. Indeed, to avoid clerical control and the evils of localism, Phillips provided that "a major part" of the trustees of Phillips Andover should be laymen and non-residents of Andover.[40] At his request the trustees appointed an instructor in theology at Phillips Exeter, but, when the minister chosen declined the appointment, the position remained vacant until 1817. Then for twenty-two years a course in theology was offered, but since 1839 no regular class instruction in religion has been required.[41] Both academies offered, even in the early days, what was more nearly a secular education than could be obtained in most secondary schools, even though it was secular education with religious, moral, and ethical purposes.

Nevertheless, the evidences of secularization in academies must not be exaggerated. The religious element was important there, as it was in life all about the academy. Even history, when it *was* added to the curriculum, was introduced to point

---

[37] *The Constitution of Phillips Academy in Andover* (1817), 12.

[38] *Ibid.*, 11.

[39] "The Constitution of Phillips Exeter Academy," in Laurence M. Crosbie, *The Phillips Exeter Academy, A History*, 307, 309.

[40] *The Constitution of Phillips Academy in Andover* (1817), 5.

[41] Ralph H. Bowles, "The Phillips Exeter Academy," *New England Magazine*, new series, XXVIII (July, 1903), 603–604.

out religious object lessons.[42] The by-law of Amherst Academy adopted in 1838 was typical of most academies in requiring all instructors to be not only "persons of good moral character" but "firmly established in the faith of the Christian religion, the doctrines of which they shall inculcate as well by example as precept."[43] In almost none of these schools could a Catholic, or deist, or atheist, or Jew obtain a position. Schools, moreover, that adopted regulations requiring students to attend daily prayers and services on the Sabbath expected all teachers not only to do likewise but to be of such "Christian character" that they would do so without a requirement. Even so, these new academies were much freer from religious control than were most American schools up to this time.

A member of a radical sect had little chance of getting or keeping a position in any school, public or private. It was during these years that Unitarianism grew up in New England as that section's tardy response to the influence of eighteenth-century liberalism. A heated feud arose. Orthodox Congregationalists looked upon the new faith as dangerously atheistical. In communities where Unitarianism had not become popular, Unitarians had slight possibility of becoming teachers. Employment of three Harvard-trained instructors in the Livingston County High School called forth a memorial in which "sundry inhabitants" begged "leave respectfully to represent, that, coming as they do from a college which has long been known to the Christian community as the fountain of the most destructive heresy, with professions of neutrality in relation to the fundamental doctrines of the Christian religion, which facts are accompanied with a train of circumstances which renders it extremely probable, if not morally certain, that they are deeply imbued with, and highly in favor of unitarian sentiments, we cannot, consistently with our duty to God, to the

[42] William F. Russell, *The Early Teaching of History in the Secondary Schools of New York and Massachusetts*, 14-15.
[43] Frederick Tuckerman, *Amherst Academy, 1814-1861*, 97.

community in which we live, and to the youth of our country either directly or indirectly support or encourage the school, while under their auspices; as we conscientiously believe, in so doing, we should be instrumental in disseminating principles which strike directly at the root of the faith, as held by *all the Christian* denominations of this country."[44] The appointment of Henry Ware to a chair of Theology at Harvard in 1805 caused a protest that fairly shook the state. When they had the chance, Unitarians retaliated in discrimination, as when they almost prevented the granting of a charter to Amherst College in 1825. Even now, more than a century after these stormy controversies, a Unitarian is seriously handicapped, if not disqualified, in getting a teaching position in many American communities.

In this period, while the average of teachers was still pretty low, more adequate educational facilities made it possible for the better schools, particularly in New England, to require higher qualifications of teachers. This meant in these more fortunate communities a rigid requirement of character. Most of the school prospectuses assured parents that their children would receive excellent training, not only by precept but by example, in "virtue and morality." Improvement of morals was an aim of all schooling. High moral character and exemplary conduct, under whatever definition the school or community gave those ever-changing concepts, were therefore demanded of teachers whenever the supply of qualified persons permitted any demands at all. In fact, a teacher's reputation for exemplary conduct was likely to be much more highly valued than intellectual qualifications. Laws often dealt with the matter. Thus a New Hampshire act required of teachers not only "a certificate from some able and reputable English grammar school-master, and learned minister . . . that he or she is well qualified to teach such school," but also "a certificate from the selectmen or minister of the town or parish to which he or she belongs, that he or she sustains a good moral character."[45] The New York Assembly in 1812 passed a measure declaring: "The respectability of every school must necessarily depend on the character of the master. To entitle a teacher to assume the control of a school, he should be endowed with the requisite literary qualifications not only, but with unimpeachable character. . . . As an impediment to bad men getting into the schools, as teachers, it is made the duty of the town-inspectors strictly to enquire into the moral and literary qualifications of those who may be candidates for the place of teacher."[46] In Virginia there was as late as 1829 a demand that the General Assembly supply qualified teachers "whose moral habits are known to the people or to the school commissioners."[47]

Secularization not only loosed the ecclesiastical hold on teachers and broadened the curriculum; it also created a keen interest in politics, which led to a new sort of restriction upon teachers. In the years preceding the Revolution, growing material prosperity, the rise of a class whose interests were primarily economic, the gradual burning out of the original religious zeal of the Reformation, all tended to create new secular interests. As a result, the earnestness and the argumentative bent of our Colonial ancestors were turned into political channels. Feeding upon the litigation caused by new economic interests, lawyers, only recently become respectable, grew into a position of power and importance once monopolized by clergymen and magistrates and gave a political and legalistic cast to popular controversies. Newly founded newspapers and printing presses helped carry the discussion to the people. Economic difficulties of the upper classes appeared to rise out of imperial restrictions, which could be best met by political changes in colonial government and imperial relations. Poor

[45] *New Hampshire Session Laws,* 1808, 34.
[46] February 14, 1812, *Journal of the Assembly of the State of New York,* 105–106.
[47] A. J. Morrison, *op. cit.,* 12.

men felt that economic hardships of the lower classes could be remedied by the attainment of a share of political power. Repudiation of debts and inflation of the currency could be won if only debtors could get the franchise and outvote their creditors. The theories of eighteenth-century liberalism, too, took a political form. This predominance of political discussion, then, at first tended to free teachers, like every one else, from the dominance of religion. But as interest in political disputes became more intense and as factions began to crystallize, political soundness came to seem as important as religious orthodoxy once had.

Men willing to die in the Revolution for their loyalty to Great Britain or for their devotion to freedom from imperial restrictions and men willing to fight to retain political privileges they monopolized or to win political rights they did not possess were unwilling to allow teachers any influence with their children, if those teachers did not hold correct views on subjects of this vital importance. Most teachers escaped notice because they taught such elementary subjects and counted so little in the community anyway that their opinions were neither asked nor expressed. Many others shared the feelings of the rest of the community. Yet "patriot" teachers suffered in loyalist neighborhoods and "loyalists" among patriots. A large proportion of the educated men of the Colonies were loyalists. In the Colonies where the Church of England was dominant, teachers were likely to be either clergymen of that Church or men trained and sent out by its Society for the Propagation of the Gospel. On the whole, these men officially connected with the Church of England were loyalists. The back country, which was usually "patriot," was at best only poorly supplied with teachers. Therefore a large proportion of the ablest teachers were neutral or loyal to England in the struggle. Many of these men were forced to keep silent and, often against their wills, to take oaths of loyalty to the patriot cause. Most states passed laws establishing patriot test oaths. Only one of these, that passed by New Jersey on October 6, 1777, specifically mentioned teachers; but the others applied to all civil and military authorities or to all males above a given age.[48] These oaths were by no means universally applied, though they remained a whip ready to be used against "loyalists" wherever a community desired to apply them. If loyalist teachers refused to swear allegiance to the Revolutionary government or if they publicly voiced their loyalty to England, they suffered financial or even bodily harm or were driven out of the country, as was President Cooper of Columbia, who fled over the college fence, half dressed, finally to escape to a British sloop. Wherever Committees of Safety functioned efficiently, little freedom was allowed to the teacher who was known to remain loyal to Great Britain. During and after the Revolution thousands of citizens were driven out of the country. Laws were passed suppressing freedom of speech. Other legislation quarantined, disfranchised, or banished loyalists, removed them from office, and confiscated their goods.[49] Since so large a proportion of educated men were loyalists there were, of course, teachers among these who suffered.

Yet after all, the interested population of the Colonies was so evenly divided between "loyalist" and "patriot" causes, and so large a portion of the people were "neutral" or indifferent, that interference with men's convictions was slight indeed in comparison with the vigorous suppression of dissent exercised during the World War. Large numbers of communities did go on about their business without supporting either side in the conflict. Though much pressure was put upon the Friends, and some arrests were made, Quaker teachers did maintain positions of "neutrality" and non-participation, even to the extent of refusing to use Continental money because it would aid the war, and yet were undisturbed to a degree that would have been impossible in 1917–1918. In the attacks upon "loyalists"

[48] Claude H. Van Tyne, *The Loyalists in the American Revolution*, 318–326.
[49] *Ibid.*, 327-341.

after the war was over, it was the property of loyalists that suffered most. Teachers as teachers were seldom singled out for attack. Where they suffered restraint or penalty it was as members of the old ruling class or as men of property, not as teachers. Since schoolmasters, as we have seen, were not wealthy or powerful or leaders in most communities, but usually obscure persons, they probably often escaped notice. In the absence of records one cannot know just what rôle they did play in the Revolution.

Our own Revolution was followed by the French Revolution and the importation of its "dangerous" and "atheistical" ideas. American parties formed partly around sympathy for and fear of French radicalism. In Federalist strongholds no teacher with dangerous French opinions was tolerated; in certain Republican centers a Federalist teacher's "pro-British," "monarchical" views were just as quickly suppressed. The French had always been regarded by many Americans as "infidels" and "free thinkers." Harvard, for instance, added a course in the French language and literature in 1787, and then during strong anti-French feeling allowed it to lapse from 1798 to 1806 until the students petitioned to have it restored. In 1798 a dialogue in French was dropped from the commencement program lest the sound of French create disorder. That year, too, the Harvard Overseers refused a proposed degree to Elbridge Gerry.[50] The violence and radicalism of the French Revolution struck terror into the hearts of conservative men all over the world. Americans who controlled schools and governments were still essentially aristocratic in the early 'nineties. It was only recently that Harvard College had ceased ranking men in each class according to their social standing.[51] The franchise and other political rights were still denied to the majority of men. Americans were divided into classes socially and economically as well as politically. Alexander Hamilton

[50] Samuel E. Morison, *Three Centuries of Harvard, 1636–1936*, 185–186.
[51] E. W. Knight, *Education in the United States*, 81.

believed that "All communities divide themselves into the few and the many. The first are the rich and well born, the other the mass of the people. . . . The people are turbulent and changing; they seldom judge or determine right." "Give, therefore," he pleaded, "to the first class a distinct, permanent share in the government."[52] He accepted the Constitution only because nothing better could be obtained. What he really wanted was a monarchy. Hamiltonian views in these days were in the ascendancy. Federalist leaders who controlled the country had no intention of surrendering economic privileges or risking them through yielding their political power to the people. *Egalité* and *fraternité* were dangerous doctrines that would destroy the very foundations of the American social order. *Liberté* had served well enough as a rallying cry against Great Britain so long as at home it remained a theoretical generalization. Yet men who had never taken Jefferson's doctrines seriously began to fear even liberty when ordinary men about them under the stimulus of the French Revolution began wishing to carry it to its logical conclusions. In the Constitution the conservatives had won a victory against the consequences of French theory. For the first twelve years they held control which they used in an attempt to prevent the spread of these "dangerous" and "subversive" doctrines.

Besides, in the 'eighties and 'nineties a great political battle was being waged in practical politics between those who believed in rule of "the rich and the well-born" and those who were trying to work out practical applications of the idealism of the Revolution in a new democratic society. Many men, some of them numbered among our most devoted patriots and greatest leaders, sincerely believed that the spread of these Revolutionary doctrines would destroy all that was good in the social and political order. Other equally public-spirited and devoted leaders believed that the future welfare and develop-

[52] June 18, 1787, *The Records of the Federal Convention of 1787* (Max Farrand, ed.), I, 299.

ment of the nation depended upon the acceptance and application of these same theories. The quarrel was bitter. Harsh names were used. The conservatives had obtained the adoption of the Constitution through minority control, and, as first drawn up before the Amendments were added, it was intended not only to protect property of the "rich and well-born" but to reserve to them political control that would hold the masses in the subordinate position to which Colonial education had sought to accustom them. In the end the conservative Federalists went to such extremes that they passed a vigorous sedition act to punish any one who so much as criticized an officer of the Government. Here, then, is an early American struggle between an old and accepted order and new and radical ideas. The conservatives did all in their power to suppress the "subversive" doctrines. "Atheist," "traitor," "destroyer of society" were shouted with all sincerity at the advocates of the new ideas. In opposing Jeffersonian rule, Theodore Dwight, brother of Yale's President, in a Fourth of July oration declared that the purpose of democracy is "to destroy every trace of civilization in the world and to force mankind back to a savage state. . . . We have a country governed by blockheads, and knaves; the ties of marriage . . . are destroyed; our wives, and our daughters are thrown into the stews; . . . Can the imagination paint any thing more dreadful on this side hell?"[53] This was not a description of Communist rule conjured up in 1920 but a prediction of the fate of America under democracy. Society was doomed, then, if these "dangerous" Jeffersonian doctrines were not suppressed. They were not suppressed but grew and blossomed into American democracy. Today men in control of schools, many of them sincere and patriotic individuals, are trying to suppress other new ideas as "dangerous" and "subversive" in the name of the very "de-

[53] Theodore Dwight, *An Oration, Delivered at New-Haven on the 7th of July, A.D. 1801, before the Society of the Cincinnati, for the State of Connecticut, Assembled to Celebrate the Anniversary of American Independence,* 20 and 29.

mocracy" that their ideological progenitors of the 1790's opposed as destructive of civilization. In comparisons between the social and political background of schools in the 1790's and the 1920's, there is appetizing food for thought.

Unfortunately, records of the effect upon schoolmasters of this controversy and desire for repression have not been preserved. It is certain, however, that in a period of such intense feeling, teachers were affected. Many of them undoubtedly shared the views of their communities. Many others conformed rather than invite trouble. What happened to the others can only be guessed. In general, however, in other fields of activity, expression of unpopular political opinion and criticism of the existing order was, in spite of the bitterness of feeling, freer than in America of the 1920's.

With the coming to power of Jefferson and the Democratic Republicans, America entered upon a period when discussion was unusually free. Local pressures and unofficial restrictions still persisted, of course, and religious control of education was by no means over, but Jefferson did have thousands of followers who devotedly believed in the principle of government that he laid down in his Inaugural when he said: "If there be any among us who would wish to dissolve this Union or to change its republican form, let them stand undisturbed as monuments of the safety with which error of opinion may be tolerated where reason is left free to combat it."[54] War is a certain test of a people's actual belief in their generalizations about freedom. Lip service is always given to liberty in peace-time, especially in spheres of activity where no vital issue is involved. In war freedom usually breaks down and most people find that their devotion to liberty does not withstand the stress and emotionalism of national combat. It is significant that criticism of the Government and opposition to war were freely and generally expressed throughout the War of 1812, as they were later during the Mexican conflict, when Abraham Lincoln introduced

[54] *The Writings of Thomas Jefferson* (Memorial ed., 1903), III, 319.

into Congress a resolution opposing the war in which his country was engaged. The people must indeed have believed in the right and wisdom of free speech, for they permitted and indulged in free discussion and criticism of the Government in 1812–1814, while that Government was engaged in armed conflict with a powerful nation that was invading its soil. Again no records of teachers' experiences remain, but, in this heyday of American freedom teachers must have been affected by the general public attitude.

Local pressures and restraints that public opinion imposes operated as strongly as ever. To them was added, as in Colonial times, the desire of those in power who helped establish schools to make them bulwarks of the *status quo.*[55] In South Carolina Governor Middleton urged upon the Legislature of 1811 "a system of general instruction," because it was "essential to the preservation of our political institutions."[56] In North Carolina, where this period saw real progress in education, Governor Smith urged elementary schools so that "the superiority of their political privileges should be infused into every citizen from their [*sic*] earliest infancy, so as to produce an enthusiastic attachment to their own country, and ensure a jealous support of their own constitution, laws and government."[57] It was this same idea of training "the people" to respect the established order that Governor Branch had in mind when, in 1818, he urged public support for education because "it is in this way, & this alone, that our Republican institutions can be perpetuated, or that radical changes can be effected in the morals and manners of the people."[58] In 1824 Governor Holmes was urging educational appropriations because "knowledge, well and generally diffused amongst every class of our citizens . . . will enable them to resist all innovations of Demagogues or

[55] See, e.g., Merle E. Curti, *The Social Ideas of American Educators,* chaps. II, III.   [56] E. W. Knight, *Public Education in the South,* 130.
[57] Benjamin Smith, Message on Education, *House Journal,* 1811, quoted in C. L. Coon, *op. cit.,* I, 80.
[58] *Journal of the House of Commons of North Carolina,* 1818, 8.

ambitious men, whose views to the constitution are inimical or subversive."[59] Governor Clinton urged education as a cure for the restlessness and disorder that pauperism brought in its train. "Half the amount," he said, "which passes from the hand of benevolence through the idle pauper to augment the funds of tippling houses, would if employed in the support of Sunday schools, free, and charity schools, . . . in a short time banish pauperism from our vicinity." This was quoted in the *Virginia Herald* in support of public education in Virginia.[60] Men who established schools for this purpose of instilling obedience to things as they were into "the people" and removing the disorders of pauperism would not approve teachers who inculcated criticism of that "republican form" of government. Nor would they tolerate teachers who aroused economic discontent that would lead "the people" to take up "the innovations of Demagogues or ambitious men." The liberal tenets of pure Jeffersonianism were, then, offset by this desire to bulwark the *status quo* with schools that would train men to appreciate "the superiority of political privileges" that denied them any voice in government unless they had paid public taxes, that permitted them to vote for state senators only if they had a fifty-acre freehold, and that forbade them to hold office unless they were land-owning, white, Protestant, fundamentalist Christians.[61]

[59] Gabriel Holmes, Message on Education, *House Journal,* 1824, quoted in C. L. Coon, *op. cit.,* I, 217.

[60] William A. Maddox, *The Free School Idea in Virginia before the Civil War,* 33.

[61] See the Constitution of North Carolina adopted in 1776. In 1835 the Constitution permitted non-Protestant fundamentalist Christians to hold office. Not until 1856 was the property qualification for voting for senators removed. The qualifications for officeholding remained until 1868. For additional evidence of the desire to bulwark the existing order through the instrumentality of the schools, see M. E. Curti, *op. cit.,* chaps. II and III.

Chapter III

THE RISE OF EVANGELICISM AND DEMOCRACY, 1800–1840

During the first four decades of the nineteenth century two phenomena of fundamental importance to American life and culture were developing—evangelicism and democracy. Both have profoundly affected American education. Certain basic concepts of each have continued to our own day to affect the whole problem of freedom in teaching.

Religion, as we have seen, had been a powerful motive in America from the beginning. Enthusiasm had waned in the late seventeenth and early eighteenth century but had been revived by the Great Awakening of the 1730's and 1740's. Then had come another lapse when politics held public attention. With the new century there now came a Great Revival, which took up the work of Edwards, Wesley, and Whitefield and once more aroused religious enthusiasm among the masses. The Church of England had never stirred America. It belonged to the old Catholic tradition that required conformity but no enthusiasm. It had merely provided a badge of respectability. An important reason for the success of the American cause in the Revolution was a revolt of the lower classes against the hierarchical control of the Church of England. In New England, Puritanism had controlled the state but had never won the devotion of all the people. The men who counted and who left records were Puritans. But in religion as in politics there had been aristocratic control; great numbers of the people had been excluded from church membership as from citizenship.[1] The theological disputations of New England Puritanism could

[1] There is good reason to believe that of the thousands of servants and other ordinary men who in history are inarticulate a goodly portion were indifferent to religion. See, for instance, the testimony of Thomas Lechford in *Plain Dealing: or, Newes from New-England* (1642).

hardly have appealed to ignorant men and thousands of Americans were both ignorant and poor. Nor could the ritualistic formalism of the Church of England win the democratic masses of a frontier community. Alongside the larger official Protestant denominations had grown dissenting sects, whose roots went back to Wyclif and Lollardism and the English dissenting tradition that had been important in fourteenth-century England before the continental Protestant Reformation. The Quakers and Baptists, the Pilgrims of Plymouth, and the Rhode Island come-outers had belonged to this English-bred dissenting tradition of the British lower classes. Then in the American frontier environment there had grown up, in the mid-eighteenth century under Edwardsian emotionalism, a native American revivalism opposed by the traditional dissenters, Baptists and Quakers alike. This really reached the masses. Even Calvinist Scotch Presbyterians who began to arrive in numbers during the Edwardsian and Wesleyan awakening were affected in their American environment by its influence. It was a combination in the pioneer background of Edwardsian emotionalism and the old dissenting tradition that, under the enthusiasm of the great revival movement of about 1800, blossomed into evangelicism as the nineteenth century knew it.[2]

The growing power of these dissenting sects among the poorer people had helped create the American Revolution. Methodism now spread over America like a prairie fire. The Baptists won converts by hundreds of thousands. New sects like the Campbellites sprang up. Great camp-meeting revivals were held all over the country. Itinerant preachers of great eloquence and physical endurance rode up and down the back country exhorting common men to repent. Less emphasis was put upon the church and more upon the Bible and the individual's following it. Here in this new dissenting-revivalistic

[2] Discussions with John M. Mecklin, professor of sociology at Dartmouth College; J. M. M. to H. K. B., Feb. 27, 1934. See Thomas C. Hall, *The Religious Background of American Culture* and John M. Mecklin's excellent study, *The Story of American Dissent.*

type of Protestantism was a form of emotional religion of the masses that profoundly affected American life.

This newer, more popular species of religion indirectly aided the spread of education. One feature of the movement was the appearance of Sunday schools. In England, the place of their origin, Sunday schools began as efforts to teach the poor not only religious tenets but the reading and writing necessary to comprehending religious doctrine. In America they originally served this same purpose, though here, where the public-school movement was beginning to reach the masses, they were from the beginning more purely religious schools than in England. Even in America, however, they promoted general education because interest could be aroused in providing religious instruction for children whose secular education was being neglected. Then many a community was convinced of the need of weekday schooling because the establishment of a Sunday school impressed it with the ignorance of the poor.[3] Evangelicism aided education, too, by creating denominational schools and colleges all through the newer regions, where it was strong.

Evangelicism thus helped in the spread of education. It has rendered other incalculable services to American culture. In communities and among classes that the more intellectual older sects could not reach evangelical religion brought comfort and sympathy into hard and dreary lives. On the frontier it served as the rallying point of respectability and decency, and it aided in bringing order and morality out of the roughness and turbulence of that environment. It softened cruelties and asperities of the frontier into humanity and kindliness. In these evangelical churches, long after the vanishing of the frontier, centered whatever cultural or esthetic values small communities might afford. Many an American in his childhood knew no other music than what he heard at church, saw no

[3] Virginius Dabney, *Liberalism in the South*, 56; Charles A. and Mary R. Beard, *The Rise of American Civilization*, I, 495–496; Frank P. Graves, *A History of Education in Modern Times*, 69; William A. Maddox, *The Free School Idea in Virginia before the Civil War*, 31–32.

other attempts at art than what the church offered, first discovered literature there, acquired there most of his ethical and
moral standards, and there received his first stimulus to spiritual or cultural growth. Even today in thousands of communities an evangelical church not only is the center of social
life but represents all that is best in the community.

Nevertheless, in spite of all that America owes to it, evangelicism has been a great force in restraint and denial of freedom.
The old dissenting tradition and native American revivalism
encouraged new ideas, nonconformity, and radicalism. Between them they gave to the evangelical movement its democratic tendencies, its new sects, its enthusiasm, its appeal to the
common man. But, as the evangelical sects grew more powerful and respectable, the influence of the dissenting tradition
waned, and the various denominations developed rigid dogmas
and became bulwarks of opposition to change. It is in this
form that they cast their shadows down the whole length of
the century. The emotionalism of evangelicism has implanted
in generations of Americans an emotional rather than an intellectual approach to important problems. In its early days it
often openly opposed intelligence and education. The Primitive
Baptists, for instance, disapproved even Sunday schools and
theological seminaries. By many of the early Primitive leaders
ignorance was regarded as a virtue, and education was frowned
upon because God did not need learning to teach the truth to
his people, and because inspiration came more readily to ignorant
than to educated preachers. Though other sects did not go so
far as the Primitive Baptists, there was a general feeling that
education beyond an ability to read the Scriptures was not
necessary to godliness and that too much learning often proved
a device of the Devil. Most members of evangelical sects would
not maintain this thesis today; but the evangelical background
in which millions of Americans have grown up has unconsciously given them a certain distrust of education as opposed to
virtue.

Furthermore, the very religious devotion and enthusiasm of the evangelical sects have tended to make them intolerant of those who differ from them. Their devotion to the Bible as the source of all that is good has developed in them a habit of acceptance of authority which extends to all spheres of life. Not only in religious matters do they live by authoritarianism but in secular matters, too, so strong has become this habit of thought. Therefore, evangelicism has tended to oppose critical analysis, discussion, questioning, reasoning, thinking. The important consideration has been what authority says on a subject. Habits of thought so fundamental as this sink deep and are passed on from one generation to another through very early training, until later schooling can overcome them only with great difficulty. The authority to which evangelical Christians turned was the authority given by God in an inspired book hundreds of years before their day. Hence the great aim of life was not to seek new authority but to preserve the old, to understand its commands and to learn to live by them. New ideas were inevitably heretical unless they arose out of the Bible itself. Evangelicism has trained men to distrust innovation, and, since thinking inevitably leads to new ideas, to distrust intelligence.

Thus, although much of the humanitarianism of the modern world has come from the social teachings of Christianity as espoused by the evangelical sects, yet there has been among the most devoted evangelical Christians a tendency to accept war, poverty, human suffering, and other social evils as the will of God, and therefore not to join in reforms and new causes that the social teachings of Jesus might otherwise make them support.

Since the evangelical denominations acquired great power with the coming of democracy, politicians learned to cater to them and educated men to bow to their superior power. The result has been a tendency on the part of Americans to place great emphasis upon emotional catchwords and beliefs without analyzing them or really believing in them. Educational institutions have always had to conform to the attitudes of the evangelical sects.[4] Schools founded through religious zeal have done so gladly.

Though evangelicism as a religion has lost its hold in recent years, still its mental habits and stereotypes have become a part of American psychology. John Dewey put it thus: "The intensity of evangelical life toned down, and the asperities of dogmatic creeds softened. But the association of the church with the moral and the more elevated social interests of the community remained. The indirect power of the church over thought and expression increased as its direct power waned. The more people stopped going to church, the more important it became to maintain the standards for which the church stood. As the frontier ceased to be a menace to orderly life, it persisted as a limit beyond which it was dangerous and unrespectable for thought to travel."[5] It is a startlingly significant fact that, where evangelical religion in its older forms still holds sway over the mass of the people, there illiteracy is greatest, schools are most inadequate, the teacher's freedom is most circumscribed, and the locally trained teacher himself feels the least desire for freedom.

It was during the early nineteenth century, too, that democracy accumulated sufficient strength to sweep Jackson into the Presidency in 1829. Without the parallel growth of democracy, the American school system could not have developed. The working man had the power to demand the schools he wanted only after he obtained the right to vote. Wealthy men who had formerly opposed taxation for schools saw that democracy could function intelligently only if the new electorate could be educated—and perhaps properly indoctrinated—in schools. Poor men, where they were well enough organized to make

[4] For their efforts to control education in early nineteenth-century Virginia see Sadie Bell, *The Church, the State, and Education in Virginia*, 205 ff.

[5] John Dewey, "The American Intellectual Frontier," *New Republic*, XXX (May 10, 1922), 304.

their newly acquired votes count, felt that only through education could they acquire the wisdom necessary to exercise
their newly won power for their own protection. Poor men,
too, desired education for the economic and social advantages
it would give them. As political democracy became a reality,
men desired social democracy also. Social democracy could be
guaranteed only by removal of the educational distinctions
that inevitably created classes as long as schooling remained a
privilege of the wealthy. Liberty itself and the very democracy
that had been won could be preserved, men felt, only through
mass education. Thus Charlestown Academy in Virginia was
established "to encourage learning and diffuse knowledge" because these were the "safeguard of liberty."[6] In North Carolina Governors Williams, Turner, Alexander, and Miller urged
general education because "with enlightened minds, and the
consequent love of freedom, . . . [our posterity] will never
cease to be free"; because "Education is the mortal enemy to
arbitrary governments"; because "[without it] the duration of
their liberties will be precarious"; because "when the sources
of information are confined to a few, it may have a tendency
to introduce into society an order of men, who . . . may be too
apt to imbibe the idea, that the people were made for them
and not they for the people"; because "if the wealthy alone be
admitted into the temple of science, the most dangerous species
of aristocracy may be apprehended, from the union of two
such powerful agents, as wealth and talents."[7] Governor Clinton in New York declared, "A virtuous and enlightened man
can never submit to degradation; and a virtuous and enlightened people will never breathe in an atmosphere of slavery.
*Upon education we must therefore rely for the purity, the
preservation and the perpetuation of republican government.*"[8]

[6] Alfred J. Morrison, *The Beginnings of Public Education in Virginia, 1776–
1860*, 129.
[7] Charles L. Coon, *The Beginnings of Public Education in North Carolina*,
31, 43, 54, 100, 103.
[8] Edward A. Fitzpatrick, *The Educational Views and Influence of De Witt
Clinton*, 48.

In a New England reader of the early years of the nineteenth century this democratic purpose of the schools, quaintly mixed with the Puritan concern for a combination of good morals and utility in one's proper sphere in life, is presented in poetic form for childish edification. After describing the college the poet continues,

> Thousands of humbler name around them rise,
> Where homebred freemen seize the solid prize;
> Fixt in small spheres, with safer beams to shine,
> They reach the useful and refuse the fine.
> Found, on its proper base, the social plan,
> The broad plain truths, the common sense of man,
> His obvious wants, his mutual aids discern,
> His rights familiarize, his duties learn,
> Feel moral fitness all its force dilate,
> Embrace the village and comprise the state.
> Each rustic here who turns the furrow'd soil,
> The maid, the youth that ply mechanic toil,
> In equal rights, in useful arts inured,
> Know their just claims, and see their claims secured;
> They watch their delegates, each law revise,
> Its faults designate and its merits prize,
> Obey, but scrutinize; and let the test
> Of sage experience prove and fix the best.[9]

If there was to be real equality as democracy urged, it must include equality of opportunity so that virtue and ability would have a chance in the world. Children of the poor could obtain an opportunity equal to that of rich men, only if the state provided them with an education. When democracy became an established fact, all men, whether rich or poor, could agree with Governor Clinton that "in [education] we must confide as the conservative power of the state that will watch over our liberties and guard them against fraud, intrigue, cor-

---

[9] Rodolphus Dickinson, *The Columbian Reader, Comprising a New and Various Selection of Elegant Extracts in Prose and Poetry, for the Use of Schools in the United States, to Which Is Prefixed an Introduction on the Arts of Reading and Speaking,* 188.

ruption and violence."[10] Democracy, more than any other factor, stimulated the spread of public education.

Yet however much the rise of democracy stimulated education, it also placed restraints upon teachers, which are effective even today. Jacksonian democracy, unlike the liberalism of Jefferson that preceded it, established the ideal of equalitarianism in American life and thought. Jeffersonian republicans were aristocrats dominated by belief in the maxim, *noblesse oblige*. They sought, by the removal of all artificial restrictions, to give the common man every chance environment could provide for him to become the equal of the leaders, who had enjoyed opportunities not open to all men. Jacksonian democrats were the people themselves. It did not occur to them that they needed opportunity to become the equals of any one. They were already the equals of any man. The *égalité* of French Revolutionary theory had been a reality on the American frontier. Their belief in the equality of men convinced Jacksonian democrats that any man was capable of filling any political office and that, if he was not, then the office ought to be changed. This same principle they applied to the schools. Training for teaching was as unnecessary as training for political office. Political appointments were rewards for friendship or for service that had nothing to do with qualification for the tasks. Teaching, too, came to be looked upon as the perquisite of "worthy" members of the community, who needed support and had powerful friends. Positions obtained under a system of local favoritism were not regarded as public trusts and opportunities for service but as rewards given to those whom the people approved. Not only the incumbent but the people themselves so regarded teaching positions and other public offices. There was no reason why a place so acquired should not again be taken from a man when he lost public approval. A teacher employed under these terms could scarcely attain a professional attitude that would make him free. Instead he sought to

[10] E. A. Fitzpatrick, *op. cit.,* 48–49.

please by any means possible the majority, which could displace him at will.

A shrewd Frenchman, Alexis de Tocqueville, traveled through America in 1835, when Jacksonian democracy was at its height, and then went home to write his impressions of democracy in action. He found many things to praise, many to criticize. "Democratic republics," he explained, "extend the practice of currying favor with the many." In America "this is more especially the case," since "the authority of the majority is so absolute and so irresistible that a man must give up his rights as a citizen, and almost abjure his quality as a human being, if he intends to stray from the track which it lays down."[11] The evils of the spoils system and insecurity of office in politics were recognized a half century ago and civil service reform was instituted. It is only recently that men have begun to see that security and training, which Jacksonian equalitarianism disregarded, are as important for the teacher as for other "public servants."

An equalitarian democracy confused literacy with education. Democracy sought, therefore, to make all men literate. Whether all normal men are educable is still a moot point, but certainly all men do not wish education beyond mere literacy. Where they think they do, they seek it because they regard higher education as a social and economic privilege. Some men who thus regard education desire it as a means of climbing out of democracy into an aristocracy, to which this privilege offers the password. Other men who so regard it resent it in others just as they resent economic, social, and political privilege. Furthermore, education beyond literacy had decidedly constituted one of the privileges of the aristocracy that Jacksonian democracy was displacing. Therefore it was under suspicion. Higher education was neither attainable nor useful to the ordinary American of Jackson's day. Nor did this ordi-

[11] Alexis de Tocqueville, *Democracy in America* (revised edition, 1899), I, 271.

nary American desire it. In fact, frontier experience had made him contemptuous of too much learning. Other qualities had served better in frontier life. Yet true democracy could brook no inequalities. Therefore it convinced itself that education was not a mark of superiority. So deep did this distrust of education sink into the soul of America that to this day most men do not regard as better than any one else's the opinion of a highly educated person unless, perhaps, that person's education is technical or practical, so that the lingering frontier consciousness is able to appreciate it.

After all, why should Jacksonian democracy have heeded the view of a single man or a small educated minority when it differed from that of a majority of the people? Jacksonian democracy was built upon the conviction that the will of the majority was both wise and righteous. The people early learned that education did not endow men with greater virtue. The basic principle of Jacksonian democracy would have been invalidated if it had endowed them with greater wisdom. Since, then, education beyond mere literacy gave no valid claim to greater wisdom or virtue, why should a majority of men, whose opinion must have been sound because they were a majority, have allowed one man to set up his opinion against theirs? Why, above' all, should a mere schoolmaster be allowed to set the will of the people at naught by disagreeing with it, when every one knew that schoolmasters were quick with their wits, to be sure, but very dull in the practical skills that helped men get on in the world. Schoolmasters were not ambitious or clever enough to be even interested in success in the material forms of which America offered an abundance. When schoolmasters came to be women, well, then certainly they could not be allowed to set up their opinions against what the majority of men knew to be correct. Unless majority rule was unsound, it was presumptuous for one person to claim a right to express a view that contradicted what a majority of people believed. To do so assumed that one man was in some way superior to a whole group of men. American democrats could only resent this egotism. In the claim of the validity of an individual opinion opposed to popular views lurked a danger of a new aristocratic attack on democracy itself, for intellectual inequalities had been one of the chief bulwarks of aristocratic society. Besides, an assumption of intellectual superiority is more galling than economic or social inequality because it is more inherent in man himself and less easily overcome by grown men whose intellectual capacity and education, whether good or bad, are already attained and not easily altered. Equalitarian democracy was, then, as much a revolt against intellectual inequality involved in the ideal of freedom of thought for minority opinion as against economic and political inequality.

In Jacksonian America communication was difficult. Once they arrived on the frontier, men traveled little save on to new frontiers. The frontier was unread. It was extraordinarily provincial. Professor Knight has pointed out that the "school district, no matter how small, was early taught to exercise its right to select and to license its own teachers, and it was encouraged by an attractive and popular political philosophy to resent any interference from a larger administrative unit. It was slow to give up any of its early rights, the jealous exercise of which discouraged standards by which good teachers and good teaching could have been had and known."[12] Besides, many of the new ideas and practices in both secular and religious life came from Europe and were distrusted by a provincialism that looked upon things foreign as probably dangerous. Democracy was the product of the frontier, and existence on the frontier was exceedingly hard and drab. Much has been written of the romantic side of frontier life. Few have recorded its failures, its heartburnings, its regrets, and its longings for what was left behind irrecoverable by men and women who could not turn back. The only recompense was to build illusions of self-importance and to dream of greatness

[12] Edgar W. Knight, *Education in the United States,* 348.

that was soon to be. The optimism of the frontier was frequently an optimism of despair. Critical attitudes clashed with this whole psychology of forced hopefulness. Questioning of the community's views of itself and its future was therefore resented. Out of all this grew a blatant sort of local pride that bred intolerance of criticism. "Nothing," declared de Tocqueville, "is more embarrassing in the ordinary intercourse of life than this irritable patriotism of the Americans. A stranger may be very well inclined to praise many of the institutions of their country, but he begs permission to blame some of the peculiarities which he observes—a permission which is, however, inexorably refused. America is therefore a free country, in which, lest anybody should be hurt by your remarks you are not allowed to speak freely of private individuals, or of the State, of the citizens or of the authorities, of public or of private undertakings, or, in short, of anything at all, except it be of the climate and the soil; and even then Americans will be found ready to defend either the one or the other, as if they had been contrived by the inhabitants of the country."[13]

The frontier was intolerant. It had no reverence for the wisdom of the past. Experience with the civilized world was unnecessary. Education and cultivation were not assets but handicaps among the crudities of new settlements. The frontier worshiped practicality. Learning was impractical. What was worse, it was effeminate. Man's place was fighting Indians, hunting, felling trees, working fields. Strong men of primitive America were contemptuous of culture. As men rose in the economic and social scale they began to be interested in the outward evidences of culture—for their womenfolk. At heart they did not regard teaching as a manly profession. On the frontier, youth and physical vigor counted most. Youth is intolerant and proud of its intolerance. Democratic America was skilful with its hands and mechanically ingenious. Theories it did not understand. Ideas that went deeper than popu-

[13] A. de Tocqueville, *op. cit.*, I, 247–248.

lar catchwords aroused suspicions. "The spirit of the Americans," wrote de Tocqueville, "is averse to general ideas; and it does not seek theoretical discoveries. Neither politics nor manufactures direct them to these occupations; and although new laws are perpetually enacted in the United States, no great writers have hitherto inquired into the general principles of their legislation. The Americans have lawyers and commentators, but no jurists; and they furnish examples rather than lessons to the world."[14] Ignorance is intolerant, and democratic America had been too busy developing her resources to educate her people. Mere literacy and a smattering of factual knowledge without training in critical judgment or familiarity with great thinkers of the past tended to increase men's dogmatism. Professor Mecklin has said, "The most dangerous weakness in a democracy is the uninformed and unthinking average man."[15] Democratic America a hundred years ago was a land of average men.

The tyranny of American democracy over ideas and opinions surprised de Tocqueville. He wrote:

The most absolute monarchs in Europe are unable to prevent certain notions, which are opposed to their authority, from circulating in secret throughout their dominions, and even in their courts. Such is not the case in America; as long as the majority is still undecided, discussion is carried on; but as soon as its decision is irrevocably pronounced, a submissive silence is observed, and the friends, as well as the opponents, of the measure unite in assenting to its propriety. The reason of this is perfectly clear: no monarch is so absolute as to combine all the powers of society in his own hands, and to conquer all opposition with the energy of a majority which is invested with the right of making and of executing the laws. The authority of a king is purely physical, and it controls the actions of the subject without subduing his private will; but the majority possesses a power which is physical and moral at the same time; it acts upon the will as well as upon the actions of men, and it represses not only all contest, but all controversy. I know no country in which there is so little true independence of mind

[14] *Ibid.*, 320.   [15] John M. Mecklin, *The Ku Klux Klan*, 103.

and freedom of discussion as in America. . . . There is but one sole authority, one single element of strength and of success, with nothing beyond it.

In America the majority raises very formidable barriers to the liberty of opinion: within these barriers an author may write whatever he pleases, but he will repent it if he ever step beyond them. Not that he is exposed to the terrors of an auto-da-fé, but he is tormented by the slights and persecutions of daily obloquy. His political career is closed forever, since he has offended the only authority which is able to promote his success. Every sort of compensation, even that of celebrity, is refused to him. Before he published his opinions he imagined that he held them in common with many others; but no sooner has he declared them openly than he is loudly censured by his overbearing opponents, whilst those who think without having the courage to speak, like him, abandon him in silence. He yields at length, oppressed by the daily efforts he has been making, and he subsides into silence, as if he was tormented by remorse for having spoken the truth.[16]

Many of the conditions that created the intolerance of democratic America have passed, but the attitudes of mind created by them have became the mental stereotypes of descendant generations.

The frontier was accustomed to settling matters by force. The self-reliance and independent spirit of the frontier frequently took the form of self-willed lawlessness and disregard for others. In primitive society an argument often ended in a fight, and physical coercion won what reason could not attain. Independence, unchecked as it was on the frontier, accustomed men to having their own way. When, therefore, a whole group of men found an individual who crossed them and differed from them, their impulse was to force him into agreement by the "manly" methods of primitive society. In men who suffered from an inferiority complex this impulse was strengthened by the secret fear that the opponent might be right and they wrong—a fear that could be overcome only by seeing the man who aroused it overpowered and humiliated

16 A. de Tocqueville, *op. cit.*, I, 267–268.

so that they could know they were superior to him. The fear of new ideas felt by untrained men in primitive communities is overwhelming. It arouses a determination to crush out the unaccustomed. Startling, indeed, is the record of hangings, mutilations, whippings, mobbings, incendiarism, sabotage, ridings on a rail, tar and featherings, shootings, lynchings, that the annals of American life present. This mob violence, often as not, has been perpetrated by generally good citizens acting under mob impulse against some one who was different from them in status or ideas and therefore disliked by them—and instinctively feared. The mob spirit has existed from the earliest settlements to the present moment and motivates officers of the law as well as "mobs."[17] It remains one of the less pleasant heritages of the frontier.

Another phase of democracy gave these attitudes particular relevance to schools. Under democracy the people owned the government and, along with it, the schools. On Jackson's inauguration day great swarms of democratic Americans overran the White House, drank the official liquor in such quantities that it had to be served in tubs, and climbed on the sofas in muddy boots. This symbolized in politics a feeling that the people had come into their own. The schools were part of their own. "In America," explained de Tocqueville, ". . . the citizen looks upon the fortune of the public as his private interest."[18] This sense of possession of all public institutions made men who knew nothing about schools or teaching feel that somehow the schools belonged to them and that they ought to control the teaching. Besides, the public paid the wages of teachers and did not this give them a right to say what those teachers should do and think on taxpayers' money? In Europe, long before popular government arose, schools

---

[17] This side of American life is not stressed in the histories, in the press, or in the public mind. The present author was as amazed as others would be at the record, when, in gathering material for a history of tolerance, he began collecting instances of mob violence.

[18] A. de Tocqueville, *op. cit.*, I, 247–248.

were established, under aristocratic control, and developed a tradition of independence generally strong enough to withstand the pressures of democratic government. In America, this tradition could not develop because education grew up under democracy itself with the common man directing its course. Great advantages have arisen out of the responsiveness of schools to the public need. Academic disregard of the world with resulting sterility has been impossible here. But the close relationship between the popular will and our educational system has been one of the largest factors in destroying teachers' freedom. It has subjected teachers to all the whims of public opinion. Under such a system teachers' actions and beliefs are dictated by the prejudices of the noisiest and most active members of the community or by mere force of numbers. Intelligence and training lose control. Professor Counts warns:

Another consequence of popular control of the school is that education will be affected by those gusts of passions which from time to time sweep through the masses. . . . The foreign observer, witnessing these instances of mob behavior, comes to the conclusion that the level of culture in the United States must be extremely primitive. The fact is that such manifestations are merely the natural fruit of the way in which public education in America is controlled. The intellectual classes, to whose care education is entrusted by tradition in the older countries of Europe, have but little to say about the conduct of the public school in the United States. Probably in no country in the world do the masses of the people believe in the theory of biological evolution, but in America those masses sit in judgment on educational policy. Thus a price must be paid for the democratization of the control of education. . . . The point to be observed is that the school must inevitably exhibit the cultural limitations as well as the ideals and purposes of the forces in control.[19]

These popular habits of thought and attitudes toward the schools that the frontier and equalitarian democracy created remain long after both frontier and primitive democracy are gone. The average American community today evidences the

[19] George S. Counts, *The American Road to Culture*, 51–52.

same belief that any one can teach, if only he has passed through certain courses in education, which give him the rules. It still appoints or refuses to appoint teachers on grounds of politics, favoritism, prejudice, and social qualities that have no remote connection with qualification for the place, but only with popular feeling toward the person. Reformers talk about security of tenure, but little has actually been done to make effective the teacher's removal from the spoils system under which Jacksonian democracy placed most public officers. Respect for the intellectual side of education has not greatly increased among the masses, though the social and economic values of it are sought after. Education is still confused with mere literacy, though in the new industrial age literacy now includes not only reading, writing, and figuring, but the use of technical tools and the ability to employ the terminology of big business, to analyze stock exchange reports, to understand the jargon of bond salesmen, and to appreciate the niceties of modern advertising. But literacy still passes as education with the average man of 1939 in this high-powered age of material possessions, as it did with the frontiersman in his cabin. America still holds the frontier attitude toward culture. To the practical man of 1939 the arts and literature still seem effeminate and theories of intellectuals amusing. Americans still dislike the unconventional. Despite all their efforts to find the new and unusual in material goods, they still fear new ideas and distrust views that differ from those of the majority. Majority support still makes right. Americans still seek to control by force what they cannot win by argument. Though forms have changed, they have inherited much of frontier democracy's intolerance. They still look upon the schools as their own, to be dominated by majority opinion. With the growth of industries that "hire" men to do their bidding, the community has built upon the old theory of public possession of schools a "hired man" theory for teachers, under which the taxpayer plays the rôle of employer. Emerson, who in many ways was the prophet of the virtues of democracy and the frontier, cried out against the equalitarianism of majority rule. "Leave this hypocritical prating about the masses," he protested. "Masses are rude, lame, unmade, pernicious in their demands and influence, and need not to be flattered, but to be schooled. I wish not to concede anything to them, but to tame, drill, divide and break them up, and draw individuals out of them. . . . Masses! the calamity is the masses."[20] "Are we," he asked, "always to be the victims of the meanest of mankind, who kill off as sentimental and visionary every generous and just design?"[21]

In our own day Professor Mecklin declares, "There is undoubtedly among the masses of the American people indifference, not to say downright opposition, to those things to which the scholar has devoted his life." But Mecklin protests that "the end of democracy is not and cannot be the dead level of vulgar, unenviable mediocrity. The goal must be a social order in which equality of opportunity is made the instrument for assuring a dynamic, progressive society based upon socially valuable inequalities."[22] Some years ago Professor Dodd asked: "Is expert opinion, trained thinking, necessarily opposed in democracies to the feelings and aspirations of the masses, who, in the final analysis, pay the bills, whereas in aristocratic societies, the reverse is true? It should seem to be so; . . . How is democracy to get the greatest good from learning and from highly trained minds?" After offering, as his solution, freedom for teachers in expressing unpopular political views, he concluded, "Such liberty exercised with scholarly balance and with the firmness of real learning might be a priceless boon to us in the way of avoiding revolutions or wars like that of 1861."[23]

[20] Ralph W. Emerson, *Works*, VI (1883), 237.

[21] R. W. Emerson, *Journals*, VIII (1849–1855), 343.

[22] John M. Mecklin, "Academic Freedom and Status," *School and Society*, III (April 29, 1916), 629.

[23] William E. Dodd, "Democracy and Learning," *Nation*, LXXXIX (Nov. 4, 1909), 430–431.

In this place democracy itself is not under appraisal either for criticism or defense; but its effects upon freedom in teaching must be analyzed. Much that is best in life Americans owe to the influence of democracy or the finer qualities of the frontier. To the frontier they are indebted, too, for their independence, inventiveness, tireless activity, buoyancy, faith in the future, and sturdy healthiness—qualities that have contributed to America's amazing prosperity and capacity for energetic living. The existence of the frontier mitigated the evils of the industrial revolution. Free land and a really democratic proximity to equality of opportunity have prevented, until recent years at least, anything akin to European class conflicts, because they enabled men to pass with ease from one group to another and made of every laborer a potential capital. Indigenous democratic practices have created high standards of living for Americans generally and, again until recently at least, have passed the fruits of prosperity around to a larger proportion of the people than in most modern nations. In fact, in education itself, some of the handicaps imposed by democracy are avoided in the schools of other nations largely because education has not been spread among all the people as it has in America but has been frankly a privilege of the upper classes. Democracy chose to give as good an education as possible to all her people instead of gaining quality by limiting most schooling to the few or providing an inferior brand for the many. Had the frontier not given the common man in America power to demand and get something approaching equal political, social, and economic opportunity, the American privileged classes would never voluntarily have surrendered their privileges, and even education would have been denied or at least long withheld from the masses. When all credit is given, however, democracy and the frontier must be held responsible for important restraints upon the schools.

The rise and fusion of evangelicism and democracy, then, in the era of Jeffersonian liberalism have greatly influenced the exercise of freedom of opinion and conduct in American life and in a peculiar way the freedom of the teacher. Jefferson declared, "I have sworn upon the altar of God eternal hostility against every form of tyranny over the mind of man." Then just when Jeffersonian liberalism was at its height, these two movements rose to contradict its basic tenets and eventually to bind it, if not actually to destroy it. Jeffersonian democracy was anti-theological and liberal; Jacksonian democracy was pious and intolerant. Jacksonianism won. Other factors have also been important. The teacher has, however, been profoundly affected by the conflict in our national life between the old liberties of Jeffersonian idealism on the one hand and the restrictions and repressions imposed by evangelicism and Jacksonian democracy on the other. The twentieth-century man and the teacher of his children have moved far from the religion and political beliefs of the Jacksonian era. Many of them have discarded its religion and have come to doubt its politics. Science has destroyed its faith, and an industrial age has destroyed much of the reality of equalitarian democracy. But the habits of mind, the attitudes toward schools, their teachers, and their teachings have persisted with a sanctity that tradition and long usage have added unto them.

Chapter IV

FREEDOM UNDER THE EDUCATIONAL REFORM-ERS AND NATIVE-AMERICANISM, 1830–1860

During the period from 1830 to 1860, great progress was made in American education. State after state appointed a superintendent of education. After long struggles,[1] and under pressure from the newly enfranchised common man, state after state in the North abandoned its partial system of schooling, discarded the idea of education as charity for the poor or a parental problem for those able to pay, and established a system of free, public, tax-supported primary education. Schools came to be regarded as an obligation of society to the next generation, as a protection of society against ignorance in power, and as the *right* of every citizen. The South, preoccupied with its economic problems, safe from the pressure of organized groups of labor, and secure in the rule of an aristocracy that had the common man completely under control, was more backward in developing education,[2] although a few Southern cities like New Orleans did keep abreast of the times. High schools increased, but were still not numerous. In the Northwest the spread of elementary education was aided by land grants, and by the absence of either an aristocratic tradition or undemocratic political institutions. It was stimulated further

---

[1] In Pennsylvania, for instance, the battle had raged for years, partly because men who controlled the state did not want to be taxed to educate other people's children and partly because the various religious sects, having built up excellent parochial schools, felt no need of public education. In 1834 the Legislature voted to provide free schools, but the measure brought such protests that repeal was about to be accomplished when strenuous efforts of the Governor and a brilliant speech of Thaddeus Stevens won the day for free schools by defeating repeal.

[2] See, e.g., William A. Maddox, *The Free School Idea in Virginia before the Civil War,* 10.

by the migration to this region of large numbers of New Englanders and Germans who brought the ideal of schooling with
them even to the frontier. Higher education also began to develop in the Northwest. In the Southwest education was handicapped by the same factors that had retarded it in the Colonial
South, and besides, so far as it concerned the masses, by the
weight of the increasingly powerful slavocratic psychology.

This was a period, too, of great improvements in the quality
of education. Men like Archibald Murphey in North Carolina,
Thomas Jefferson in Virginia, and James G. Carter in Massachusetts had prepared the way. The humanitarian movement
and intellectual awakening of the 1830's and 1840's aroused
public interest. Great educational reformers provided the leadership. The careers of Henry Barnard in Connecticut and
Rhode Island, Horace Mann in Massachusetts, Calvin H.
Wiley in North Carolina, and Caleb Mills in Indiana need no
recapitulation here. These men analyzed the faults and needs
of American education. They studied European school systems. They aroused public opinion. They campaigned for
funds, converted reluctant taxpayers, and stormed legislatures
for appropriations. They realized the importance of planning,
of expert supervision, and of trained officials. They sought and
produced improved textbooks. They recognized the importance
of well-qualified teachers and professional attitudes, and they
founded normal schools to create a trained teaching profession.
By improving the quality of both schools and teachers, these
educational reformers of the mid-century performed the
groundwork without which no superstructure of freedom for
teachers could have been erected.

Important as was the work of these men, its immediate effects must not be exaggerated. The reformers had charted the
way and made a start. But it took generations to fulfil their
hopes. Even yet thousands of American children get what
education they can in schools and under teachers as bad as the
worst with which Barnard, Mann, or Wiley dealt. The influ-

ence exerted by these men upon educators was profound; the average American of their day would not, however, have known who they were.

Educational legislation was passed in many states, but practice lagged far behind the requirements of statute books. Perhaps the greatest service rendered by legislative enactments was to provide an ideal and to encourage practical people who were seeking to improve the schools. Southern apologists point with pride to the excellent training of leaders of the aristocracy of this period, or to individual schools. Even in money spent, they present statistics of comparative per capita expenditures not unfavorable to Southern schools.[3] Nevertheless, these happier accounts of Southern education ignore two important facts. In no consideration of Southern education was her largest labor group—Negro slaves—included. They were almost universally excluded from all education, whereas in this period Northern education was being extended to the laboring classes. In the second place, Southern expenditures largely benefited private institutions, which served only certain classes of even the white population. Since Southern schools served very limited groups, schools that did exist could be of good quality and yet leave general education very backward. Far more common than the glowing picture presented by men who considered only the large planters was the situation depicted by the state superintendent of Louisiana, who complained in 1859: "Under the present law nearly every planter has a school at his house and draws the pro rata share out of the public treasury. The poor children have not the benefit of these schools, and in this parish, which pays about $14,000 in school tax, there is consequently not enough in the treasury to pay the expense of a single school at the parish seat, where it ought to be."[4]

Characteristic of the newer West was the schoolhouse in

[3] See, e.g., George W. Dyer, *Democracy in the South before the Civil War*, 66–68.   [4] Edgar W. Knight, *Public Education in the South*, 246.

Iowa described by an early settler. "It was built of round logs, the spaces between them chinked and then daubed with mud. . . . There was no danger of burning the floor, as there was none. The seats were made of stools or benches constructed by splitting a log, hewing off the splinters from the flat side and then putting four pegs into it from the round side for legs. The door was made of clapboards. On either side a piece of one log was cut out and over the aperture was pasted greased paper, which answered for a window. Wooden pins were driven into the log running lengthwise immediately beneath the windows, upon which was laid a board, and this constituted the writing desks."[5]

The reports of commissioners of education even in New England repeatedly complain of the unspeakable physical conditions of schoolhouses in the most prosperous towns, of the continued failure of towns to provide any schools at all in spite of clear legal requirements, and of shortness and irregularity of terms even in the better schools. The physical equipment was still so crude in New England schools as to require most of a teacher's time and effort to accomplish the meagerest results. The quality of schools, as late as 1830–1860, usually prevented any real chance for the exercise of freedom. James Russell Lowell declared that Americans were "the most common-schooled and least educated" people in the world.[6] It was promising, however, that there were now state commissioners of education who could report these deficiencies to an increasingly interested public.

Complaints about the quality of teachers continued. Though normal schools were now turning out some well-equipped teachers, they were not numerous enough seriously to affect the teaching personnel. Besides, most communities paid salaries too low to obtain trained teachers had trained teachers been

[5] Leonard F. Parker, *Higher Education in Iowa*, 15.
[6] S. K. Ratcliffe, "America and Fundamentalism," *Contemporary Review*, CXXVIII (September, 1925), 291.

available. Increased protests over the lack of qualified teachers do not necessarily mean that teachers were of poorer quality than formerly; they probably indicate, on the contrary, that standards had improved and that the public was more awake to the need of good teachers. None the less, the average teacher had as yet little training. On his journey through that region in 1853–1854, Olmsted testified of the South: "The teachers are, generally, totally unfitted for their business; [they are] young men . . . not only unadvanced beyond the lowest knowledge of the elements of primary school learning, but often coarse, vulgar, and profane in their language and behavior, who take up teaching as a temporary business, to supply the demand of a neighborhood of people as ignorant and uncultivated as themselves."[7]

In 1843 a Virginia correspondent complained, "Good men deem . . . [teaching] disreputable; . . . In the schoolhouse . . . there is often installed a man with a heart of stone, and hands of iron; too lazy to work, too ignorant to live by his wits in any other way, whose chief recommendation is his cheapness and whose chief capacity to instruct is predicated by his incapacity for other employment. . . . Of the progress of the pupils in these temples of indolence but little inquiry is made."[8] A mid-century governor of South Carolina complained that teachers were "grossly incompetent to discharge their high and sacred functions." "With but few exceptions," he declared, "they are very ignorant and possess a very easy morality. With the poor pay allowed them, we cannot reasonably calculate upon a better state of things. The men who take charge of our public schools, and accept so miserable a pittance as the reward of their labors, are they who cannot get employment on any other terms. . . . It is now in South Carolina a reproach to be

---

[7] Frederick L. Olmsted, *A Journey in the Seaboard Slave States in the Years 1853–1854*, I, 407.

[8] E. W. Knight, *Public Education in the South*, 294–295. See also *ibid.*, 202–204, 252; Cornelius J. Heatwole, *A History of Education in Virginia*, 115; R. A. Hamlet, "History of Public Education in Campbell County," *Virginia School Report*, 1885, part III, 61.

a teacher of a free school, as it is regarded as prima facie evidence of want of qualification."[9] President Caldwell of the University of North Carolina exclaimed:

Is a man constitutionally and habitually indolent, a burden upon all from whom he can extract support? Then there is one way of shaking him off, let us make him a schoolmaster. To teach school is, in the opinion of many, little else than sitting still and doing nothing. Has any man wasted all his property, or ended in debt by indiscretion and misconduct? The business of school-keeping stands wide open for his reception, and here he sinks to the bottom, for want of capacity to support himself. Has any one ruined himself, and done all he could to corrupt others, by dissipation, drinking, seduction, and a course of irregularities? Nay, has he returned from a prison after an ignominious atonement for some violation of the laws? He is destitute of character and cannot be trusted, but presently he opens a school and the children are seen flocking into it, for if he is willing to act in that capacity, we shall all admit that as he can read and write, and cypher to the square root, he will make an excellent schoolmaster.[10]

Through the West and North the story was the same. "Teachers were so scarce," explained Superintendent C. C. Camp in Kansas, "that I had *to be very careful not to reject* any one who was sent by a school board for examination."[11]

Religious training remained an important function of education. Many schools were still directly or indirectly controlled by religious denominations. The Quakers, the Scotch-Irish, and the German sects had early established schools. The religious enthusiasm of the newer sects led them to set up others.

[9] E. W. Knight, *Education in the United States,* 353–354.

[10] Charles L. Coon, *The Beginnings of Public Education in North Carolina,* II, 560–561.

[11] [Board of Directors of the Kansas State Educational Exhibit,] *Columbian History of Education in Kansas,* 124–125. See also "Annual Report of the Superintendent of Public Instruction," Michigan Senate and House of Representatives, *Joint Documents,* 1843; Edward W. Hall, *History of Higher Education in Maine,* 15; Louise G. and Matthew J. Walsh, *History and Organization of Education in Pennsylvania,* 163, 167–169; Hugh B. Eastburn, "The Early County Superintendency of Bucks County," Bucks County Historical Society, *Collection of Papers,* II (1909), 255–256; Horace Mann, "Seventh Annual Report of the Board of Education," *Common School Journal,* VI (1844), 153.

In states where they no longer predominated and in New England where they were developing strength, the Episcopalians founded schools of their own. Catholic schools also sprang up. In all of these institutions the tenets of the sect in control formed an important portion of the curriculum, and a teacher's orthodoxy was carefully inspected.

The secular academies and female seminaries, now growing in numbers, continued free from sectarian influence. The public schools were usually unhampered by required sectarianism. In fact, this period showed a tendency to resent sectarianism in its schools, particularly in the West, where sects were pretty thoroughly intermingled. In 1833, for instance, when Alton Seminary applied for a charter, the Illinois Legislature refused to grant one requiring that trustees be Baptists and establishing a theological department.[12] In the same year in the North Carolina Legislature charters for two denominational schools were contested because of a strong feeling that allowing a religious sect to control a school violated the constitutional prohibition against the establishment of religion. One of the schools was finally approved after its charter had been amended to make the board of trustees self-perpetuating instead of allowing the Orange Presbytery to fill vacancies.[13] In chartering academies at Independence and at Troy, the Missouri Legislature provided: "No preference shall be given, or any discrimination made [in the choice of trustees, professors, teachers, or students] on account of religious sentiments; nor shall any trustees, professors or teachers, at any time, make by-laws, ordinances or regulations that may, in any wise, interfere with or in any manner control the rights of conscience, or the free exercise of religious worship."[14] The first Arkansas law incorporating an academy included the proviso "That as the dissemination of useful knowledge ought to be the only object

---

[12] As the trustees refused to accept the amended form, no charter was granted until later. John W. Cook, *Educational History of Illinois*, 302–303. In 1836 a compromise charter was agreed upon.
[13] C. L. Coon, *op. cit.*, xl.   [14] *Missouri Session Laws*, 1834–1835, 6.

contemplated by this institution, no preference shall be given, nor any discrimination be made, in the choice of trustees, professors, teachers, or students, on account of religious sentiment."[15]

Laws prohibiting sectarian teaching in public schools increased in number. For instance, Louisville in her first city school provided that pupils should not be taught a catechism or any particular form of religious belief.[16] In 1838 the Pennsylvania superintendent of schools drew up a model law in which he included a guarantee that *"the religious predilections of the pupils and their parents or guardians shall be sacredly respected,"* and a rule that *"no catechism, creed, confession, or manual of faith,* shall be used as a school book nor admitted into the school; sectarian instruction not being the province of the school master, but of the parent or guardian, and the spiritual teacher selected by him."[17] In 1846–1847 Virginia provided that "no book shall be used nor instruction given in the public schools, calculated to favour the doctrinal tenets of any religious sect or denomination."[18] Wisconsin's Constitution of 1848 forbade "sectarian instruction" in the schools.[19] Alabama in 1853 decreed that "no sectarian religious views" should be inculcated.[20]

While sectarianism was increasingly discouraged, practically all schools still included religion in their curricula. School opened with prayer. The Bible was read and portions of it memorized. Hymns were sung. The principles of Protestant Christianity, so far as they were accepted by all Trinitarian sects, were instilled into children. Boarding schools required their pupils to attend religious services, usually twice on the Sabbath. Where the parents expressed a preference, they were

[15] Josiah H. Shinn, *History of Education in Arkansas*, 23.
[16] [Reuben T. Darrett,] "Public Schools," *Louisville Courier-Journal*, Jan. 9, 1881.
[17] Thomas H. Burrowes, *Draft of a Revised Common School Law and of a Law Relative to the Preparation of Common School Teachers; . . .*, 54.
[18] *Virginia Session Laws*, 1846–1847, 36.
[19] Article X, section 3.   [20] *Alabama Session Laws*, 1853, 9.

sent to the local church of parental choosing, otherwise to the service preferred by the head of the school. Prospectuses and catalogues give repeated assurance, first, that the religious needs of the children will be amply provided for and the principles of Christianity taught, and, second, that no sectarian teaching will be forced upon children of sects other than the prevalent one.[21] Even religious schools in their bids for children of other denominations promised not to proselyte. Strict observance of the Sabbath, however, was almost always provided in the school rules, usually including a prohibition against leaving one's room except to attend public worship and against reading anything save the Bible or other religious books.

In general, then, religion was insisted upon, but sectarianism was barred. L. S. Everett expressed the prevailing attitude when he said:

Our common schools are supported by the taxable members of the community. The community is composed of individuals of various religious views; and charity inclines us to admit, that all are sincere and honest in their religious preferences. Our public schools are *common property;* no one sect has a better right to them than another. It should be the endeavor of all good friends of Education, to keep them free from every thing of a sectarian character, so that all may reap the advantages of them, without having their feelings, or their religious prejudices offended. Religion—if by that we understand strict morality, may be taught *in* school as well as *out* of school; and ought to be, in an early day, taught to every human being. *Theology* is quite another thing. That may be taught in Sabbath schools, in churches, in Theological Seminaries —at whatever places parents may please to send their children— with this understanding, that our *common schools* shall be a kind of *neutral ground,* where the children of all parents may be sent, to learn *science,* and nothing else, with the exception of that morality, without which science would be like a jewel in a swine's mouth.[22]

---

[21] The author has examined a great many pamphlet catalogues and prospectuses of nineteenth-century schools.

[22] L. S. Everett, "Essays on Education," *Philadelphia Liberalist,* I (March 30, 1833), 170.

These religious requirements of schools decidedly affected teachers. In religious schools where children were now allowed to attend the worship of their parents' choosing, teachers were still expected, on the contrary, to adhere to the denomination that controlled the school. In many communities local public opinion, even in the face of a state prohibition of sectarianism for the pupils, still required public-school teachers to be orthodox according to the local conception of orthodoxy. In places where the sects were mixed, sectarian restrictions disappeared, but a teacher still had to be a fundamentalist Protestant Christian without Unitarian taint. Most states had constitutional provisions guaranteeing religious liberty. But this had not yet come to mean religious equality. If it had really been interpreted to mean what it said, most early state constitution-makers would have opposed as destructive of the integrity of the state that provision of the Wisconsin Constitution of 1848 that declared that "no religious test shall ever be required as a qualification for any office of public trust under the State."[23] But "religious tests" usually meant only sectarian tests among Protestant Christians. Most original constitutions included restrictions that violated this principle in regard to important state functionaries. It is doubtful whether local public opinion permitted its fulfilment in regard to teachers even in Wisconsin in 1848. In any case, the public-school requirements concerning religious instruction, Bible reading, and prayers would have made it impossible for the teachers to accept, and unwise for the school to offer, a position to any but orthodox Protestant Christians. Even to these, if they were not deeply religious, the religious routine left little freedom in method of teaching. The strict religious observances required of pupils were, of course, expected of the teacher as well. Not only his orthodox Christian teaching inside the classroom but his active participation

[23] Article I, section 19. Ohio did include such a provision in its Constitution as early as 1802. Early constitution-makers were willing to remove sectarian tests among Trinitarian Protestant Christians but not those barring Catholics, non-Christians, and the godless.

in church activities outside the school, had to measure up to the practices and convictions of the devout members of the community. In matters like Sabbath observance the teacher was expected to teach as much by example as by precept.

All would have been well, however, in the best of Protestant school worlds, had not this period brought a great influx of Roman Catholic immigrants who objected to Protestant schools and who had the power in some cases to make men heed their objections. There had always been a few Catholics, a few Jews, a few deists, and many who were indifferent to religion. But the indifferent had not objected to a system that excluded them from teaching and taught their children Protestant Christianity. The indifferent had merely accepted the situation, because, after all, religion did no harm. The Jews, Catholics, and deists had accepted the situation because they did not have power to alter it. The Protestant sects, therefore, had been able to meet the religious problem by agreeing to teach in the schools not the sectarian dogmas on which they disagreed but the Protestant Christian principles upon which they could unite.

The Catholics had always had a few schools of their own. As democratic influence increased their desire for education, they built more. When thousands of new Catholics arrived from Europe, they built still more. In days when all education was in private hands, this arrangement had been satisfactory. Their teachers and their children had been on equal terms with Protestants. Under a system of public education, however, they contributed in taxes to the support of schools in which their teachers were not allowed to teach and could not have taught the required subjects anyway without violating their own consciences. Furthermore, the Catholics were not satisfied to have religion excluded from the schools. Like the Protestants they wanted to teach religion to children, but, again like the Protestants, they wanted to teach their own religion. Since in America Catholic control of the public schools seemed impossible, they preferred a parochial-school system in which each denomination trained its own children and supplied its own teachers. If, however, they were to be taxed for the support of public schools, then, since schools that taught Protestant religion could not satisfy them, they demanded a share of the school fund to pay their own teachers to teach their own children in schools that taught Catholic doctrine. There were American precedents for state aid to religious schools. But Protestants objected to having public tax money used to spread "dangerous" Papist power, and nationalist democracy objected to contributing to schools that were controlled neither by the local community nor by the nation but by a "foreign sovereign." Unless some compromise could be reached, two groups of the population would continue to demand that the schools teach at one and the same time two mutually exclusive and contradictory sets of doctrine. As a religious exercise for children neither would teach the Bible of the other nor allow it to be read. One solution tried at this time was to excuse during the reading those who objected to the school version of the Bible. Protestants, however, objected to this yielding to Papist power and Catholics objected to the "unequal" treatment of their children through a school curriculum that included anything they could not study.

In some places, the dilemma was met by granting state aid to religious schools. New Jersey did this under laws of 1830 and 1831.[24] In 1830, Lowell, Massachusetts, granted money to Catholic parochial schools, and in 1835 took two such institutions into the school system and maintained them as part of it.[25] As late as 1849 Pennsylvania passed a law providing that "when a free school of the common grade in any district, shall be maintained under the care and direction of any religious society, it shall be lawful for the [school] directors of such district, to cause to be paid to the proper person or per-

[24] Ellwood P. Cubberley, *Public Education in the United States,* 177.
[25] *Ibid.,* 178–179.

sons for the support of such school, any portion of the school funds of the district which they may deem just and reasonable."[26]

In New York City a Public School Society had been established in 1805, which, under a law of 1812, shared with certain parochial institutions the public-school money. In 1825 the Legislature turned over to the New York City Council that city's share of the state school funds. The Council put the money and the schools into the hands of the Public School Society, permitted it to levy a local school tax, and excluded all religious schools from a share in school funds. But the Public School Society was a completely Protestant organization that taught Protestant Christianity. In fact, it had been chartered to teach in its schools "the sublime truths of religion and morality contained in the Holy Scriptures." The quarrel in New York is typical. As the Catholics became stronger, they protested more vigorously against the injustice of paying taxes to support schools in which really loyal Catholics could neither teach nor be educated. They appealed in 1840 to the City Council for a portion of the school funds. After a hearing in which they were ably represented by Bishop Hughes and in which the various Protestant denominations came to the support of the Public School Society, the Council rejected the Catholic petition. Then the controversy was carried to Albany and became a political issue. Governor Seward supported the Catholic cause with an appeal to the Legislature to allow foreign children to have separate public-supported schools, in which their own teachers might instruct them in their own religion in their own language. This proposal was not enacted into law, but in 1842 a state law took the New York City schools out of the hands of the Public School Society, made regular public schools of them, and forbade public support of any religious or sectarian schools.[27]

[26] *Pennsylvania Session Laws*, 1849, 446.
[27] John B. McMaster, *A History of the People of the United States*, VII, 159–

In 1842 Bishop Kenrick of Philadelphia protested because Catholic children were required to read the Protestant Bible and join in Protestant religious exercises. The Philadelphia School Board then excused Catholic pupils during religious exercises. In 1843 a school director, seeing the disorder caused by the retiring of Catholic pupils, told the principal of a Kensington school that she had better stop reading the Bible than create such confusion. She refused. The community became aroused over this "Papist attack" on the Bible. Bishop Kenrick denied that he wanted the Bible excluded and maintained that he merely objected to requiring Catholic children to read a Protestant version. Terrific riots then broke out in an atmosphere already tense with strife between Native-Americanism and Catholicism.[28] During the rioting several Catholic schools were burned.

These were the years of the violent anti-Catholic feeling that gave rise to Native-Americanism and Know-Nothingism. The controversy could not have ended favorably for the Catholics. Public sentiment was thoroughly against them, wherever justice lay. A convention of Presbyterians and Congregationalists, meeting in Cleveland in 1844, approved a resolution that declared: "The liberty to *worship* God according to the dictates of conscience, conceded to our citizens by the Constitution, cannot, by any principle of legitimate interpretation, be construed into a right to embarrass the municipal authorities of this Christian and Protestant nation in the ordering of their district schools."[29]

About this time a hundred Catholic children were expelled

160; E. P. Cubberley, *op. cit.,* 177–178; Thomas O'Gorman, *History of the Roman Catholic Church in the United States,* 369–374; *New York Session Laws,* 1842, 187. In 1851 the prohibition against state aid to sectarian schools was renewed. *Ibid.,* 1851, 745.

[28] J. B. McMaster, *op. cit.,* VII, 376–383; H. J. Desmond, "Native Americanism," *American Catholic Quarterly Review,* XXVII (October, 1902), 758; T. O'Gorman, *op. cit.,* 356–360.

[29] Mark Mohler, "The Protestant Church and Religious Tolerance," *Current History,* XXVI (April, 1927), 43.

from the Elliot School in Boston for refusal to participate in school religious exercises.[30] In 1858 a Catholic child was severely flogged in Boston for refusing to read the Protestant Bible.[31] In 1855 the Know-Nothing party introduced an anti-Catholic bill into the Massachusetts Legislature requiring all teachers in private schools to submit to examination by a school committee.[32] This bill did not pass, but one requiring "the daily reading of some portion of the Bible, in the common English version, . . . in the public schools"[33] did become a law —the only official Massachusetts answer to the Catholic complaints.

In Rhode Island a memorial was presented to the Legislature protesting because Bible reading and prayer in the schools violated rights of conscience. The legislative committee reported, however, that a majority of the local community had the power to decide that the Bible ought to be read. No action was taken in 1838. After years of controversy the state superintendent of schools ruled in 1854 that "all public religious exercises, by which I mean prayer and the reading of the Bible, or any religious book by the teacher and the whole school, the school boy being required to listen to it, can only be had by general consent. And it does not remove the difficulty to authorize a scholar who has conscientious objections, to leave the school room while the exercises are proceeding." He pointed out that where objection was raised, which would not be often, each child could read his own Bible, as a separate assignment.[34]

In Ellsworth, Maine, Bridget Donahoe was expelled from school for refusing to read from the Protestant Bible. In 1854 the Maine Supreme Court, in denying redress, declared, "The

[30] Leon Whipple, *The Story of Civil Liberty in the United States,* 64.
[31] *Loc. cit.*
[32] George H. Haynes, "A Know-Nothing Legislature," American Historical Association, *Annual Report,* 1896, I, 182.
[33] *Massachusetts Session Laws,* 1855, 810.
[34] Edward Field, *State of Rhode Island and Providence Plantations at the End of the Century,* II, 244.

right, as claimed, undermines the power of the State. . . . If the several consciences of the scholars are permitted to contravene, obstruct or annul the action of the State, then power ceases to reside in majorities, and is transferred to minorities. . . . If Locke and Bacon and Milton and Swift are to be stricken from the list of authors which may be read in schools, because the authorities of one sect may have placed them among the list of heretical writers whose works it neither permits to be printed, nor sold, nor read, then the right of sectarian interference in the selection of books is at once yielded, and no books can be read, to the reading of which it may not assent."[35]

In San Francisco the first Board of Education required prayer and Bible reading in the schools. But in 1853 Bible reading was discontinued because "under the conditions of a cosmopolitan city, in which there were large numbers of the children of Catholics and Jews, it was an unwise policy." When the parochial and public schools were fused in 1854, however, the question broke out again, got into Know-Nothing politics, and was not settled until many years later, when a rule was finally adopted forbidding religious exercises in the city schools altogether.[36] In Louisiana the Catholics did obtain a law in 1855 providing that if, in any district where there was no public school, children attended a private one, the teacher of that private school should receive the same compensation from the state for each child as if he taught in a public school.[37] In Ohio the Catholics won a doubtful verdict from the State Commissioner of Common Schools implying that, if objection were raised, religious exercises might be forbidden in the schools. The Commissioner evaded a direct decision, however, by saying, "Let it be distinctly understood that if no objections are raised against religious exercises in school, if the exercises are of reasonable length, and if the teacher takes care

[35] *Donahoe* v. *Richards et al.,* 38 Maine 407, 409.
[36] John Swett, *Public Education in California,* 115.
[37] *Louisiana Sessions Laws,* 1855, 425.

to avoid the discussion of all controverted points, or sectarian dogmas, he may conduct those exercises during school hours."[38]

Another effect of the Catholic agitation against Protestant religion in the schools and of the newly aroused anti-Catholic excitement was a batch of prohibitions against the long-established practice of contributing public funds to sectarian schools instead of establishing public ones. "In no case," declared the Minnesota Constitution of 1857, "shall . . . any public moneys or property, be appropriated or used for the support of schools wherein the distinctive doctrines, creeds, or tenets of any particular Christian or other religious sect are promulgated or taught."[39] Michigan in 1835, Indiana and Ohio in 1851, Kansas and Massachusetts in 1855, and Oregon in 1857 adopted similar constitutional provisions.

A few thoughtful men questioned the wisdom of requiring Protestant religious exercises in the schools because if Protestantism could be established there by law, then, by the same logic Catholicism or infidelity or anything else could be, too.[40] Horace Mann stood for secularization, but Mann was attacked for this by religious forces just as the Catholics were. He was accused of sponsoring "Godless schools." Vigorous efforts were made to abolish his State Board of Education. Press and pulpit denounced him.[41]

The net result of all this agitation was that the status of the teacher remained about what it had been. A Catholic teacher was still barred from the public schools, as was a Jew and in many places a deist or a Unitarian. Trinitarian Protestant Christians, however, retained the liberty to teach the Bible and the general principles of Protestant Christianity in the schools with no further restraint upon them than the prohibitions against sectarianism. Here was freedom for a par-

---

[38] Charles N. Lischka, *Private Schools and State Laws, 1924,* 210.

[39] Article VIII, section 3.

[40] See, e.g., "The Prospects Which the Present Age Presents to the Cause of Religious Freedom," *New Englander,* III (July, 1845), 405.

[41] E. P. Cubberley, *op. cit.,* 175–176.

ticular group—freedom that in many places is denied today, but freedom exercised at the expense of other groups. In this controversy, the first blows were struck in a struggle that was to bring sufficient secularization of the school curriculum so that some day men could be qualified to teach in the public schools whatever their religious views might be.

Morality was still a chief objective of schooling. In fact, as religious dogma became less important, the practical effects of religion upon personal conduct became in this age of humanitarianism and reform a major concern of educators. "The young," declared L. S. Everett, "are almost passive in our hands. . . . Yes—I say it reverentially—*we* have the power in our own hands, to say who shall, and who shall not, . . . be the thieves and murderers of the next generation—who shall, and who shall not, be the tenants of our prisons, and victims of the halter for the approaching fifty years!"[42] North Carolina sought funds for education in 1838 because "ignorance and vice generally accompany each other and the only effective method of reclaiming the vicious is by operating upon the mind."[43] Many parents were alarmed because, while reform movements were arousing their interest in practical morality, secularization of the schools was removing from their children the religious control that had been looked to as a guarantee of morality. It is not surprising, then, that the records show a close scrutiny of the moral qualifications of teachers during this period. Certification always included character as well as ability to teach the necessary subjects, and character was more carefully investigated than ability. A typical law in 1846 instructed school directors before employing a teacher to require "a certificate of qualification and good moral character."[44] A West Virginia law of 1863 went so far as to specify that "profanity, obscenity and intemperate habits"

[42] L. S. Everett, *op. cit.*, 127.
[43] C. L. Coon, *op. cit.*, II, 861.
[44] *Illinois Session Laws*, 1846, 136.

should always disqualify a teacher.[45] But school boards were often negligent in demanding high standards. In 1843 the New York superintendent complained that "moral qualifications have been disregarded, and teachers notoriously intemperate have been employed"; and when their dismissal has been urged by the deputy, "the ready reply is, 'he has got a certificate from the town inspectors, and keeps sober enough in school hours to manage his pupils.' "[46]

Very careful censorship of books a teacher might use was maintained. Eugène Sue, George W. M. Reynolds, Tom Paine, and others who might, "perchance, injure youthful morals or principles of belief" were banned. "Indeed," declared one Southern writer, "many are so very careful on this point as to taboo many of the political and general newspapers of the day, lest their frequent recital of crimes and enormities may prove prejudicial."[47] In these days nude statues were carefully clothed or else barred altogether. The word "leg" was too indecent for use in mixed company. At least one girls' school draped piano legs. Nicknames were forbidden even in boys' schools. Bundling had now been laughed out of court even in the back country, and a properly brought up young lady considered it vulgar to address a young man by his Christian name or raise her eyes from the floor while talking with him, or at least her mother did, and she never saw a young man without her mother present—if her mother knew it. A people just emerging from a struggle for existence to more comfortable living was trying desperately to become "genteel," and the most obvious way was to acquire the pruderies and outward artificialities of manners that to untutored eyes appeared to be the qualities of gentility. Most people still saw no use in educating girls at all except for the morality

---

[45] *West Virginia Session Laws*, 1863, 255–256.

[46] *Documents of the Assembly of the State of New-York*, I (1843), no. 14, 116.

[47] J. W. Morgan, "Our School Books," *De Bow's Review*, XXVIII (April, 1860), 436–437.

and good manners it might give them. The newly powerful evangelical sects, too, placed great emphasis upon strict behavior. The Scotch Presbyterians, Puritans, and Friends had always urged austerely correct living. Methodists and Baptists now carried strict views of behavior to masses of people who never before had been able to afford the luxury of proper manners and morals. The schools sought to instil these correct views of morality. The restrictions, then, upon the books a teacher might fittingly use and upon his own personal conduct were rigid indeed.

Criticism of the social and economic order was not popular in those days, and, in communities well enough organized to know what their teachers believed, would not have been tolerated in teachers. Political discussion there was. As we have seen, savage criticism of the Government was indulged in during the Mexican War. But more fundamental questioning of prevailing institutions was not allowed. Emerson cried out in despair in 1841 because "every proclamation, dinner speech, report of victory, or protest against the government ... betrays its thin and watery blood."[48] Criticism in the schools was hardly to be expected. The argument of educators, which won taxpayers, was that schooling would provide an antidote to Jacksonian democracy and would protect, against the menace of ignorant voters, men who would never have paid taxes to educate children of unenfranchised poor men. Besides, as Beard puts it, "Education was also offered as a panacea for every other ill—for pauperism and for the revolutionary distempers imported from Old World monarchies, for the growing radicalism among the ranks of American labor, for the spread of socialistic and anarchistic ideas, and for the opposition of the ignorant to the new scientific requirements of public health."[49]

[48] Ralph W. Emerson, *Journals*, VI, 88.
[49] Charles A. and Mary R. Beard, *The Rise of American Civilization*, I, 812–813.

Men frankly stated their determination that education should prevent the growth of a radicalism that might endanger the *status quo*. Thus L. S. Everett in Philadelphia declared, "The safety of our civil, moral, literary, and religious Institutions, depends upon the manner in which our children shall be educated. . . . It is in vain to talk about a virtuous, intelligent, and happy community, unless the individuals composing it are virtuous, intelligent, and happy. Those who are growing up among us . . . are soon to have charge of those institutions, —are soon either to enjoy, or abuse those privileges, for which *our* fathers toiled, bled, and died. These blood-purchased blessings, can never be safe in the hands of those who know not their value. And none can place a fair estimate upon them but the intelligent and virtuous."[50] In North Carolina, where, a generation earlier, governors were urging education that free men might protect their liberties, it was now being urged because it would protect men of substance against the restlessness of the people. A legislative committee reported in 1827: "Your committee cannot but contrast the sullen discontent of an ignorant people, brooding over evils which do not exist, and wrongs never sustained, with the happy condition of a well-informed people, whose sound judgments discriminate between the declamatory froth of a demagogue, and the sound doctrines of political philosophy."[51] The *Raleigh Register* in 1839 promised that the bill establishing common schools "will be the downfall of error and corruption. Popular demagogues can no longer stand up before [an] honest and well meaning constituency, and rail against measures calculated to advance the prosperity of their State."[52] By 1856 De Bow was telling the South that "the State is *not* required to provide education for the great bulk of its laboring class," but that "it *is* required to afford that degree of education to every one of its white citizens which will enable him intel-

50 L. S. Everett, *op. cit.*, 127.
51 C. L. Coon, *op. cit.*, I, 377.   52 *Ibid.*, II, 897.

ligently and actively to control and direct the slave labor of the State."[53]

In this period the idea grew that education of the masses would help general prosperity. The North Carolina and Virginia press told its readers that in other more flourishing states prosperity was due to the general diffusion of knowledge. In bringing prosperity to the state, declared one correspondent, "The intellectual improvement of the lower classes must constitute the adamantine basis of the whole superstructure. Do this, and agriculture will feel its genial influence; commerce will wave its flag."[54]

A natural result of this desire to make education serve the economic well-being of the nation was a demand for vocational training. Ignorance of agriculture, Governor Wise of Virginia believed, had ruined more men than "any other cause known to me, except brandy, fox-hounds and horse-racing."[55] De Bow complained because "scarcely anything is ventured for the benefit of the great mass who are reared and intended neither for the professions nor the politer walks of literature, but the plodding, busy, active life which opens upon them as they step from college walls and enter the world beyond."[56] This period consequently saw the founding of three agricultural schools in Virginia, Rensselaer Polytechnic in New York, Massachusetts Institute of Technology in Boston, a farmers' high school in Philadelphia, and numerous other institutions for instruction in practical subjects.

Men who looked to schools to stimulate economic prosperity by training sons of poorer men to work industriously would not have been pleased with teachers who put "ideas" into children's heads that made them dissatisfied with the place in

[53] "The States' Duties in Regard to Popular Education," *De Bow's Review,* XX (February, 1856), 148.

[54] C. L. Coon, *op. cit.,* 255; C. J. Heatwole, *op. cit.,* 122.

[55] E. W. Knight, *Public Education in the South,* 214.

[56] [J. D. B. De Bow,] "Commerce and Agriculture Subjects of University Instruction," *De Bow's Review,* III (June–July, 1847), 502.

society for which they were meant. Men who had been persuaded to support free public schools because they would help protect society against the "declamatory froth of a demagogue" did not purpose to allow this aim to be subverted by putting teachers into those schools who did not hold "right" ideas. Had they not established schools to prevent popular restlessness? These men whose consent needed to be won before schools were possible at all were such substantial citizens that it was necessary to maintain their continued good will. They had every intention of seeing that the schools served those purposes that had persuaded them to agree to their establishment out of public taxes.

Chapter V

FREEDOM UNDER THE RULE OF THE SLAVOCRACY, 1830–1861

The great conservative force of ante-bellum America was the slave system. Extreme abolitionists, whose vehement attacks on slavery impressed themselves on the public mind, were interested chiefly in the moral evils of slavery. After the war, a victorious North rationalized the complex causes of conflict into a simple moral issue. A defeated South sought to idealize its ante-bellum life. These factors have combined to blind men to the fact that the slavery issue was more than a moral question. The slavocracy was a political aristocracy almost feudal in nature. It was a distinct culture based on highly trained intelligence and rich enjoyment of the world's art and literature for the few, and appalling ignorance for the multitude. It was a social organization of sharp class distinctions in which a small topmost group enjoyed the life that romanticists picture as typical, while the two lowest and largest classes lived in perhaps no more distressing but much more hopeless squalor than even the mill operatives in the slums Northern industry was building. It was an economic system in which a few wealthy men held vast power not only over the Negro labor, which they owned, but also over the poorer white population, which their great holdings in land and labor subjected almost completely to their will. Though the social and cultural and political elements were important, the power of Southern aristocrats was at root an economic one based upon possession of property in land and Negroes, the chief sources of production.

Many men in the South who did not belong to this small ruling class retained independence and self-respect. On many subjects they held distinct views of their own. In minor matters they quarreled with the powerful planter. They might disagree with him in politics. They often grumbled about his manners toward them, his political power, and his business practices. But where the basic economic problem of slavery was involved, all whites were united by the poorer man's fear of a free Negro and by the power of the great slaveholder, which invaded every phase of Southern economic life. Furthermore, through its power to buy or refrain from buying, this greatest business interest of that day held many a Northern firm or community where it did not dare offend the slave power. Besides, since they held the nation's greatest property interest, the members of the slave-owning class were concerned with social stability and, consequently, could depend upon the support of the conservative business groups throughout the North, who also wished to preserve order and favorable business conditions. Through its own power in the South and its allies in the North, this great slavery interest controlled the schools of both sections. As the agitation by critics of its morals, its ethics, and its business and labor practices increased, it became more and more determined to crush out all criticism, which, through talk of a juster and better economic order, might endanger the smooth functioning of slavery. The slavocracy's power over teachers was exerted in several ways that effectively restricted their freedom.

1. Teaching of Negroes

In the first place, teachers were generally not permitted to instruct Negroes. Difficulties first arose in Colonial days, when missionaries sought to save the souls of Negroes. The Friends and emissaries of the Anglican Society for the Propagation of the Gospel were particularly eager to teach Negroes the elements of Christianity. Throughout Colonial days these men clashed with masters who feared the effects of Christianity upon their slaves. In these early days it was believed by many Negroes and feared by many masters that conversion to Christianity would free slaves. There had once been an English belief that no Christian could be held as a slave. It was early abrogated, but even when it became thoroughly understood that Christians could be held in bondage, other difficulties remained. Admission that a Negro could be converted to Christianity implied that he had a soul. This might lead to regarding him as a human being. Holding a human being in bondage and maintaining that Christianity freed his soul but not his body raised implications that could be avoided as long as the slave was a savage pagan. Conversion, it was believed, developed ideas of religious equality, which made slaves dissatisfied and hard to manage. Recently arrived Negroes were savages regarded as little better than beasts. A Swedish traveler, Peter Kalm, reported masters afraid to see their slaves converted because equality at the communion table raised in them a pride dangerous to the social order.[1]

Various methods were used to discourage the teaching of slaves. Mere social pressure usually sufficed. Many a minister who wished to teach slaves to read the Bible was deterred by fear of the displeasure of wealthy planters. Those who had the courage to face planter disapproval were apparently not molested. In 1680 Virginia prohibited meetings of Negroes in large numbers under penalty of "Twenty Lashes on the Bare Back well laid on."[2] Maryland passed similar laws in 1695 and 1723. A teacher who gathered Negroes together was fined one thousand pounds of tobacco.[3] Other colonies followed

---

[1] Marcus W. Jernegan, *Laboring and Dependent Classes in Colonial America, 1607–1783*, 26, 35, 36; Booker T. Washington and W. E. Burghardt DuBois, *The Negro in the South*, 215.

[2] *Acts of Assembly Passed in the Colony of Virginia, 1662–1715*, 136.

[3] *Laws of Maryland, 1692–1784* (Kilty revision), 1695, chap. VI; *ibid.*, 1723, chap. XV; *A Compleat Collection of the Laws of Maryland, 1692–1699* (Wm. Parks revision, 1727), 245, 246.

this lead, New York, for example, in 1702,[4] and Georgia in 1765.[5] These acts could be used to dissolve Negro schools, or churches for that matter, but where no strong desire to suppress schools existed, these "insurrection laws" were not applied to that kind of gathering. South Carolina in 1740 and Georgia in 1755 enacted laws prohibiting all men from teaching Negroes to write. The South Carolina law laid a penalty of one hundred pounds upon any one "who shall hereafter teach, or cause any Slave or Slaves to be taught to write, or shall use or employ any Slave as a Scribe in any manner of Writing, whatsoever."[6]

Many Colonial masters, however, were eager to have their slaves converted to Christianity. It salved qualms of conscience about enslaving Negroes to feel that slavery was freeing them from the bonds of savage paganism and providing eternal salvation. Benevolence led many masters to seek Christian teaching for their house servants. Others found a Negro able to read, write, and figure a valuable asset. Therefore, many slaveholders provided Christian teaching for some of their slaves and taught ambitious ones to read and write.[7] The Friends, impelled by humanitarianism, were, however, the first to instruct slaves. Their efforts were resented in the South from the first, because they also preached abolition of slavery. In New Jersey, Pennsylvania, and New York, however, they met less opposition, and it was there that men first enjoyed the privilege of teaching Negroes. The Society for the Propagation of the Gospel made a still more systematic attempt to instruct slaves and early sent out not only clergymen but

[4] *Colonial Laws of New York, 1664–1776*, I, 520.

[5] "An Act for the better ordering and governing Negroes and other Slaves in this Province, . . . ," March 25, 1765, sections III, IV, XLV, *Laws of Georgia, 1759–1770* (Johnston printer).

[6] *South Carolina Session Laws*, 1740, 23; *Acts Passed by the General Assembly of the Colony of Georgia, 1755–1775* (Wormsloe, 1881), 94–95. Georgia passed another prohibitory act in 1765, "An Act for the better ordering and governing Negroes and other Slaves in this Province, . . . ," March 25, 1765, section XLVI, *Laws of Georgia, 1759–1770* (Johnston printer).

[7] Carter G. Woodson, *The Education of the Negro Prior to 1861*, 2–3.

schoolmasters.[8] That a few Colonial slaves could read and write is evidenced by the advertisements for runaways.[9]

In 1790 the African Free School for Negroes was opened in New York City. In 1810 the New York Legislature made it compulsory for masters to teach minor slaves to read the Scriptures. By 1773 Newport, Rhode Island, had a Negro school. In 1798 one was established in Boston. In North Carolina the Friends' schools early taught slaves. Two Episcopal schools for Negroes were opened in Philadelphia in 1760, a Friends' school in 1770. By 1797 Philadelphia reported seven private Negro schools. In 1822 a public school was opened to Negroes. Taylor and Varnod, missionaries of the Society for the Propagation of the Gospel, taught slaves in Charleston with assistance from the slaves' masters and mistresses. The Society bought two slaves, educated them, and in 1744 opened in Charleston a school for slaves under their tuition, which purposed to educate other slaves each year who should carry home knowledge and diffuse it among their fellow-bondsmen. The school continued for a number of years. Later the prosperous free colored people of Charleston maintained their own schools with Negro teachers. Eighteenth-century masters there seem not to have prevented it. When an early nineteenth-century law prohibited Negroes from teaching, the blacks hired white teachers. In 1747 a Georgia convention recommended that masters educate their slaves. In 1801 the Abolition Society of Wilmington, Georgia, began providing instruction for Negroes one day each week. In 1816 a regular Negro school was established in Wilmington, under a Negro teacher. In this same year the Friends opened a two-day-a-week school in North Carolina, where Negroes were taught "to read, write, and cipher as far as the Rule of Three." In Baltimore an adult Sunday school was established in 1820 where in the face of

[8] *Ibid.*, 4, 25–26, 43–44, 46–47.
[9] See, e.g., "Eighteenth Century Slave Advertisements," *Journal of Negro History*, I (April, 1916), 170, 177, 187.

some opposition Negroes were taught to read. In New Orleans a large group of prosperous free Negroes and Creoles with Negro blood maintained schools for their own children. Certain parochial schools instructed Negroes and whites together. In Norfolk, Richmond, and other Virginia towns were a few schools where favorite slaves and Negro children of white masters were taught to read and write until this practice was forbidden in 1819. In the 1820's the Presbyterians established a number of schools for slaves in Kentucky. Until 1829 a Santo Domingan Negro, Julian Troumontaine, taught a Negro school in Savannah.[10]

While these Negro schools were exceptional, it is important that in Colonial days men who taught Negroes were frowned upon rather than punished. Toward the end of the Colonial period, the spread of eighteenth-century liberalism through the South provoked contradictory reactions. Some men were impelled by it to grant greater privileges to Negroes, to encourage or provide teachers for them, and to talk of freeing them.[11] Other men became alarmed at the effect Locke's and Rousseau's views would have upon slaves who were able to read them. On the whole, however, the years of Revolution and Jeffersonian liberalism provided the greatest freedom ever enjoyed under slavery by teachers of Negroes.

[10] John B. McMaster, *A History of the People of the United States,* V, 360–361; U. S. Commissioner of Education, *Special Report on the Condition and Improvement of Public Schools in the District of Columbia, 1870* (*House Ex. Docs.,* 41 Cong., 2 sess., vol. XIII, ser. no. 1427, doc. no. 315), 362, 394; U. S. Bureau of Education, *Negro Education* (*Bulletin,* 1916, no. 38), I, 246; C. G. Woodson, *op. cit.,* 46, 50, 93–121, 128–129; Benjamin Brawley, *A Short History of the American Negro,* 104; Mary S. Locke, *Anti-Slavery in America from the Introduction of African Slaves to the Prohibition of the Slave Trade* (*1619–1808*), 28, 108; Edwin R. Embree, *Brown America,* 60–68; Asa E. Martin, *The Anti-Slavery Movement in Kentucky Prior to 1850,* 37; *Third Annual Report of the Female Union Society for the Promotion of Sabbath Schools,* 22, 24; James P. Wickersham, *A History of Education in Pennsylvania,* 249–254; John S. Bassett, *Slavery in the State of North Carolina,* 66; [U. S. Army,] Dept. of the Gulf, Board of Education for Freedmen, *Report . . . 1864,* 3.

[11] New Jersey, for example, enacted a law in 1788 requiring all masters to have slaves under twenty-one taught to read. *New Jersey Session Laws,* 1786–1793, chap. CCXLIV, sec. 6, 488.

Indeed, during the first decades of the nineteenth century, before the slavery issue fixed racial prejudice upon the South, one Negro, at least, conducted a school in North Carolina that white boys attended. He was John Chavis, who had acquired his education in part by unofficial study at Princeton under President Witherspoon of that institution. Among the pupils of this cultivated Negro were such prominent white North Carolinians as United States Senator Willie P. Mangum, Governor Charles Manly, Abraham Rencher, congressman and governor of New Mexico, the Reverend William Harris, and two sons of Chief Justice Henderson.[11a]

The discovery of the cotton gin, the increasing economic importance of the slave system, the beginnings of abolition criticism from the North, the Nat Turner insurrection in 1831, a gradual realization that the slave section was falling far behind the free states in population and economic power, and the new slave philosophy that the South built up as a defense mechanism against world humanitarianism's indictment of slavery, combined to intensify the struggle. With the widening of the suffrage in the half century following the Revolution, the alarm of a newly vocal non-slaveholding white group desperately afraid of free Negroes was added to the slaveholders' desire to maintain the slave system. Until about 1830 the South was divided about slavery. Gradually criticism died away. Belief in slavery came to be a mark of Southern patriotism.

The religious leaders, who had been numbered among those most eager to teach Negroes, gradually ceased to oppose and came to support the slave philosophy. Formerly religious in-

11a James C. Ballagh, "John Chavis," *Dictionary of American Biography,* IV, 44–45; Edgar W. Knight, *Public Education in the South,* 86–87, and *Education in the United States,* 380; "A Negro Teacher of Southern Whites," *Baltimore Sun,* Dec. 8, 1929, and "Notes on John Chavis," *North Carolina Historical Review,* VII (July, 1930), 326–345; Booker T. Washington and W. E. Burghardt Du Bois, *The Negro in the South,* 146–147; Carter G. Woodson, *The Education of the Negro Prior to 1861,* 116–117; E. W. K. to H. K. B., Oct. 8, 1934.

struction had involved learning to read and write. Now the various evangelical sects contented themselves with oral instruction in religious beliefs. The Catholics and Friends alone continued to try to teach Negroes to read and write, and they were not numerous in the South.[12]

After 1830, Southerners felt more and more keenly the dangers of allowing Negroes to be taught. The poor white feared the competition of educated Negroes. The slaveholder felt that education of slaves menaced the whole slave system. Slavery was justified partly upon the theory that the Negro was uneducable and therefore capable of nothing better. The slaveholder inwardly feared that this might be disproved if men were allowed to try to educate Negroes. More serious, however, was the fact that with the growing effectiveness of escapes, ability to write enabled the slave to make out passes and, if questioned, to establish his freedom by proving he could write. Worst of all, reading would give a Negro "dangerous ideas," which would destroy his contentment and happiness, make him restless, and unfit him for slavery. As abolitionist literature increased in volume, fear of literate Negroes grew.[13] "Instead of reading the Bible," wrote De Bow, "slaves would have placed in their hands those 'other documents, books, and papers' inculcating insubordination and rebellion, and thus placing the lives of our families in imminent peril. If with the ability to read you could impart true religion, or even a desire or disposition to read the bible, the

[12] C. G. Woodson, *op. cit.*, 11, 181–183; J. S. Bassett, *op. cit.*, 67.

[13] Hermann E. von Holst, *The Constitutional and Political History of the United States*, II, 96; "Eighteenth Century Slave Advertisements," *Journal of Negro History*, I (April, 1916), 178, 181; Ulrich B. Phillips, "The Central Theme of Southern History," *American Historical Review*, XXXIV (October, 1928), 32–33; E. W. R. Ewing, *Northern Rebellion and Southern Secession*, 260; Ivan E. McDougle, *Slavery in Kentucky, 1792–1865*, 79; Charles S. Johnson, *The Negro in American Civilization*, 224; C. G. Woodson, *op. cit.*, 7–8, 170; Charles L. Coon, *Beginnings of Public Education in North Carolina*, I, 479; Oliver Johnson, *William Lloyd Garrison and His Times*, 122–123; "Negro Emancipation," *De Bow's Review*, XX (January, 1856), 92; [U. S. Army,] Department of the Gulf, Board of Education for Freedmen, *Report . . . 1864*, 4.

danger would be largely diminished. But if a judgment may be formed from the known conduct of white readers, we may reasonably conclude that the majority of blacks would prefer other books than the Bible. Is there any great moral reason why we should incur the tremendous risk of having our wives and children slaughtered in consequence of our slaves being taught to read incendiary publications?"[14] Ability to read and write made the communication of plots of insurrection easier. An "incendiary" publication of one Walker of Boston seeking to arouse Negroes to improve their condition was a large factor in the passage of the North Carolina law forbidding the teaching of Negroes.[15] The Nat Turner insurrection led to the immediate exclusion of all Negro children from white Sunday schools in Washington.[16]

Teaching of Negroes was, then, vigorously forbidden throughout the South. Berry declared in the Virginia House of Delegates in 1832, "We have, as far as possible, closed every avenue by which light might enter . . . [the slaves'] minds. If we could extinguish the capacity to see the light, our work would be completed; they would then be on a level with the beasts of the field, and we should be safe. I am not certain that we would not do it, if we could find out the process, and that on the plea of necessity."[17] A Virginia law of 1805 forbade overseers of the poor to require black apprentices to be taught reading and writing. Another in 1819 prohibited the teaching of Negroes or free mulattoes and provided for the punishment of the teacher, black or white, with a fine of three dollars and costs or twenty lashes on the bare back. In 1831 the fine was increased to a maximum of one hundred dollars.[18] In 1800 South Carolina forbade the teaching of Negroes "in

[14] "Ought Our Slaves Be Taught to Read?" *De Bow's Review*, XVIII (January, 1855), 52.
[15] J. S. Bassett, *op. cit.*, 100–101.
[16] U. S. Commissioner of Education, *op. cit.*, 200.
[17] William Goodell, *The American Slave Code in Theory and Practice*, 323.
[18] *Virginia Session Laws*, 1804–1805, 9; *Virginia Revised Code* (1819), I, 424–425; *Virginia Session Laws*, 1831, 107–108.

a confined or secret place of meeting, or with the gates or doors of such place of meeting barred." An 1834 enactment allowed a white teacher of free Negroes or slaves to be punished with a fine as high as one hundred dollars and six months' imprisonment, a free Negro teacher with a fifty-dollar fine and fifty lashes on the bare back, and a slave teacher with fifty lashes.[19] A Savannah ordinance of 1818 punished the teacher with a fine of thirty dollars if white and thirty dollars plus thirty-nine lashes if black. In 1833 the penalty was increased.[20] In 1829 Georgia imposed a fine and a whipping upon Negro teachers and a five-hundred-dollar fine and imprisonment upon white teachers.[21] In 1818 and again in 1829–1830 the North Carolina Legislature rejected an anti-teaching bill. But in November, 1830, it forbade teaching slaves "to read or write, the use of figures excepted." The punishment for a white teacher was a fine of one to two hundred dollars; for a free Negro teacher, a fine, imprisonment, or a whipping; for a slave, thirty-nine lashes.[22] In 1832 Alabama enacted a fine of two hundred fifty to five hundred dollars for any teacher of free Negroes or slaves. In 1833 this law was modified to allow any one licensed by the mayor of Mobile to instruct children of "free colored Creoles" in Baldwin and Mobile Counties whose ancestors resided there when Louisiana was purchased from France in 1803.[23] Missouri passed an anti-teaching act in 1847.[24] Louisiana in 1830 penalized teach-

---

[19] *South Carolina Session Laws*, 1800, 36–38; *ibid.*, 1834, 13.

[20] W. Goodell, *op. cit.*, 321; Kelly Miller, *Race Adjustment*, 248–249.

[21] *Georgia Session Laws*, 1829, 171. The law was reënacted in 1833. *Ibid.*, 1833, 202. In 1850 a series of Savannah newspaper articles by Mrs. F. C. Adams urged repeal of the law against teaching slaves, because schooling would increase the slave's value to his master. The subject was debated in an Agricultural Convention at Macon. In 1852 a repeal bill passed the House and was defeated in the Georgia Senate by only two or three votes. U. S. Commissioner of Education, *op. cit.*, 339.

[22] C. L. Coon, *op. cit.*, I, 178; J. S. Bassett, *op. cit.*, 100; *North Carolina Session Laws*, 1830–1831, 11.

[23] *Alabama Session Laws*, 1831–1832, 16; *ibid.*, 1833–1834, 68.

[24] *Missouri Session Laws*, 1846–1847, 103.

ing slaves by one to twelve months' imprisonment.[25] Tennessee, Kentucky, and Maryland were the only slave states east of the Mississippi where teachers could lawfully instruct slaves.[26]

Yet in spite of these rigid laws some men did teach Negroes. In New Orleans, the private schools of Negro Creoles were tolerated "because of the freedom, wealth, respectability and light color of the parents, many of whom were nearly white, and by blood, sympathy, association, slave-holding, and other interests, [were] allied to the white rather than the black."[27] Virginia had a few Negro schools despite the prohibitory law. In Alexandria, then a part of the District of Columbia, a freedman named Parry conducted a night and later a day school despite a local anti-assembly ordinance. When arrested, Parry pleaded his good reputation but to no avail. The Mayor declared that his consent for teaching Negroes would never be given though the teacher were "as pure as the Angel Gabriel." Then the Mayor proceeded to wink at Parry's teaching, and Parry took the precaution of hiring a white man to be present at his night school.[28] Tennessee had a few Negro schools. Kentucky had more. Lexington, Richmond, Maysville, Danville, Louisville each possessed at least one school where masters permitted their slaves to be taught.[29] In Baltimore slaves occasionally went to school with white children; one large community center for Negroes housed several schoolrooms; a Catholic order of colored women conducted a school for colored girls.[30]

[25] *Louisiana Session Laws*, 1828–1831, 96.
[26] Delaware did not specifically forbid it; but a strict anti-assembly law in 1863 made holding school impossible. C. G. Woodson, *op. cit.*, 165, 168–169.
[27] [U. S. Army,] Department of the Gulf, Board of Education for Freedmen, *Report . . . 1864*, 3.
[28] U. S. Commissioner of Education, *op. cit.*, 283.
[29] Charles E. Hedrick, *Social and Economic Aspects of Slavery in the Transmontane Prior to 1850*, 74–75.
[30] Benjamin Drew, *A North-Side View of Slavery: The Refugee*, 110, 114; C. G. Woodson, *op. cit.*, 144; George W. Williams, *History of the Negro Race in America*, II, 161.

Nevertheless, openly conducted schools for Negroes were exceptional. Negroes were usually taught privately by masters or clandestinely without the masters' knowledge. A master occasionally found it useful to educate slaves trusted with responsibility and slave children who were constant companions of the master's children. It was a New Orleans custom for a master to send illegitimate children by slave mothers abroad or to the North for a good education, but they received their elementary training at home. Often the master himself taught the slave. Sometimes it was a kind-hearted mistress; sometimes the master's children, while they were themselves studying. Occasionally, Negro children were allowed to sit in on the lessons of the white children. Many Negroes learned to read or write at Sabbath school. Stonewall Jackson, for instance, taught a Negro Sunday school while a professor in Lexington, Virginia. Nat Turner got his education in Sunday school. Abundant records evidence a not uncommon practice of privately teaching certain household slaves.[31] Planters apparently regarded the laws as applying not to themselves but to non-slaveholders or Negroes or Northerners who wished to teach their slaves.[32]

More often the teaching was done clandestinely.[33] Frederick Douglass's white playmates were his teachers.[34] One slave obtained a spelling-book with a ninepence a man gave him for holding his horse, studied in the hayloft on Sundays, and got white children to hear his lessons.[35] Sarah Grimké

[31] U. S. Bureau of Education, *Negro Education* (*Bulletin*, 1916, no. 38), I, 245–246; *Report of the U. S. Commissioner of Education*, 1902, I, 200; "Religious Instruction of Slaves," *De Bow's Review*, XXVI (January, 1859), 107–180; C. G. Woodson, *op. cit.*, 13–14, 205–206, 210, 214–215, 220, 221; Booker T. Washington, *The Story of the Negro*, II, 123; K. Miller, *op. cit.*, 246; [Mrs.] L. H. Hammond, *In Black and White, an Interpretation of Southern Life*, 184–185.

[32] See, e.g., Jabez L. M. Curry, *Education of the Negroes since 1860*, 8.

[33] See, e.g., [U. S. Army,] Department of the Gulf, Board of Education for Freedmen, *Report . . . 1864*, 4; C. G. Woodson, *op. cit.*, 13; G. W. Williams, *op. cit.*, 471.

[34] Frederick Douglass, *Life and Times*, 101.

[35] B. Drew, *op. cit.*, 97. See also *ibid.*, 45, 89.

as a girl in South Carolina taught in the colored Sabbath school, but was allowed to instruct the Negroes only orally. She longed to teach them to read, but argue and plead though she did, this was forbidden. Therefore, "I took almost malicious satisfaction," she wrote, "in teaching my little waiting maid at night, when she was supposed to be occupied in combing and brushing my long locks. The light was put out, the keyhole screened, and flat on our stomachs before the fire, with the spelling-book under our eyes, we defied the laws of South Carolina."[36] In 1851 Fredrika Bremer reported two Negro schools in Charleston. In Savannah the Union Army found a Negress named Deveaux who for thirty years had conducted a school undetected.[37]

Regular schools were frequently conducted surreptitiously. A District of Columbia mulatto named Mrs. Peake taught a school secretly by night in her cabin.[38] A Fredericksburg Negro named De Baptiste turned his home into a school, where his children and relatives were taught first by a Negro and then by a Scotch-Irishman. The police became suspicious and watched the home but were never able to get evidence sufficient to take action.[39] Two English women in Fredericksburg who ran a secret school kept on hand a supply of splinters and a match preparation so that, if any one surprised them, the children could be learning to make matches.[40]

More often, however, teaching of Negroes was discovered and stopped. The experience of the future Negro bishop, Turner, in South Carolina was typical. He managed to buy a spelling-book and got a white boy to teach him to spell, but the boy's brother learned of it and forbade it. Turner then employed a white woman to teach him on Sundays, but her

[36] Catherine H. Birney, *The Grimké Sisters*, 11–12.

[37] C. G. Woodson, *op. cit.*, 216–219.

[38] Augustus F. Beard, *A Crusade of Brotherhood*, 122.

[39] C. G. Woodson, *op. cit.*, 217–218.

[40] W. B. Hartgrove, "The Story of Maria Louise Moore and Fannie M. Richards," *Journal of Negro History*, I (January, 1916), 24–25.

neighbors learned of it and prevented her continuing. Finally, he went to work for some lawyers who allowed him to use their books and taught him to read and write.[41] Frederick Douglass's mistress began to teach him to read the Bible, but when his master heard of it and explained the dangers of educating a slave, she not only stopped the instruction but thereafter watched Douglass's every movement and rushed at him in wrath and took away his book or newspaper whenever she caught him reading.[42] When it was discovered that Mrs. Caroline Hill, then a slave nursemaid in Tennessee, was learning from memory the lessons her charges recited, she was kept apart from them while they were studying or reciting.[43]

In Charleston, schools conducted by clergymen for free Negro children were closed. While in that city, an English traveler named Benwell who went to a meeting in the home of a prosperous free Negro to discuss the organization of a school for Negroes was warned by the proprietor of his hotel that he had been shadowed because of interest he had expressed in the school and that it was known he had attended the school meeting. He was urged for his own safety to write a letter to the press repudiating all interest in the matter. When he refused, the proprietor "related several instances of mob law, which had been enacted within the twelve months preceding, which, he said, were quite necessary to maintain Southern rights." The school was opened but "the virulent conduct of the constables, supported by some of the citizens and the civil authorities," forced it soon to close.[44]

In North Carolina, where public opinion had once been favorable to Negro education, a Sunday school run by two Friends, Levi and Vestal Coffin, was attacked in 1821 as dan-

---

[41] C. G. Woodson, *op. cit.*, 212.   [42] F. Douglass, *op. cit.*, 94–95, 101.
[43] Hallie Q. Brown, *Homespun Heroines and Other Women of Distinction,* 104.
[44] J. Benwell, *An Englishman's Travels in America,* 194–198; J. B. McMaster, *op. cit.*, VI, 280.

gerous. Slaveholders were persuaded to withdraw their slaves. Finally, the school was forced to close. In a few more years the "patrols" were ordered to search every Negro house in the state for books and prints, particularly Bibles and hymnals.[45]

After the retrocession of Alexandria to Virginia in 1847, the Virginia laws came into effect and Negro schools, which hostile public opinion had forced into hiding even under the District rule, were now broken up by vigorous searching of suspected houses.[46] In Norfolk, Mrs. Douglas, a white South Carolinian, conducted a school for Negro children for a year without molestation, and, according to her defense, without knowledge of the prohibitory law. Then she was arrested, convicted, and imprisoned for thirty days.[47]

Even in Kentucky, where there was no prohibitory law, the Louisville school of a Baltimorean named Gibson, in which about a hundred slaves with their masters' written permissions were learning to read and write, was closed upon complaint of a slaveowner whose bondsman had attended despite his master's prohibition.[48] Another Louisville school was taught by a Friend named Hethers. Three slaveholders, suspicious of him, hired a Negro slave barber to ask Hethers to write a "free paper" for him to use in getting to Canada. When the barber asked Hethers's price for a "free paper," he replied that if he were to write one he would not charge anything. At that moment the three slaveholders, concealed under the barber's counter, seized Hethers. He was thrown into jail and his school was successfully broken up.[49]

Violence was sometimes used. By this method, the school of an Ohio free Negro was broken up in Halifax County, North Carolina,[50] and Frederick Douglass's Sabbath school for fellow-Negroes was twice dissolved. Once Douglass was helping a white man conduct a Sabbath school in the home of

[45] J. S. Bassett, *op. cit.*, 66–67; C. G. Woodson, *op. cit.*, 114; W. Goodell, *op. cit.*, 324.   [46] U. S. Commissioner of Education, *op. cit.*, 284–285.   [47] James W. Massie, *America*, 88.   [48] B. Drew, *op. cit.*, 180–181.   [49] *Ibid.*, 241–242.   [50] *Ibid.*, 276.

a free Negro when a mob of white church members armed with sticks and missiles rushed in and drove them away. One of them accused Douglass of trying to be another Nat Turner and threatened that he would share Turner's fate if he did not desist. Another time his secretly teaching a Sabbath school under a large tree was discovered by a mob with missiles. Douglass and his pupils were threatened with flogging if they met again.[51]

But violence or the threat of violence was not usually necessary. Even the laws prohibiting teaching were important chiefly as evidence of overwhelming popular sentiment. Public opinion completely dominated by the slave psychology was the really effective restriction against the teaching of Negroes. That this was effective is abundantly proved by the testimony of Negroes like Booker T. Washington and Frederick Douglass who wanted an education,[52] and by the dense ignorance men confronted in the Negro population when, after emancipation, they set out to establish a system of Negro education.[53]

So thoroughly did the slavocratic psychology possess the country that even in the North there was strong opposition to teaching Negroes. This was based partly upon unwillingness to spend money upon them, partly upon a feeling that a Negro school was not quite respectable and would ruin a community, partly upon the belief that education spoiled a Negro if it did not make him dangerous, but, more than anything else, upon the fear that allowing Negroes to be educated would bring an influx of them into the community. Northerners were not fond of Negroes. Ohio, Illinois, and Oregon enacted laws forbidding the migration of free Negroes into those states. Other state laws discouraged it. Public opinion frowned on anything that would encourage them to come. Most Northern states had no law prohibiting teaching them.

[51] F. Douglass, *op. cit.*, 136–137, 187.
[52] See, e.g., B. T. Washington, *op. cit.*, I, 115; B. Drew, *op. cit.*, 41, 105.
[53] See the testimony of J. L. M. Curry of the Peabody Fund, J. L. M. Curry, *op. cit.*, 9, and E. R. Embree, *op. cit.*, 68.

Yet a year after Alabama imposed her two-hundred-fifty to five-hundred-dollar fine for teaching Negroes, Connecticut forbade the private teaching of out-of-state Negroes or the admission of out-of-town Negroes to any school without the consent of the "civil authority" and "the select-men" and provided a fine of one hundred dollars for the first violation, two hundred for the second, and four hundred for the third.[54] Ohio in 1829 forbade teachers and school directors to admit Negroes to the public schools.[55] The African Colonization Society opposed education because it would encourage Negroes to refuse to be colonized back to Africa. Even in Canada escaped slaves found opposition to their being educated.[56] In rejecting a proposal in 1853 in the Indiana Legislature for the education of Negroes, the opposition insisted that it was "better for the weaker party that no privilege be extended to them" since education "might . . . induce the vain belief that the prejudice of the dominant race could ever be so mollified as to break down the rugged barriers that must forever exist between their social relations."[57]

In the North resentment toward the teaching of Negroes led to forcible closing of schools, driving out of teachers, and burning of buildings.[58] In Cincinnati, Augustus Wattles who resigned a professorship at Lane Seminary to teach Negroes and four young women who volunteered as helpers "were daily hissed and cursed, loaded with vulgar and brutal epithets, oaths and threats; filth and offal were often thrown at them as they came and went; and the ladies especially were assailed by grossest obscenity, called by the vilest names, and subjected to every indignity of speech which bitterness and diabolism could frame." Rooming houses in which they lived lost other tenants, and landladies, on learning their occupation, set their trunks upon the sidewalks. No one had "ac-

[54] *Connecticut Session Laws*, 1833, 426.
[55] *Ohio Session Laws*, 1828–1829, 72–73.
[56] C. G. Woodson, *op. cit.*, 15, 175–176, 261–262; B. Drew, *op. cit.*, 341–342.   [57] C. G. Woodson, *op. cit.*, 332.   [58] *Ibid.*, 10–11, 242–243.

commodations for nigger teachers." Finally they had to club together, rent a house, and board themselves. They were threatened with violence. They received letters enclosing pictures of hearts thrust through with daggers, bloody tongues hanging from mouths spouting blood, decapitated heads, or cut throats. Now and then their schools were closed entirely by mob violence.[59]

Elias Neau, a missionary of the Society for the Propagation of the Gospel, established a Negro school in New York City in 1704. At first opposition forced him to go from house to house to teach his pupils, but soon he was able to gather them at night into his own home. For four years the school prospered. Then a group of Negro incendiaries tried to burn the city. Neau was accused of complicity. The Governor visited his school and gave it his full sanction. Neau was cleared of all suspicion in the trial that followed. The guilty slaves were found to be those whose masters had forbidden their education. None the less the council passed an ordinance prohibiting Negroes from being out after dark without lanterns or candles. Since Negroes could not afford these, the school was henceforth seriously handicapped.[60] When in 1790 another Negro school was opened in New York, prejudice was so great that it had difficulty surviving. After the New York School Society in 1834 took over the Negro schools formerly under the Manumission Society, they were badly neglected.[61]

But New England, the heart of abolitionism, provided the most famous cases of suppression of freedom to teach Negroes. In Canaan, New Hampshire, Noyes Academy was founded in 1834 with a constitution admitting colored pupils. Undeterred by the threat of a town meeting resolution barring intercourse with any one who taught blacks, the school opened in

[59] O. Johnson, *op. cit.*, 171–172; U. S. Commissioner of Education, *op. cit.*, 371.
[60] *Ibid.*, 361; C. G. Woodson, *op. cit.*, 26–27.
[61] *Ibid.*, 96–97; U. S. Commissioner of Education, *op. cit.*, 364, 366.

1835. Another town meeting then appointed a committee to remove the Academy. A mob of several hundred men and nearly a hundred yoke of oxen dragged the seminary to a swamp, left it there in ruins, and drove the teacher from town.[62] Then the town meeting solemnly voted: "The Abolitionists must be checked and restrained within constitutional limits, or American liberty will find a speedy grave."[63] Apparently this was not accomplished without criticism because Kate Brousseau in a French treatise quotes the New Hampshire *Patriot* as caustically reporting "qu'on le déposa intact à l'angle près duquel était située la maison de réunion des Baptistes, où il se dresse aujourd'hui, non pas comme le monument de Bunker Heights, élevé à la mémoire des héros disparus, qui combattirent et tombèrent dans la lutte pour la liberté, mais comme un monument élevé à des vivants qui combattent pour détruire ce que nos pères ont conquis."[64] Yet no one was punished and no property restitution was made. In fact, this violence was ordered by formal town meeting vote of the "best citizens."

In 1830 the First Annual Convention of the Colored People of the United States, meeting at Philadelphia and aided by Arthur Tappan and the Reverend Simeon Jocelyn of New Haven, decided to erect a manual labor college for Negroes at New Haven. The citizens of that city in alarm gathered and resolved: "That the founding of colleges for educating colored people is an unwarrantable and dangerous interference with the internal concerns of other States, and ought to be discouraged"; that the establishment of such a college in New Haven "is incompatible with the prosperity if not the existence of the present institutions of learning, and will be de-

[62] *Ibid.*, 400; H. von Holst, *op. cit.*, 97–99; Rev. F. A. Cox and Rev. J. Hoby, *The Baptists in America, A Narrative* . . . (London ed., 1836), 343–344; Amos Hadley, "New Hampshire in the Fourth Decade of the Passing Century," New Hampshire Historical Society, *Proceedings*, III (1895–1897), 49.

[63] Leon Whipple, *The Story of Civil Liberty in the United States*, 118.

[64] Kate Brousseau, *L'Education des Nègres aux Etats-Unis*, 44.

structive of the best interests of the city"; and that "the Mayor, Aldermen, Common Council and Freemen will resist the establishment of the proposed college in this place by every lawful means." The plan was finally abandoned.[65]

In the village of Canterbury, Connecticut, in 1831, Sarah Harris, daughter of a respectable Negro farmer, asked admission to the school of Prudence Crandall. Miss Crandall, knowing the sentiment of the town, hesitated but was finally impelled by her Quaker conscience to admit the girl. Her pupils apparently did not object, but some of the parents and many of the townspeople did. The opposition was led by a wealthy Democratic politician and later judge of the United States District Court, Andrew T. Judson, whose house stood next Miss Crandall's school on the village green. Warning was given that if Sarah was not dismissed, the white pupils would be withdrawn. Miss Crandall, knowing that it probably would mean loss of property and ruin to her school, finally decided to keep Sarah and to advertise in the *Liberator* for Negro girls. She was interviewed, argued with, threatened, insulted. When this failed, a town meeting on March 9 passed resolutions condemning the school and appointed a committee to persuade Miss Crandall to abandon the project. The resolutions protested that the school would "collect within the town of Canterbury large numbers of persons from other States whose characters and habits might be various and unknown to us, thereby rendering insecure the persons, property and reputations of our citizens." Mr. Judson declared: "The colored people never can rise from their menial condition in our country; they ought not to be permitted to rise here. They are an inferior race of beings, and never can or ought to be recognized as the equals of the whites. . . . The Constitution of our Republic . . . settled forever the status of the black men in this land."

[65] O. Johnson, *op. cit.,* 119–124; J. B. McMaster, *op. cit.,* VI, 77–78; C. G. Woodson, *op. cit.,* 288–291.

In April fifteen or twenty Negro girls arrived. An attempt to frighten the pupils with an old vagrancy law imposing a fine and ten stripes on the naked body failed. Non-intercourse agreements were made. No one would sell to Miss Crandall. She bought her supplies in neighboring towns. The stage-driver refused to carry her pupils. Boys threw filth into her well and her neighbors refused her a pail of water. Stones and rotten eggs were repeatedly thrown at her home. She and her pupils were insulted and threatened whenever they appeared on the street. Finally in May, an act of the Legislature made it a punishable offense for her to teach Negroes. In June she was arrested, confined in the common jail in the cell just vacated by an executed murderer, and in August brought to trial. The judge put aside the defense arguments and declared the law constitutional, but the jury disagreed. In a second trial in October Miss Crandall was convicted. She appealed and in July, 1834, the highest court evaded a decision on the constitutionality of the law by quashing the indictment on a technicality. The infuriated citizens of Canterbury then set her house on fire at daybreak. She and her pupils persisted in their school. Finally, late one night, a mob of men attacked the house with heavy clubs and iron bars, broke in all the windows and doors, and seriously damaged the first floor. Then the school was abandoned. The most significant feature of this whole episode is that the attacks on Miss Crandall were inspired and led by the wealthiest and "best" citizens of the town.[66]

Even in the nation's capital under the federal ægis a teacher was not free to instruct Negroes. In 1835 mobs of white men attacked the Negro schools of the District, demolished several

[66] See *infra*, 172–175; Samuel J. May, *Recollections of the Anti-Slavery Conflict*, 39–72; Ellen D. Larned, *History of Windham County, Connecticut*, II, 490–502; Anna T. McCarron, "Trial of Prudence Crandall for Crime of Educating Negroes in Connecticut," *Connecticut Magazine*, XII (summer, 1908), 226–232; G. Smith Wormley, "Prudence Crandall," *Journal of Negro History*, VIII (January, 1923), 72–80.

of the buildings, destroyed the furniture in the others, threatened the white teachers and leading Negro residents, and ransacked the homes of Negroes. Nearly all of the teachers —white women—abandoned their teaching after this. One of them, Miss Miner, when warned by one of a mob that her school was about to be destroyed, asked, "What good will it do to destroy my school-room? I shall only get another and go right on." Her school continued for many years. About 1843 the school of John H. Fleet was burned. In 1845 a Georgetown ordinance was passed, but never rigidly enforced, forbidding all meetings of Negroes except for religious instruction by whites. In 1858 two teachers from England and five white supporters of their schools were expelled from white churches of Washington and insulted; their schools were burned; and finally they were driven from the city. In 1860 Miss Miner was again threatened by a mob but again defied it. Finally, her school was set on fire, though she escaped.[67]

2. SECTIONALISM

The slavocracy sought not only to prevent teachers from instructing Negroes but also to bar Northerners from its schools and to force Southern teachers to obtain their training in Southern institutions. After 1830 the slavocracy was on the defensive. Earlier there had been uncertainty about the value of slavery, free discussion of slavery, and even apology for it. Now disagreement about the necessity of slavery was less frequently found, except in the border states. Freedom of speech was so thoroughly suppressed that doubts that did exist could not be voiced. The more ardent slavocrats worked out a slave philosophy in politics, in economics, in morals, that ceased to apologize for slavery as a necessary evil and taught instead its manifold blessings. Many non-slaveholding whites who had objected to slavery had moved to free territory to escape

[67] U. S. Commissioner of Education, *op. cit.*, 65, 201, 209, 214, 310; J. W. Massie, *op. cit.*, 87; C. G. Woodson, *op. cit.*, 266–267.

it. Many who remained had become convinced that their only safety lay in keeping the Negro controlled by keeping him a slave. Others who stayed behind after their more independent and ambitious fellows had left fell so completely under the political, social, economic, and ideological power of the large slaveholders that they ceased to think for themselves. They were thoroughly dependent upon the possessors of great plantations for what livelihood they did have. They might dislike the slave, but they feared the free Negro. Conditions of life might be hard, but nobody knew how bad they might become if the slave system were destroyed and chaos followed. At least conditions under the slave system were known; those with slavery abandoned were untried. Man is afraid of change. Besides, many poor whites still hoped some day to become slaveholders. Those who suffered from it as well as those who profited by it thought in terms of slavery. The non-slaveholding population therefore supported large planters in defense of the slave system.

In spite of all this, however, Southern institutions were on the defensive. The most serious symptom of ill-health and weakness was the South's fear of free discussion. Most mid-century Southerners professed the political ideals of Jefferson; they gave lip-service to freedom. Yet on the subjects that really mattered, they were afraid to allow criticism or discussion. In Congress, in state politics, in literature, in economic discussions, in morals and ethics, they suppressed freedom wherever it touched Southern institutions. The slavocracy, entrenched and powerful though it was, bravely though it talked, was at heart afraid to face facts about itself. It had lost confidence in the efficacy of truth to overcome error in a free field because, though individuals would not admit it even to themselves, it had lost faith in itself. Deeply rooted as it was, with great property interests at stake, it could do only what every social system does when it becomes decadent—stave off disaster by not admitting that disaster was possible.

The South saw itself falling far behind the North in population, agricultural output, shipping, railroads, manufacturing, wealth, and standards of living, in all of the elements that make prosperity. Northern ships carried Southern goods to market. Northern factories made much that the South bought and they turned its own cotton into cloth, which they sold back to it. In schools, literacy, newspapers, magazines, publishing houses, higher institutions of learning, all of the agencies that dominate intellectual life, the North, originally only its equal, was forging far ahead of the South. Southerners read Northern periodicals; they bought Northern books; they sent their sons North to school if they could afford it.[68] Not only the North but most of the civilized world looked upon the South's social system as harsh and unjust. The South maintained it was not, but was afraid to let unrestrained public discussion decide. Southerners were wrathful at Helper's *Impending Crisis* and suppressed the book, but all through the 1850's they had been seeking in Southern commercial conventions to remedy shortcomings in their economic system that were causes of the very economic inferiority Helper portrayed. Many slaveholders were eager, too, to ameliorate the cruelties of slavery. The South was not entirely uncritical of itself; it did discuss and suggest economic reforms. But human inertia and the concern of each individual with immediate personal advantages, which in any society handicap reform, prevented action. Convention proposals that would have benefited Southern society got no farther than incorporation into resolutions.

That many Southerners perceived faults in their economic system is evidenced by the discussions of a decade of Southern commercial conventions. Yet no one ever did anything about the difficulties after the conventions passed their resolutions and adjourned. The efforts to remedy minor faults in the

[68] Except when they bought English books and, if very wealthy, sent their sons to English schools.

slave system were vitiated by a deep-seated unwillingness to admit any evils inherent in slavery itself. All discussion remained superficial because it had to stop short of the possibility that the economic and social order on which all depended was itself inferior to that of the North. The faults of slavery might have been remedied if thoroughly analyzed and frankly faced. But the men who controlled the slavocracy had too much at stake to risk such an analysis. That would have required courage, clear thinking, and social-mindedness. It was easier and more human to refuse to admit that there could be any fundamental faults, to blame critics of the system for shaking confidence in the South rather than the system itself, and to suppress as subversive to society and disloyal to the South any person or written matter that suggested fundamental defects. Men who do not have faith in themselves and their social institutions always resort to denunciation of their critics and their critics' motives when facts and reason fail them.

It is easy to understand why Southerners did not want slaves taught to read and write and thereby brought into contact with ideas that books contained. The more ardent slavocrats, however, were afraid to have whites, even sons of slaveholders, exposed to ideas and practices that were not Southern-bred. They sought, not too successfully, to persuade the slavocracy to keep Southern youth at home for its education, to exclude Northern periodicals, books, and teachers, and to develop their own publishing houses, authors, and teacher-training institutions. This was difficult to accomplish, since Southerners had long depended upon the North in these matters. Nevertheless, though only partially successful, the more extreme slavocrats and the exigencies of the situation did together create a pronounced sectionalism, which seriously affected teachers in Southern schools.

There had long been a dislike of Northerners that grew partly out of natural sectional differences and partly out of certain characteristics of New-England-trained teachers, which

Southerners regarded as priggishness. In the first quarter of the nineteenth century, the South had been invaded by a swarm of Northern teachers who "caused our boys to guffaw over their weary platitudes and formal manners." This "class of stiff, formal pedagogues" was despised by Southern boys "because they represented so little that appealed to the human side of the normally healthy boy."[69]

As sectional antagonism increased, protests against hiring Northern teachers grew louder. "Men cannot come to reside temporarily among us," declared a Mississippi minister, "and pass away like birds of the season, and build up permanent interests."[70]   Edwin Heriott asked, "While we are striving to enforce the correctness of the principle, that the State should evince a decided preference for the results of the studies and labors of her own sons, in all other departments of industry, is it too much to expect of her that she should recognize the responsibility resting upon her, also, in determining to whom she is willing to commit the mental discipline and training of her children? . . . Is it not enough that our school-books are brought from unfriendly latitudes? Must we have Northern teachers, also, to enforce and give authority to the lessons they inculcate?"[71]

In the Southern Commercial Conventions repeated protests were voiced against the hiring of Northern teachers. "Let us look to our schools and academies," R. G. Payne of Tennessee urged the Knoxville Convention, "and see whether our youthful minds are trained by Southern teachers, or whether we have imported Yankeedom teachers to train them. Go to your sacred desks and see whom you have there. Guard and protect the rising generation from Northern influence."[72]

[69] Edgar W. Knight, *Education in the United States,* 354.
[70] "Home Education at the South," *De Bow's Review,* XVIII (May, 1855), 656.
[71] Edwin Heriott, "Wants of the South," *ibid.,* XXIX (August, 1860), 219.
[72] *Official Report of the . . . Southern Commercial Convention Assembled at Knoxville, Tennessee, August 10th, 1857,* 55.

The Memphis Convention in 1853 earnestly recommended to Southerners "the employment of native teachers in their schools and colleges."[73] The next year the Charleston Convention urged the "Universities, Colleges, and other scholastic institutions . . . to discriminate in the election of all professors and other teachers in favor of Southern talent and education."[74]

In 1857 J. D. B. De Bow of Louisiana rejoiced at Knoxville that "A growing preference is now manifested for Southern teachers over Northern ones, and in a notable instance it was found to be impracticable to retain at the head of a great institution of learning in one of our States, a gentleman, whose virtues were not to be questioned, but whose nativity was beyond Mason and Dixon's line."[75] In 1859–1860 the teaching staff of fifteen in the Norfolk schools included persons from New York, Philadelphia, New Jersey, Kentucky, Portsmouth, and Williamsburg, and only three natives of Norfolk. The next year loud protests were raised against the Northern teachers. The *Daily Southern Argus* averred: "If we are unfit to train our children, we are unfit to have them." Norfolk taxpayers asserted that fully qualified native applicants were rejected merely because they were not from the North. The school commissioners were threatened with repudiation by the people if they did not exclude from "temples dedicated to the moral and intellectual training of youth" all who had been educated "in that boasted land of political piracy and religious dearth."[76]

These protests and growing popular feeling barred North-

[73] "The Memphis Convention," *De Bow's Review*, XV (September, 1853), 268.

[74] "The Great Southern Convention in Charleston," *ibid.*, XVI (June, 1854), 638.

[75] *Official Report of the . . . Southern Commercial Convention Assembled at Knoxville, Tennessee, August 10th, 1857*, 15.

[76] L. Minerva Turnbull, "Early Public Schools in Norfolk and Its Vicinity," *William and Mary College Quarterly Historical Magazine*, XII (January, 1932), 8.

erners from many a Southern school. Yet in 1857 De Bow
lamented that "in organizing the Charleston Free Schools,
the other day, a troop of Northern teachers was imported,
when no one doubts there are sons of the South sufficient for
the work."[77] In July, 1860, William Gregg declared, "Professing as we do to be a highly intelligent people, it is strange,
nevertheless true, that we are in a great measure indebted to
the Northern people for teachers to instruct our children."[78]
The Convention Committee appointed to study the textbook
situation in 1856 reported: ". . . we have permitted, from the
unwillingness of Southern men to become teachers, our schools
and colleges to pass almost entirely into the hands of Northern men."[79] Edwin Heriott felt that Northern teachers were
hired, not because Southerners were incompetent or Northern training was better, but because of new fads in education.
"In plain English," he averred, ". . . our best qualified native
teachers are incapable of learning thoroughly, in a few months
or weeks, a system which has but little beyond the charm of
novelty to give it eclat, of which gymnastics and pantomime
are prominent characteristics, and to which a kind of pseudo-
military organization among the juveniles, imparts, to the
eye of the superficial observer, an aspect of order and uniformity!"[80] The *Richmond Enquirer,* on the other hand, found the
explanation of Northern teachers in an analogy of North and
South with Greeks and Romans. "The dignity and energy of
the Roman [Southern] character," the *Enquirer* pointed out,
"conspicuous in war and in politics, were not easily tamed
and adjusted to the arts of industry and literature. The degen-
erate and pliant Greeks [Northerners], on the contrary, excelled
in the handicraft and polite professions. We learn from the
vigorous invective of Juvenal, that they were the most useful

[77] *De Bow's Review,* XXII (May, 1857), 556.
[78] William Gregg, "Southern Patronage to Southern Imports and Southern
Industry," *ibid.,* XXIX (July, 1860), 79.
[79] "Future Revolution in Southern School Books," *ibid.,* XXX (May-June,
1861), 606–607.   [80] E. Heriott, *op. cit.,* 219–220.

and capable of servants, whether as pimps or professors of rhetoric. . . . The people of the Northern States of this confederacy exhibit the same aptitude for the arts of industry.— They excel as clerks, mechanics, and tradesmen, and they have monopolized the business of teaching, publishing, and peddling."[81]

In spite of the opposition to them, Northerners continued to teach in the South. After deploring the folly of sending Southern youths North for an education, De Bow in 1861 concluded, "Those who were left behind endured a worse fate, in being left to the tender mercies of peripatetic Yankees—a class which one of their own poets has so aptly described as,

> Wandering through the Southern countries, teaching
>   The A. B. C. from Webster's spelling-book,
> Gallant and godly, making love and preaching,
>   And gaining—by what *they* call *hook* and *crook*,
> And what the *moralists* call overreaching—
>   A decent living. The Virginians look
> Upon them with as favorable eyes
>   As Gabriel on the devil in paradise."[82]

Added to jealousy of Northerners' possession of the teaching positions was dislike of their ideas. "We should beware," said an Alabama correspondent, "of those who, under the garb of religion, poison the minds of the weak and credulous. Still more should we beware of teachers who instill into the minds of our children principles averse to our institutions."[83]

Northern ideas were almost as obnoxious, however, when transmitted by Southern teachers educated in the North as when inculcated directly by Northerners teaching in the South. In an address at the University of Virginia in 1851 R. H. Garnett denounced the "second-hand history and shallow

[81] Leonard Marsh, *A Bake-Pan for the Dough-Faces*, 7.

[82] "Future Revolution in Southern School Books," *De Bow's Review*, XXX (May–June, 1861), 608–610.

[83] *De Bow's Review*, IX (July, 1850), 123.

philosophy" of men who went North for an education. He protested:

> They joined the place-hunting politicians in an outcry against Southern indolence, and its fancied cause, Southern slavery; they pointed us to Northern opulence and the growth of Northern cities, not as what they really are, the fruit of the tribute that has dwarfed our own cities, but as examples of their superior enterprise and industry, until at last we began to believe, what has so often been dinned into our ears, that slavery was the moral, social and political evil they pretended. . . . Mr. Jefferson saw this danger, and designed the University to prevent it. . . . *The line of division lately marked out between different portions of our confederacy, is such as will never, I fear, be obliterated,* and we are now trusting to those who are against us in position and principle, to fashion to their own form the minds and affections of our youth. . . . This canker is eating in the vitals of our existence, and if not arrested at once, will be beyond remedy.[84]

De Bow and his *Review* persistently urged Southerners not to seek their training in the North. "Let our young and rising generation," the *Review* urged in 1849, "seek the light, as it is reflected from their own hill tops and through their own valleys. Let not a tyrant necessity subject them to periodical banishment from home, and its associations, at the tenderest period, to form among a distant people, habits, feelings, and thoughts at variance, frequently, and frequently *opposed,* to those they have left behind. Is it thus that we would rear up men to battle for the rights and institutions which belong to them, and which have come down to them from their fathers as an inheritance?"[85] In 1852 the *Review* quoted Jefferson as warning that the education of "southern youth, in the southern states, is necessary if the states are to remain sovereign and independent."[86] In the 'fifties North Carolinians were urged not to send their children North to schools hostile

---

84 *Ibid.,* X (April, 1851), 476–477.
85 "The Commercial Age," *ibid.,* VII (September, 1849), 229.
86 "Southern School-Books," *ibid.,* XIII (September, 1852), 261–262.

to slavery. Harvard especially was condemned as anti-Southern.[87] Before his death Calhoun, though himself a graduate of Yale, had advised that "boys intending to reside at the south, should be educated at the south."[88]

The Reverend C. K. Marshall of Mississippi told the New Orleans Convention,

We are in the habit of sending our sons and daughters to the north, far from their homes and home influences, there to be exposed to those which we believe dangerous to our interests, and damning to our peace. . . . It is not possible for southerners to be safely educated at the north. [Applause.] They cannot come back with the proper feelings toward their families and their people. Our sons and daughters return to us from their schools and colleges in the north with their minds poisoned by fanatical teachings and influences against the institution of slavery, with erroneous religious opinions on the subject, and with the idea that it is a sin to hold slaves. . . . Men for the south must be educated in the south; then they will rejoice in their own institutions, advance the integrity and strength of their own native States.[89]

The Memphis Convention in 1853 earnestly recommended to Southerners the education of their youth at home as far as practicable.[90] The Charleston Convention in 1854 urged "all parents and guardians . . . to consider well that, to neglect the claims of their own seminaries and colleges, and patronize and enrich those of remote States, is fraught with peril to our sacred interests, perpetuating our dependence on those who do not understand and cannot appreciate our necessities and responsibilities, and at the same time fixing a lasting reproach upon our own institutions, teachers, and people."[91] The con-

[87] Newspapers quoted in J. Carlyle Sitterson, "The Secession Movement in North Carolina" (Ph.D. dissertation at the University of North Carolina), 124.

[88] John Perkins, Jr., "Southern Education for Southern Youth," De Bow's Review, XIX (October, 1855), 464.

[89] "Home Education at the South," ibid., XVIII (March, May, 1855), 430–431, 656. See also Edwin Heriott, "Educational Reform at the South," ibid., XX (January, 1856), 67.

[90] "The Memphis Convention," ibid., XV (September, 1853), 268.

[91] "The Great Southern Convention in Charleston," ibid., XVI (June, 1854), 638–639.

ventions at New Orleans and Richmond in 1855, and Savannah in 1856 repeated the warning.[92]

If Southern teachers were to receive training in the South, colleges and normal schools capable of giving them that training had to be developed, for after all the South hired Northern teachers and sent its sons North for schooling largely because of the inadequacy of Southern institutions. This the men who urged patronage of Southern schools realized. *De Bow's Review* determinedly urged financial aid to existing Southern institutions and the establishment of new ones.[93] A University of New Orleans was advocated. The greatness of the University of Virginia was pointed out to Southerners. Elaborate plans were made for a great Central Southern University supported coöperatively by all the slave states, devoted to "thoroughly Southern" teachings and "pledged to the defence and perpetuation of that form of civilization peculiar to the slave-holding States."[94] The commercial conventions repeatedly passed resolutions urging the ample endowment of existing colleges, universities, and schools and the establishing of new ones, particularly normal schools where Southern teachers could be trained in the South to teach Southern ideas and culture.[95]

[92] *De Bow's Review*, XVIII (May, 1855), 655; "Southern Convention at Richmond," *ibid.*, XX (March, 1856), 351; "Southern Convention at Savannah," *ibid.*, XXII (January, 1857), 100.

[93] *De Bow's Review*, IX (July, 1850), 123; E. Heriott, "Education at the South," *ibid.*, XXI (December, 1856), 658; E. Heriott, "Educational Reform at the South," *ibid.*, XX (January, 1856), 75–76; "Ross on Slavery and Stiles' Modern Reform," *ibid.*, XXIV (April, 1858), 305–306; "Public School System of Georgia," *ibid.*, XXVI (January, 1859), 109; W. Gregg, *op. cit.*, 79–80.

[94] "Central Southern University," *De Bow's Review*, XXIII (November, 1857), 490–496; "Rights of the South," *ibid.*, IV (October, 1847), 211; "Universities," *ibid.*, V (March, 1848), 231; "Common Schools and Universities, North and South," *ibid.*, XVIII (April, 1855), 549; "The University of the South," *ibid.*, XXVI (May, 1859), 538–539; "The Education, Labor, and Wealth of the South," *ibid.*, XXIII (September, 1857), 268; D. H. London, "Enfranchisement of Southern Commerce," *ibid.*, XXVIII (March, 1860), 323–324.

[95] See, e.g., resolutions passed: at Memphis in 1853, "Memphis Convention," *ibid.*, XV (September, 1853), 273; at Charleston in 1854, *ibid.*, XVI (June, 1854), 638–639; at Savannah in 1856, *ibid.*, XXI (November, 1856),

In the West there was occasional prejudice against Eastern teachers. For example, the schools opened in Michigan by the Reverend David Bacon and his wife did not thrive because "the prejudice against the Yankees reached even to a Yankee education."[96] But the prejudice was not nearly so strong as that found in the South, and after all New England school teachers were found all through the West. In the North, generally, sectionalism was not much talked of in the teaching world. Very few Southerners taught in Northern schools. The North did not exclude them. It just did not hire them any more than it sent its children South to school or college. Northerners would have said this was merely because Northern teachers and schools were better than Southern.

In one way sectionalism did affect Northern teachers. Northern schools and colleges depended for support in part upon their Southern students. They did not wish to close this supply of students by offending them. Therefore many Northern schools and colleges discouraged the expression of views on controversial sectional issues. This is one reason why many Northern schools were not stirred, as one would have expected, by the great sectional controversy until the War actually broke out.

3. ABOLITIONISM

Northern ideas were bad enough when free from abolitionism. Abolitionism itself was not tolerated in the ante-bellum South. Until about 1830 there had been Southern emancipationists. In the 1820's a number of Southern newspapers advocated freeing the slaves. In 1831–1832 Virginia very nearly enacted a proposal for gradual abolition. The newspapers of the state almost unanimously urged it, the *Whig* among them. Yet by 1846 sentiment had so changed that Pleasants, editor of the *Whig,* challenged Ritchie, editor of the *En-*

552–553; at Knoxville in 1857, *ibid.,* XXIII (September, 1857), 315; at Vicksburg in 1859, *ibid.,* XXVII (July, 1859), 102–103.

[96] Andrew C. McLaughlin, *History of Higher Education in Michigan,* 14.

quirer, to a duel and was killed by him because the *Enquirer's* charge that Pleasants was planning to found an abolitionist paper was by 1846 a deep insult. In North Carolina William Swaim, editor of the abolitionist *Patriot,* declared in 1826 that no paper in the state was earnestly engaged in defending slavery. By the 1840's every North Carolina editor had either lapsed into profound silence or had become a vigorous advocate of slavery. Dabney believes that an abolitionist paper would not have lasted a week in any Southern state in the 'forties. Its editor would have been driven North and its presses "dumped into the nearest river."

Southern clergymen who criticized the slave system were expelled from their churches and from the South. Southern churches almost without exception defended slavery. Ministers did as ministers usually do—served the powerful business interests of that day by conforming Christianity to a defense of the economic and social system of the time. One of the most prominent clergyman of the day, Benjamin M. Palmer of New Orleans, declared in 1860 that it was the "providential trust" of Southern Christians "to conserve and perpetuate the institution of domestic slavery as now existing." "The position of the South is at this moment sublime," he told his slaveholding congregation. Dabney believes that Breckinridge and Fee were almost the only ministerial denouncers of slavery who succeeded in remaining in the South in the 'fifties. Even in the national capital Moncure D. Conway was driven from the Unitarian Church in 1856 because of his anti-slavery views.

"During the three decades immediately preceding the Civil War," Dabney summarizes, "the atmosphere in the South was not conducive to the free play of ideas. The intense preoccupation of the section with the slave question made it so morbidly sensitive to criticism and so intolerant of the views of those who found fault with its peculiar institution that free speech was stifled."[97] In this atmosphere it would have been

[97] Virginius Dabney, *Liberalism in the South,* 85, 90–92, 116–118.

surprising if teachers had spoken out against slavery. The vast majority of them had no desire to criticize slavery. In the ante-bellum South, as in most communities in any period, teachers shared and reflected the views of those around them. To "teach" views on slavery was perfectly acceptable to slavocrats, provided one taught the "right" views. Most schoolmasters were teaching elementary subjects; they were on the whole poorly trained; their facilities were entirely inadequate. Most of them therefore were too busy imparting the rudiments of knowledge to bother about slavery. If they thought at all about purposes of education, most of them unquestioningly wished to teach their children proper ideas of life, which, in a Southern community, meant indoctrinating them with slavocratic views. Southern extremists were probably needlessly alarmed, too, about the average Northern teacher. A Yankee teacher did undoubtedly teach many of the attitudes of his own Northern community. Usually, however, he came not to prophesy a new order or to reform the South but merely to earn a peaceful living in a section where the scarcity of native teachers made it easy to find positions. Teachers with this attitude either had no positive views about slavery, or, if they did when they came, refrained from expressing them if voicing them would cause trouble.

A minority of Northern teachers and a few Southern ones objected strenuously to slavery. It is to such a minority that freedom really matters. In the ante-bellum South they were effectively silenced.

Practically all Southern states rigidly prohibited the circulation of abolition literature. Mere possession of it was proof of crime. When an Oberlin student named Amos Dresser went South in 1835 to earn money by selling Bibles to complete his education, he protected his Bibles from rubbing by packing old anti-slavery tracts, religious newspapers, and temperance almanacs between them. At Nashville he left his books at the Inn and sent his buggy to be repaired. In it were found a few of the abolition papers. He was arrested, convicted of inciting insurrection, given thirty lashes on his bare back, and forced to flee in disguise abandoning three hundred dollars' worth of books and his buggy.[98] Being found with a book or newspaper with even one item derogatory to slavery was enough to label one an abolitionist. A teacher was therefore handicapped in what he could read. If a Northerner, he had to be particularly careful. If he had any "discretion," he kept his views to himself. All around him were warnings.

With most men pressure of public opinion was sufficient to prevent expression of unpopular views. James G. Birney was a man of courage and independence. Yet, after dismissal from a teaching position in Kentucky for anti-slavery beliefs, he wrote Theodore Weld of the great "pressure upon me at home." "My nearest friends," he lamented, "though hating slavery in the abstract, and wishing there was none of it, think it very silly in me to run against the world *in a matter that cannot in any way do me any good.* . . . I do not believe I can remain in Kentucky. . . . I shall (probably) be compelled to become a citizen of Illinois. . . . My nearest friends here are of the sort that are always crying out: 'Take care of yourself—don't meddle with other people's affairs—do nothing, say nothing, get along quietly, make money.' "[99]

There was no doubt about Southern sentiment. De Bow voiced a common attitude when he said, "Slavery educates, refines, and moralizes the masses by separating them from each other, and bringing them into continual intercourse with masters of superior minds, information, and morality. The laboring class of Europe, associating with nothing above them, learn nothing but crime and immorality from each other.

98 Wilbur G. Burroughs, "Oberlin's Part in the Slavery Conflict," *Ohio Archæological and Historical Quarterly*, XX (April–July, 1911), 281–282. See also U. S. Commissioner of Education, *op. cit.*, 308–309.

99 William Birney, *James G. Birney and His Times*, 144.

. . . Slavery is necessary as an educational institution, and is worth ten times all the common schools of the North. Such common schools teach only uncommonly bad morals, and prepare their inmates to graduate in the penitentiary, as the statistics of crime at the North abundantly prove."[100]

Mob violence was common. In 1835 members of a Charleston mob attacked the federal post office, rifled the mail, and made a bonfire of all the abolition literature they found. Instead of punishing them, the South cheered them, and a Southern president in the White House sent a message to Congress demanding a law prohibiting the sending of anti-slavery literature through the mail.[101] Congressman Hammond of South Carolina in 1836 spoke for the slavocracy when he said: "I warn the abolitionists, ignorant and infatuated barbarians as they are, that if chance shall throw any of them into our hands, they may expect a felon's death."[102] When, for a speech Sumner had made, Preston Brooks of South Carolina attacked him as he sat defenseless at his desk in the Senate and caned him so severely that he was incapacitated for several years, the South applauded loudly. The University of Virginia and other colleges presented Brooks with canes.[103] Helper's *Impending Crisis* was burned in the South. In North Carolina charges and countercharges of possessing a copy figured importantly in the gubernatorial election of 1859, for mere possession of it would have been politically disastrous.[104]

The Southern press and Southern politicians carried on a "war against Abolition teachers." The *Richmond Examiner* urged its readers "to *crush out,* really and truly, the Freesoil

[100] "Southern Thought Again," *De Bow's Review,* XXIII (November, 1857), 454.

[101] The measure did not become a law, but Congress, controlled by slave-holders, did actually pass a "gag" law in 1836 that automatically laid all anti-slavery petitions on the table without debate, without printing, without reference to committees. [102] V. Dabney, *op. cit.,* 105–106.

[103] Henry Wilson, *History of the Rise and Fall of the Slave Power in America,* II, 489. [104] John S. Bassett, *Anti-Slavery Leaders of North Carolina,* 15.

and Anti-slavery fanaticism . . . 'CRUSH IT OUT!' should be the shibboleth and watchword."[105] *De Bow's Review* warned its readers: "The disorganizing doctrines of abolition-ism are now taught from the pulpit and in the common schools, both orally and in text books. Hatred to the slave-holder, for abolitionism resolves itself into that at last, is indirectly inculcated as the highest civil and religious duty."[106] "Why," J. W. Morgan asked De Bow's readers, "should we wish that the rising generation, who are to frame and control public opinion, after we have passed from being, should be, on this question of vital importance, taught doctrines which are in direct conflict with what we now believe? Common sense, the dictates of self-preservation, the interests of what we deem to be the truth and the right, all equally forbid such a line of policy."[107] The *Richmond Examiner,* once an anti-slavery sheet, went farther. "The South," it shrieked, "has for years been overrun with hordes of illiterate, unprincipled graduates of the Yankee free schools, (those hot beds of self-conceit and ignorance,) who have by dint of unblushing im-pudence, established themselves as schoolmasters in our midst. These creatures, with rare exceptions have not deserved the protection of our laws.—They bear, neither in person nor in mind, a very strong resemblance to human beings. So odious are some of these *'itinerant ignoramuses'* to the people of the South; so full of abolitionism and concealed incendiarism are many of this class; so full of guile, fraud and deceit, that the deliberate shooting of one of them, in the act of poison-ing the minds of our slaves or our children, we think, if re-garded as homicide at all, should always be deemed *perfectly justifiable; and we imagine that the propriety of shooting an abolition schoolmaster, when caught tampering with our slaves, has never been questioned by any intelligent South-*

[105] L. Marsh, *op. cit.,* 14.

[106] "Reply to Abolition Objections to Slavery," *De Bow's Review,* XX (June, 1856), 646.

[107] J. W. Morgan, "Our School Books," *ibid.,* XXVIII (April, 1860), 436.

ern man. This we take to be the unwritten law of the South.
. . . Let all Yankee schoolmasters who propose invading the
South, endowed with a strong nasal twang, a long Scriptural
name, and Webster's lexicographic book of abominations, seek
some more congenial land, where their lives will be more
secure than in the vile and 'homicidal Slave States.' "[108]

Under such conditions only courageous teachers ventured
to express abolition views. Records of such teachers in colleges
are scant, in lower schools, non-existent. What happened to
men who did openly oppose slavery can, then, only be imagined from the general temper of the South. A few college
cases of dismissal are famous: President Alden Partridge of
Jefferson College, Mississippi, dismissed in 1832 for his
slavery views complicated by other factors; James G. Birney
of Centre College, Kentucky, forced out in 1834 for his abolition views; Benjamin S. Hedrick of the University of North
Carolina, dismissed, burned in effigy, and threatened with
tarring and feathering in 1856 for supporting Frémont;[109]
Henri Harrisse ousted for supporting Hedrick. Francis Lieber
was defeated for the presidency of the College of South Carolina in 1855 and left voluntarily in 1856 because his anti-
slavery views made him too unpopular for comfort. The whole
faculty of Berea School was driven out in 1859 for abolitionism.

In the national capital, Reuben Crandall, M.D., a teacher
of botany, was arrested and thrown into prison in 1835 for
alleged circulation of abolition literature. Although it was
proved that the "abolitionist" newspapers found in his trunk
were merely wrappings for his botanical specimens and that
the "incendiary" pamphlets were nothing more dangerous
than articles opposing slavery and maintaining the right of
free Negroes to live in America, the District Attorney sought
his execution on a capital offense. The jury cleared him, but

[108] L. Marsh, *op. cit.,* 6.
[109] For an account of the episode see J. G. de Roulhac Hamilton, *Benjamin
Sherwood Hedrick,* and J. Carlyle Sitterson, *op. cit.,* 126–127.

eight months in damp confinement caused his death of tuber-
culosis.[110] Oberlin students often went South to teach, but
were in danger if it became known that they were from
Oberlin.[111] Angelina Grimké, a Charlestonian Quakeress
teaching in the North, had written an anti-slavery tract. When
she tried to return to her native city to visit her family, she was
warned by the mayor that she would be arrested and imprisoned the minute she landed.[112] In 1857 the Reverend J. C.
Richardson, schoolmaster in the Kentucky mountains, was
seized by a mob because in his school library was found a
collection of Wesley's sermons containing one against the sin
of slavery. The mob bound him, beat him, and threw him
into a cabin guarded by two of their number, expecting
to return and further punish him later. Two of his pupils
rescued him and held off the pro-slavery mob with their rifles
while the schoolmaster and his wife escaped northward. A
little later Vestal, another schoolmaster of the American Missionary Association, was forced to flee from North Carolina.[113]

John Fee, a native Kentuckian, preacher, abolitionist, and
schoolmaster, was more persistent than most teachers. In 1855
he founded an avowedly abolitionist school in the mountains,
away from the slaveholders. In Rockcastle County he was
greeted by a riot; in Pulaski County his school was burned.
In all he was mobbed twenty-two times and twice left for
dead. Finally, after the John Brown raid, a mob of seven hundred men, "many of them wealthy and honorable," marched
on his school and drove him and the other teacher and their
families from the state. Three times Fee tried to return; three
times he was driven back. Finally, during the War, he did
return under protection of Union soldiers and reëstablished
the school that later became Berea College.[114]

110 J. W. Massie, *op. cit.*, 92–93.
111 W. G. Burroughs, *op. cit.*, 287.   112 C. H. Birney, *op. cit.*, 149–150.
113 *History of the American Missionary Association* (1891 ed.), 60–61, 10.
114 E. R. Embree, *op. cit.*, 76–77, 79, 81–84; *History of the American Missionary Association*, 7; H. Wilson, *op. cit.*, II, 669; Alvin F. Lewis, *History of
Higher Education in Kentucky*, 185.

After the War broke out, De Bow could write with pride, "We have expelled the whole brood of them from our borders, and are fast eradicating the false sentiments and ideas which they introduced and labored so assiduously to impress upon the minds of the young. They have left behind them a legacy of school books. Let us complete the work by banishing them, too, from our land."[115]

There were, of course, notable examples of men who could and did express their dislike of slavery. George Tucker of the University of Virginia pronounced slavery a "social, economic and political" evil; he declared as late as 1843 that it made slaveholders "idle, indolent, proud, luxurious and improvident." President Henry Ruffner of Washington College published a pamphlet in 1847 urging gradual abolition. In 1848, the Virginia historian, R. R. Howison, said that the majority of Virginians regarded slavery as an "enormous evil." In 1856, Robert E. Lee pronounced it "a moral and political evil."[116] Cassius M. Clay in Kentucky was outspoken in his abolitionism. The Berea School did continue until 1859. These things would have been practically impossible, however, farther south. The men involved were prominent, respected Southerners. They sought no action but merely expressed views. Those who dared give public expression to views like these were exceptional even in Virginia and Kentucky.

In the North the views of teachers on slavery caused much less excitement than in the South. The North had far less at stake. Yet during the 'thirties and in many places through the 'forties and 'fifties, abolitionists were extremely unpopular in the North, even in New England where they bred most prolifically. The 'thirties held them not really respectable, just fanatics and radicals, disruptive of society. They were insulted. Mobs pelted them with rotten eggs, vegetables, sticks, and stones, and broke up their meetings. In New York in-

---

[115] "Future Revolution in Southern School Books," *De Bow's Review*, XXX (May–June, 1861), 610.   [116] V. Dabney, *op. cit.*, 110.

surance companies refused to insure Arthur Tappan's property, and banks to discount his notes. William Lloyd Garrison was hounded through the streets of Boston by a mob and finally put in jail for protection. Another mob raised a gallows in front of his house with a halter on it for him. Whittier was stoned by an angry crowd in New Hampshire. Owen Lovejoy's press was destroyed, and he himself was killed by an Illinois mob.

In certain Northern colleges abolitionism was openly professed by the faculty. Illinois College in Jacksonville, Franklin College at New Athens, Ohio, Oberlin in the old Western Reserve, and New York College at McGrawsville were ardently anti-slavery in sentiment. They survived the pressure of antagonistic public opinion around them. But this popular hostility to abolitionism made their careers stormy ones.

In the majority of schools and colleges slavery was not discussed. So controversial a question endangered the growth and well-being of institutions seeking friends, not enemies.[117] Indeed, colleges were desperately afraid of being regarded as abolitionist. Conway, a Southern pro-slavery student in a Northern college who later turned against slavery, testified that, in 1847, "it would not have been easy . . . to find a professor in any American college willing to shield Negro slaves."[118] Miami University and Kenyon College forbade anti-slavery societies among their students. At Lane Theological Seminary in 1834 President Beecher, after promising to preside over a debate on slavery, was persuaded by the trustees to stay away. Most of the faculty had from the first advised against discussing the subject. Now the trustees forbade any meetings, save for devotional purposes, and dissolved both the Anti-Slavery Society and the Colonization Society.

---

[117] For instance, Vernon F. Schwalm ("The Historical Development of the Denominational College of the Old Northwest to 1870" [MS. dissertation at the University of Chicago]) found little evidence of discussion of the slavery question even in denominational colleges.

[118] Moncure D. Conway, *Autobiography*, I, 47–48.

One anti-slavery professor, John Morgan, was removed. At Franklin and Marshall College in Pennsylvania students were forbidden to attend political lectures. At Yale students of Southern sympathies broke up abolition meetings. Harvard students mobbed with rotten eggs a hall where Emerson was giving an anti-slavery lecture. At Harvard, too, Professor Charles Follen was dismissed for his anti-slavery activity. Bowdoin College in Maine gave an LL.D. to Jefferson Davis in 1858.[119]

Records of schools are ill preserved, but they were even more controlled by community pressure, and most communities disliked abolitionism. Phillips Andover, for instance, forbade its students to form an anti-slavery society.[120] The Missionary Institute, a preparatory school at Quincy, Illinois, lived under constant attack because of its anti-slavery views. It was finally burned by a mob from Missouri.[121] In 1850 three of the buildings of the Eleutherian Institute of Lancaster, Indiana, were burned as a protest against its abolitionism. In 1852 pro-slavery men tried to force the school to close by arresting two of its teachers, John G. Craven and James Nelson, on a charge of harboring Negroes.[122] Private schools needed students and endowment gifts and could not afford to offend Southern pupils. Public schools needed tax funds, which would not be voted if they got the reputation of being trouble-breeders. Where the pressure of public opinion was strong, teachers either shared the local views or thought it advisable to conceal their disagreement. Where public opinion was divided, the safest procedure was to keep the school and its teachers free

[119] L. Whipple, *op. cit.*, 121–122; H. Wilson, *op. cit.*, 264–265; O. Johnson, *op. cit.*, 166–169; George W. Knight and John R. Commons, *History of Higher Education in Ohio*, 60; W. G. Burroughs, *op. cit.*, 271; Joseph H. Dubbs, *History of Franklin and Marshall College*, 224–226; Edward W. Bemis, "Academic Freedom," *Independent*, LI (Aug. 17, 1899), 2195; Kuno Francke, "Charles Follen," *Dictionary of American Biography*, VI, 491; Louis C. Hatch, *History of Bowdoin College*, 116.   [120] L. Whipple, *op. cit.*, 121.

[121] G. W. Williams, *op. cit.*, II, 490, 492.

[122] William G. Thompson, "Eleutherian Institute," *Indiana Magazine of History*, XIX (June, 1923), 111–112.

from the controversy. Besides, abolitionism hurt business. Any town with Southern commercial relations was sensitive about conduct that might encourage the growing Southern dislike of trading with the abolitionist North. A Cincinnati placard posted on James G. Birney's press expressed the views of many Northern towns:

> ABOLITIONISTS BEWARE. The Citizens of Cincinnati, embracing every class, interested in the prosperity of the city, satisfied that the business of the place is receiving a vital stab from the wicked and misguided operations of the Abolitionists, are resolved to arrest their course. . . . The plan is matured to eradicate this evil which every citizen feels is undermining his business and property.[123]

When the Lane trustees forbade anti-slavery societies and all political discussion in 1834, they did so because such discussion had "a bearing upon a divided and excited community," because slavery was a subject of "great national difficulty and high political interest," and because the seminary debates had been "conducted in a manner to offend needlessly public sentiment."[124]

In Pennsylvania an "abolitionist" was sustained under great pressure in Dickinson College, which had not one abolitionist among students most of whom were from the slave states. Professor M'Clintock protected a Negro woman in a riot caused by the Court's returning three runaway slaves to their master. The Southern students arose against him in wrath and threatened to leave. But ultimately the students were pacified and he was retained.[125]

If abolitionism was prohibited in many schools and colleges, pro-slavery views were, too—sometimes because the institution was controlled by abolitionists, more often because of a desire to avoid controversy altogether. At Franklin College in Ohio, President Joseph Smith was forced out because he was not an abolitionist. At Illinois College in 1857 a student was

---

[123] L. Whipple, *op. cit.,* 101–102.   [124] O. Johnson, *op. cit.,* 175–176.
[125] M. D. Conway, *op. cit.,* I, 50–53.

forbidden to deliver an oration proclaiming that agitation of the slavery question was injurious to the country. Princeton students maltreated a Southern fellow-student so severely that the faculty had to suspend three of them, but the faculty warned the Southern boys against further "inflammatory utterances." Though Harvard disliked abolitionists, it had by 1855 become so anti-slavery in its views that it dismissed Judge Loring from a lectureship in its law school because as federal judge he enforced the fugitive slave law and returned a Negro to his master in the Burns case.[126]

Several factors concerning this issue in the schools are significant. Teachers seem to have played little part in the slavery controversy. They surely were not leaders in the new movement. Indeed, it is not the fact that scattered teachers got into trouble that is impressive, but the smallness of the number of teachers who held views on this greatest controversial issue of the day that would have caused them trouble. Pronounced opinions would have aroused criticism in most communities. Teachers were not of the stuff that made abolitionists. Most of them seem to have accepted slavery and drifted along with the sentiment of their community. It is significant, too, that most of the cases of difficulty over abolitionist views arose in the 'thirties or early 'forties. By the 'fifties the South had so crushed out opposition that it had no trouble, and in the North the anti-slavery movement had become so respectable as seldom to provoke attack. For instance, when Frederick W. Gunn opened a school in Washington, Connecticut, in 1837, he was denounced by the minister, driven from the church, and made so thoroughly uncomfortable that he had to give up his school and leave town—all because he was an abolitionist. In 1847 he returned to the

---

126 G. W. Knight and J. R. Commons, *op. cit.*, 204; Charles H. Rammelkamp, "The Reverberations of the Slavery Conflict in a Pioneer College," *Mississippi Valley Historical Review*, XIV, 450–453; L. Whipple, *op. cit.*, 145; J. Perkins, *op. cit.*, 465; James F. Rhodes, *History of the United States*, I, 504–505.

same school in the same town and taught without interference, because the attitude of the community toward slavery
had changed in the interval.[127]   Finally, in both North and
South, teachers were expected to indoctrinate the children
with the community attitudes toward slavery, wherever the
community as a whole had one, or to avoid the subject
entirely. Schools were looked upon as the people's agencies,
whose duty it was to foster the business interests and the
provincialisms of the locality that supported them. No effort
was made to use them to train citizens capable of critical
analysis of the economic system of that era. It did not occur
to men of slave days that, by training children to substitute
reason for emotion, teachers might increase human understanding and bring about a reasonable solution of sectional
differences.

4. TEXTBOOKS

The Southern press deplored the dependence of the South
upon Northern textbooks and publishers, particularly upon
Harper and Appleton and their books.[128]   "We do not remember," declared *De Bow's Review* in 1852, "a single text-book of
the schools printed or published south of Mason and Dixon's
line unless it be Peter Parley's at Louisville. If there are such,
they have but slight circulation. The Southern booksellers are
literally in a state of 'peonage' to the 'barons of Cliff-street'
and others of that ilk."[129]   "Let us not be content," urged
Morgan in 1860, "to banish the wandering, incendiary Yankee
schoolmaster, but let us also send his incendiary schoolbooks
to keep him company. What earthly improvement a girl,
not yet 'in her teens,' or a boy not yet free from the reign of
the 'round-about,' can derive from reading works wherein

[127] Bernard C. Steiner, *The History of Education in Connecticut*, 59.
[128] See, e.g., "Southern School Books," *De Bow's Review*, XIII (September,
1852), 258–266; E. Heriott, "Education at the South," *ibid.*, XXI (December,
1856), 650–659; and J. W. Morgan, *op. cit.*, 434–440.
[129] "Southern School-Books," *ibid.*, XIII (September, 1852), 259.

they are constantly informed that their fathers, and ancestors generally, for the last two hundred years, have been a heartless, cruel, bloody-minded set of robbers, kidnappers, and slave-whippers, I cannot imagine. . . . We forbid the abolitionist an abode in our midst, whenever he dares openly to declare and promulgate his opinions. Why should we be more considerate and forbearing toward his published or written sentiments than we are toward his spoken ones? We guard, by heavy penalties, against the possibility of his tampering with our slave population. We allow no interference with them on his part. Shall we be less careful when our youth, the growing, future rulers of our country, are concerned?"[130] One of the editors of the *North Carolina Journal of Education* urged: "Let every book in which the individual sentiment and moral of our section is disparaged, be at once published and repudiated in all our schools of every grade."[131] C. K. Marshall warned that the Union may break asunder at any time. "What if that sad catastrophe should fall upon us?" he asked. "What condition would our schools and academies be found in, with scarcely a book to study, except such as are written with a view to arraying children against their parents and consequently parents against their children, or such as are printed and published by establishments which are as hostile to our interests as the maddest fanatic who longs for a brand to fire the temple and sanctuary of freedom."[132]

Since the South produced very few good texts, it was necessary not only to banish Northern books but to subsidize Southern authors and publishers to produce others. The Charleston Convention of 1854 passed resolutions calling for patronage of Southern texts and publishers and urging legislatures to help create a supply of Southern books. It appointed a committee to draw up a list of proper Southern

[130] J. W. Morgan, *op. cit.,* 436, 439.
[131] J. Carlyle Sitterson, *op. cit.,* 123.
[132] C. K. Marshall, "Southern Authors—School Books and Presses," *De Bow's Review,* XXI (November, 1856), 519–520.

books. The New Orleans, Savannah, Knoxville, Montgomery, and Vicksburg conventions all appointed committees, passed resolutions, and discussed means of carrying them into effect.[133] Little resulted, however, except resolutions.

There were Southern texts. Simms had written a geography and a history of South Carolina, Adams a moral philosophy, and Mason a reader. In 1846 B. M. Norman advertised a "Series of Southern School Books." A text on bookkeeping was already in use, a history of Louisiana with a history of Texas appended was in preparation, and others were to follow. But these books did not sell. "Every Southern author, editor, or compiler," complained Heriott, "who has had the temerity to try the experiment on his own hook, of appealing to that dernier res[s]ort, 'Southern patronage,' has been compelled to pay the piper for his patriotism, instead of being paid for his industry."[134] The *Richmond Whig* bemoaned the fact that Southern men would not patronize a Southern book. "The North usually scowls at it, ridicules it, or damns it with faint praise; and the South takes on a like hue and complexion and neglects it. . . . The last chance now of getting a Southern book sold, is to manage to secure the favorable notice of the Northern press, and then the South buys it."[135]

Geographies were particularly criticized for inculcating the notion that the South was inferior to the North, for insidiously teaching that slavery was evil, and for overstressing the North and ignoring the South. "What," asked De Bow, "is to be done with geographies that tell pupils 'States are divided into *towns* and counties?' as if, out of New England, the use

---

[133] For the Charleston Convention, see *ibid.*, XVI (June, 1854), 632–641; for New Orleans, *ibid.*, XVIII (March, June, 1855), 430–432, 749–760; for Savannah, *ibid.*, XXII (March, 1857), 312–313; for Knoxville, *ibid.*, XXIII (September, 1857), 298–320, and *Official Report of the . . . Southern Commercial Convention Assembled at Knoxville . . . August 10th, 1857;* for Montgomery, *De Bow's Review*, XXIV (June, 1858), 574–606; for Vicksburg, *ibid.*, XXVII (July, 1859), 94–103.

[134] E. Heriott, "Education at the South," *ibid.*, XXI (December, 1856), 650–651.

[135] F. L. Olmsted, *A Journey in the Seaboard Slave States, 1853–1854,* I, 192.

of town as synonymous with parish, district, or township, was usual; that devote *two* pages to Connecticut onions and broom-corn, and ten lines to Louisiana and sugar?"[136] Mitchell's *Geography* was criticized because in its listing of the resources of Southern states, "reference to their provision for popular education is either studiously omitted, or else bestowed in so superficial a manner, without comment of any kind, as to leave the impression that the few [Southern universities] which are considered worthy of being named in passing, have never attained the smallest celebrity," and because it gives New England universities "the credit . . . of having contributed to the Union many of its most distinguished men."[137] Woodbridge and Willard were denounced because their *Geography* stated that "Massachusetts is considered the best cultivated State in the Union, except Pennsylvania, and much advance has been made by means of Agricultural Societies, and the premiums offered by them." "In all the States lying south of Pennsylvania," on the other hand, "the land is tilled almost entirely by slaves. In consequence of this, agriculture is much more imperfect than in the Northern States." They further offended by saying that "New England is more amply supplied with colleges than other parts of the Union, and receives a great number of students from other States," and that "The Southern States are not so well provided with literary institutions, and a large number of their youth are educated in the Northern States."[138] The slavocracy was very sensitive about even facts when facts were unfavorable. Gilbert's *Atlas* was disapproved as "abolition matter." *Appleton's Complete Guide of the World* was denounced as "a sort of literary and scientific infernal machine, . . . containing hidden lessons of the most fiendish and murderous character that enraged fanaticism could conceive or indite." The following

[136] "Southern School-Books," *De Bow's Review*, XIII (September, 1852), 262.
[137] "Educational Reform at the South," *ibid.*, XX (January, 1856), 75.
[138] E. Heriott, "Education at the South," *ibid.*, XXI (December, 1856), 656.

passage in Appleton is typical of the kind of school text that alarmed slaveholders:

In the southern States, . . . the field-labor is, for the most part, performed by Negro slaves—a race of beings who we understand to be worse treated in the American States than in any other part of the world. They are very numerous, and as they are aware of the black government in Hayti, and the emancipation of the black population in Jamaica and the other British colonies, the severe yoke, under the burden of which they have long groaned, must become more and more galling to them every day. Nor is there any doubt that the time is rapidly approaching when they will, by their own bravery, wrest their independence from their American masters, upon the very same principle and with the same justice that the Americans wrested their independence from the British Government.[139]

Northern histories were equally objectionable. They were attacked for sectional bias, which they undoubtedly had. Of course the loyal Southerner did not want unbiased history. He merely wished to substitute his own Southern for the historian's Northern prejudices. Peter Parley's *Pictorial History,* used all through the South, was particularly criticized. "It devotes an instructive chapter," said one critic, "to the history of slavery in the country, and the very benevolent and painfully philanthropic efforts of those who first introduced it to prevent its further extension southward after they had pocketed the profits of their own enterprising exertions. See page 220."[140] The following passage was a Northern textbook writer's idea of history:

But for what purpose, was [the slave] . . . forced from the scenes of his youth, and from the cool retreats of his native mountains? Was it, that he might witness the saving knowledge of the gospel? That he might become a Christian? Did they desire to open his prospects into a future life? to inform his clouded soul of immortal joys; and aid him in his pilgrimage to heaven? No. . . .

[139] "Home Education at the South," *ibid.,* XVIII (March-May, 1855), 431–432, 661.
[140] "Educational Reform at the South," *ibid.,* XX (January, 1856), 72.

He was placed among those who hate and despise his nation; who undervalue him, even for that of which he is innocent, and which he could not possibly avoid! He is detested for his complexion, and ranked among the brutes for his stupidity. His laborious exertions are extorted from him, to enrich his purchasers; and his scanty allowance is furnished, only that he may endure his sufferings for their aggrandizement. Where are the incentives, that may induce him to become a Christian? Alas! they are crushed beneath a mountain of desperate and hopeless grief; his views of happiness are depressed, so that he must almost doubt of his natural claim to humanity! . . . Hapless children of men! when shall light and order pervade the cheerless regions, where you dwell? What power shall heave the adamantine bars which secure the gates of your dungeon, and bring you forth? When shall the cherub hope smile on you from heaven, and, with a compassionate voice, call you to the pleasures of reason? to the delights of immortality? . . . Your deliverer must be a being of almighty power, wisdom and goodness. To that Being, then, let me commend you—to his favor—to his grace—to his everlasting mercy.[141]

One critic complained:

A very large proportion of the histories used in our schools are built upon this plan. They are filled with praise and glorification of the first settler of the New-England and Northern States generally, as a set of incorruptible patriots, irreproachable moralists, and most exemplary models for future imitation. And their descendants are depicted as fully equalling the standard set for them by their distinguished ancestors of unexceptionable demeanor. On the other hand, the individuals, who organized society in the Southern States, are pictured as a race of immoral reprobates, who have handed down all their vices and evil habits to their descendants of this day. While the institution of slavery, and its introduction into our country, are made the occasion of much violent invective, there is but slight effort at rebuke, and a large amount of apology is offered, for the amusements of burning witches, hanging Quakers, and banishing Baptists, formerly so very popular in New-England. While we, who now support and defend the institution of slavery, are either denounced or pitied, the residents of the Northern States, who have always been the chief prosecutors of the slave-trade, are allowed to pass uncensured. Such is the state of the histories.[142]

[141] Samuel Whelpley, *A Compend of History*, II, 159, 161.
[142] J. W. Morgan, *op. cit.*, 438.

De Bow complained in 1858 that the history teacher at the Citadel in Charleston was using as a text Willson's *United States,* which declared:

Of the state of manners and morals in Maryland, Virginia, and the Southern colonies generally, we cannot give so gratifying an account. While the upper classes of the inhabitants among the Southern people were distinguished for a luxurious and expensive hospitality, they were too generally addicted to the vices of card-playing, gambling, and intemperance, while hunting and cock-fighting were favorite amusements with persons of all ranks. . . . It cannot be denied, however, that New England colonial character and New England colonial history furnish, on the whole, the most agreeable reminiscences, as well as the most abundant materials for the historian. . . . Schools and churches [in the South] were necessarily rare, and social intercourse but little known. The evils of the state of society thus produced still exist to a considerable extent, in the southern portions of the Union. The colonization of New England was more favorable to the improvement of human character and manners. . . . The North, with unyielding firmness, rejected [in 1850] any compromise of human rights for the interests of slavery; and the South, with a zeal blind to the dreadful consequences, proclaimed adherence to her position, even to the alternative of disunion. . . . The hydra-heads of the old controversy will ever and anon start up anew while slavery exists among us.[143]

Northern books on "Moral Science," particularly those of Wayland and Hicock, aroused indignation. These inevitably included a chapter on slavery. A Northerner could scarcely have written on the morals of slavery to the satisfaction of a slaveholder, but usually these books denounced slavery as morally evil. One wonders not that leading slavocrats complained of them, but that they ever got into Southern schools at all. A teacher in one Southern school told one pupil that Wayland's chapter on slavery was "heretical and unscriptural" and that she would not be examined on it, but De Bow has a secret suspicion that such warning may not have deterred her from reading it.[144] In 1856 Wake Forest College in North Carolina

---

[143] *De Bow's Review,* XXV (July, 1858), 117; *ibid.,* XXII (May, 1857), 557.
[144] "Home Education at the South," *ibid.,* XVIII (May, 1855), 661.

dropped Wayland's book as inimical to Southern institutions.[145]

Readers, speakers, and orators were the worst of all. They were used by younger children and their attacks were more subtle. The *American First Reader,* the *English Reader,* Mandeville's *Course of Reading,* the *National Reader,* the *Village Reader,* the *Young Ladies' Reader,* the *Columbian Orator,* Lovell's *United States Speaker,* the *National Orator,* Scott's *Lessons,* even Noah Webster's spellers, were denounced as abolitionist propaganda. The selections in the orations were mostly Northern, often anti-slavery eloquence. In the *National Orator,* for instance, were printed orations carefully learned and declaimed by Southern schoolboys on "The Atrocity of Slavery," "The Evils of Slavery," "The Horrors of the Slave Trade," and also Curran's speech in England on "The Irresistible Genius of Universal Emancipation." Mandeville printed an essay on "The Existence of Slavery Inconsistent with Our Principles and Institutions." "Even in the spelling books," complained one critic, "are found allusions, more or less covert, and observations, more or less disparaging, according to the policy of the author, upon our peculiar institutions."[146] Readers teach that any spelling but Noah Webster's is "vulgar" and "not used in good society," protested another.[147] "It is stupid," declared a third, "to condemn the works of George Sand, and allow children to devour the abominable sophistries and jingling rhymes of Stowe and Whittier."[148] Even the poetry sang odes to New England or lamented the wrongs of the slave.

These repeated complaints of Southern slaveholders took effect in the form of greatly modified textbooks. Northern publishers could not afford to lose their Southern book trade.

---

[145] *North Carolina Standard,* Nov. 5, 1856, quoted in J. Carlyle Sitterson, *op. cit.,* 123.

[146] J. W. Morgan, *op. cit.,* 438–439.

[147] "Southern School-Books," *De Bow's Review,* XIII (September, 1852), 262.

[148] J. W. Morgan, *op. cit.,* 436–437.

Northern periodicals, unless they catered especially to anti-slavery patronage, avoided the issue. Publishing articles on slavery might lose Southern subscribers. In 1842 the editor of *Graham's* declared that no Philadelphia periodical dared allow the word "slavery" to appear in it. The *Knickerbocker* printed only innocuous material. During the 'fifties the *North American Review* declined all articles of a controversial nature.[149] Publishing houses assumed the same attitude. Harper, Scribner, Appleton, and all the other "regular publishers" refused to print Helper's *Impending Crisis* because it would alienate Southern trade. James Harper, himself an abolitionist, frankly told Helper that he agreed with Helper's views and thought the book should be published, but that after consultation with his business partners, he must decline to undertake it, because it would cost Harper's at least twenty per cent of its annual trade.[150] Some publishers sent the Northern books south with merely the title page changed to give a Southern imprint, but this was likely to be discovered.[151] Others carried two sets of books, one for Northern, the other for Southern trade, with objectionable passages all carefully deleted from the latter. Still others, and these the majority, omitted from all textbooks passages that would offend Southern sensibilities. This accommodating practice of Northern publishers undoubtedly explains why Southern extremists could not get Southern texts into their schools. English works, when reprinted in this country, were carefully censored with a business eye on slaveholders. Even the American Tract Society, the American Sunday School Union, and the Methodist Book Concern resorted to this expedient. Southern publishers, indeed, sometimes merely took Northern texts and deleted objectionable passages. In the first·issue of the *Southern Educational Journal,* for instance, a series of readers was advertised

149 V. Dabney, *op. cit.,* 134.
150 J. S. Bassett, *Anti-Slavery Leaders of North Carolina,* 43.
151 "Educational Reform at the South," *De Bow's Review,* XX (January, 1856), 77.

"carefully revised and freed from all objectionable pieces."[152] Gradually, then, in spite of the contrary impression given by extremists' complaints, textbooks were modified under pressure of the slave power, to suit slavocratic tastes. In 1854, for example, a Georgia woman whose uncles and aunts had used the *Columbian Orator* declared: "The books now used . . . show plainly that a great change has come over public opinion. They contain speeches against abolition. The writer has frequently heard persons in Georgia, not over fifty years of age, say they remembered when at school-boy examinations, speeches against slavery were not uncommon, and it was a frequent subject of discussion in school-boy debating societies."[153] By 1861 even De Bow admitted that Southerners were now sufficiently aroused that the anti-slavery *Compendium of American Literature* by Cleaveland could not possibly have circulated anywhere in the South.[154]

5. THE SLAVOCRACY AND BIG BUSINESS: A COMPARISON

A close parallel exists in their attitudes toward teachers and the schools, between the great "slave power" of yesteryear and "big business" of today.[155] Then it was commercial conventions of slaveholders. Now it is chambers of commerce and associations of utility men and manfacturers. The business of that day was badly organized and poor in ready cash. Business today is highly efficient and able to throw huge sums into the control of teaching. Slaveholders operated crudely and by vituperation. Big business today works subtly and with finesse. The teacher's position, however, is much the same under

[152] See, e.g., W. Goodell, *op. cit.*, 214–215; O. Johnson, *op. cit.*, 185; *A Brief Notice of American Slavery and the Abolition Movement*, 14–15; E. W. Knight, *op. cit.*, 445.
[153] [A Lady of Georgia,] "Southern Slavery and Its Assailants," *De Bow's Review*, XVI (January, 1854), 52.
[154] "Future Revolution in Southern School Books," *ibid.*, XXX (May-June, 1861), 612–613.
[155] See H. K. Beale, *Are American Teachers Free?* 98–173, 533–536, 545–577.

twentieth-century owners of industry and nineteenth-century owners of slaves. Both look upon the schools as instruments of indoctrination with ideas that serve the current order, help preserve it, and increase its prosperity. Both look upon teaching, not as development of thinking individuals with critical judgments but as a passing on of facts and attitudes, and a development of emotional loyalties to things as they are. The slaveholder did not want his slave taught to read and write because it would incite him to insurrection; the captain of industry wants vocationally trained workmen and clerks but does not want "radical tendencies" put into the people's heads. Neither can brook criticism of its fundamental tenets. Both put pressure on teachers and on textbooks with subversive tendencies, abolitionism in the one case, socialism in the other. Most teachers under both systems reflect community attitudes. Those who do not are forced to maintain silence on really vital subjects. Textbooks are criticized and then changed to please the ruling power of the day. Both resort to repression instead of reason to carry their points. Both call names when argument fails. What a familiar sound to men of the 1920's have the names hurled by the great slaveholders at their critics: "abolitionist," "infidel," "sabbath-breaker," "woman's rights fanatic." The parties to the conflict, declared President J. H. Thornwell of South Carolina College, "are not merely abolitionists and slaveholders—they are atheists, socialists, communists, red republicans, jacobins on the one side, and the friends of order and regulated freedom on the other."[156]

Freedom is allowed on questions that do not matter. But on the burning issues of that day or this, on which the teacher might be expected to provide leadership and to guide opinion in calm and rational consideration of society's problems toward a reasonable and peaceable solution, teachers are expected not to express views. Teachers played a very small part in the

[156] V. Dabney, *op. cit.*, 117–118; "Educational Reform at the South," *De Bow's Review*, XX (January, 1856), 74.

slavery controversy. Since schoolmasters were not allowed freedom, children grew up in blind faith in the slave system, incapacitated for peaceful solution of the slavery problem both by unfamiliarity with critical views of slavery and by psychological incapacity for critical analysis. Finally, the whole system blew up in bloody civil war with its train of chaos and suffering and irrational and unwise forced reforms of the slave system from which the South is only recently recovering. Professor Dodd, the great historian of the Old South, believes that if it had not been for the shutting off of all "authoritative objection to the dangerous trend of the plantation system" by denying to "teachers and scholars the function of free criticism," "one of the most cruel and most needless of wars" might not have come. America of 1932 he urged to profit by the South's folly. "Not many men," he says, "have the vigor to oppose openly the unsocial efforts of their own benefactors. But they must do so in the hope that society may not drift into war or economic collapse."[157]

[157] William E. Dodd to the editor, *Chicago Tribune*, July 15, 1932.

Chapter VI

FREEDOM UNDER WAR, RECONSTRUCTION, AND INDUSTRIALIZATION, 1861–1917

The period from 1865 to 1917 witnessed extraordinary growth and improvement in American schools. Elementary schools spread to almost every hamlet in the nation. Free public high schools sprang up through the North and West until almost every child there could reach one. Reconstruction democratized Southern schools, and Northerners in the South and Southerners themselves, under great hardship, stimulated popular education. But war and the Reconstruction experience impoverished the South. Because Northerners and Reconstruction legislatures had insisted on equal treatment of Negroes and often on racial coëducation, the white Southerner, when he regained control, undid or remodeled much that had been attempted under Reconstruction and began anew, handicapped by poverty and a late start. Then, too, aristocratic ideology deprived the South of the long-established tradition of general popular education that was bearing fruit so abundantly in the North. The South, none the less, made considerable progress, and, by the end of the period, had provided elementary schools for its white population and high schools for most of them. It was rapidly changing its attitude toward Negro schooling.[1]

In quality, too, this period witnessed a notable advance. Experimentation brought new methods. For instance, kindergarten technique was developed. New and improved texts now supplemented the old but still widely used McGuffey. The advance of science and general culture brought new objectives. William T. Harris, Charles A. McMurry, William

[1] For a discussion of Negro schools see H. K. Beale, *Are American Teachers Free*, 430–463.

James, John Dewey, and a score of others began a re-analysis of educational theory. The roots of progressive education go far back into this period. Normal schools sprang up all over the country so that, for the first time, training could be demanded of teachers. Later schools of education arose to train not only teachers but trainers of teachers. Laboratory schools were opened to experiment in educational method. A group of great college presidents raised some of our institutions of higher learning to legitimate collegiate rank and created great universities for research. During this period, too, the social studies came into new importance in the school curriculum. At the same time students of history, economics, government, and sociology evolved a trained scholarship with professional objectives and techniques.

This educational development profoundly affected the teacher's freedom. In many places teachers now were freed by adequate equipment from the handicaps that had always limited their choice of method. Replacement of the ungraded one-teacher school by a graded school with a teacher to each grade permitted specialization and freed thousands of teachers from one of the worst limitations upon choice of method. More adequate appropriations emancipated teachers, in the North at least, from the handicap of poverty and overwork. Increased salaries and better training schools removed another of the worst limitations upon freedom—a teacher's own inadequacy of preparation. Higher standards could now be required. In larger towns throughout the country, even in many small places in the North, teachers could now be obtained who were capable of exercising freedom if given the opportunity. The growth of scholarship in higher institutions began, late in this period, to develop critical attitudes in teachers of the social studies. These critical attitudes set teachers to thinking and developed in a few social philosophies that gave them both the need and the capacity for freedom.

Offsetting these tendencies to greater freedom inherent in

a more highly organized school system were certain tendencies that restrained the teacher. Administrative organization
accompanied the improvement of the schools. As the technique
and personnel of administration developed, its control over
the teacher became greater. Centralization, standardization,
more efficient supervision, growing slavery to pedagogical theory,
too great a faith in the power of "scientific" method to make up
for other inadequacies in a teacher, all tended to neutralize some
of the gains for freedom.

Growth was, in any case, a slow process. Many schools
and many teachers were still extraordinarily inadequate.[2] The
ultimate effects of improved schools upon freedom became
evident only toward the end of the era. Through most of
it, teachers, school trustees, and public were too preoccupied
obtaining schools and then raising the quality of those schools
to a decent level to think much about freedom or restraint of
freedom. Furthermore, the new critical attitude of the universities toward the social studies penetrated down to the schools
only slowly, scarcely at all until the end of the period. It takes
a whole new generation of teachers trained in new attitudes to
affect teaching in the lower schools. It requires even longer to
capture school textbooks and bring them into conformity
with the results of new scholarship.

Community attitudes toward life had not changed appreci-
ably. America was still a nation of religious folk, much concerned over strict standards of conduct. Dancing, card-playing, smoking, drinking, theater-going, and Sabbath-breaking

[2] S. E. Beach, for example, who was a county superintendent in Kansas from
1866 to 1868 testified: "I was frequently requested by the school boards to be
a little easy in the examination. . . . I sometimes found it difficult to select
questions easy enough to elicit any correct answers, as I did not like to grant
a *first*-grade certificate without getting some correct answers. . . . Of one lady
candidate for a teacher's certificate I asked the question, 'What is a noun?'
She replied that she did not know, as she had studied grammar but little. I
then asked her a few questions in geography, all of which she failed to answer,
until I asked her to name the capital of Kansas, when she promptly replied,
'Humboldt!' I gave her a certificate." [Board of Directors of the Kansas State
Educational Exhibit,] *Columbian History of Education in Kansas*, 175.

were still regarded by multitudes as sinful. Modesty still tabooed much that the World War generation took for granted in both conduct and conversation. The teacher was expected in all these matters to be exemplary. "He may find of a sudden," Royce wrote in 1883, "that his non-attendance at church, or the fact that he drinks beer with his lunch, or rides a bicycle, is considered of more moment than his power to instruct."[3] Thwing expressed a well-nigh universal attitude when he wrote in 1910, "The character of most teachers is an inspiration to right living. The example of their life is more potent than the significance of the precepts of the lips or of the textbook. Orderliness, punctuality, frugality, conscientiousness, thoroughness, persistence, represent elements in the life of the schoolroom which are of primary worth in the life and the character of the people. They embody foundations and forces, constantly acting, which penetrate into and form the springs of being."[4] Complaints were now seldom heard of the moral depravity and drunken habits of teachers. Improved schools and a more adequate supply of persons trained for the profession made it possible to demand and obtain conduct "proper" according to strict small-community standards. This was, however, no great handicap to most teachers, because teachers came from families that believed in the community standards. It was only toward the end of this period, when urbanization created communities no longer homogeneous in mores and beliefs and cultural backgrounds, that conflicts over conduct became serious. It has been in the succeeding period that teachers have most frequently found themselves restrained and limited by community demands. Then the World War had broken down old standards and left rapidly changing, chaotic concepts of morals in place of the older certainties; coincidentally teachers had come to share com-

[3] Josiah Royce, "The Freedom of Teaching," *Overland Monthly,* II (September, 1883), 239.
[4] Charles F. Thwing, *A History of Education in the United States since the Civil War,* 175.

munity standards less frequently than formerly. The period, 1865–1917, in conduct as in many other matters, was one of comfortable certainty and peace and community homogeneity.

During this period of development of American education, several major movements in American life decidedly reacted upon the teacher in the schools. First came the Civil War, then the turbulence and military rule of Reconstruction, then Darwinism with its doubt-raising teachings, than a new wave of secularization, then various reform movements, and, with great significance for education of the future, the growth of industrialism and big business. Each in its own way affected the freedom of teachers.

1. THE CIVIL WAR

The Civil War brought general repression of freedom. There is no indication that teachers were more eager in urging armed conflict than were other groups or, on the other hand, that they exercised any influence in restraining the emotional un-reason of war in favor of a more intelligent method of settling the sectional controversy. Teachers as a group made no stand for freedom of expression.

A few outstanding cases of violation of freedom occurred in the colleges.[5] No records remain to tell what happened to teachers in the lower schools who opposed the Civil War. Undoubtedly the great majority shared their community's views. Just as the imprisonment of a few newspaper editors was sufficient to gag many others, so the threat of punishment or the fear of popular disapproval unquestionably silenced

[5] For instance, Richard M. Johnston was forced out at the University of Georgia for opposing secession, Professor Totten at the University of Iowa for "disloyalty," President Woods at Bowdoin College for sympathy with the South and disapproval of the War, and President Lord at Dartmouth for support of slavery and criticism of the purposes of the War. E. Merton Coulter, *College Life in the Old South,* 308; Leonard F. Parker, *Higher Education in Iowa,* 87–88; Louis C. Hatch, *The History of Bowdoin College,* 123; John K. Lord, "Nathan Lord," New Hampshire Historical Society, *Proceedings,* IV (1900), 89–91; G. G. Bush, *History of Education in New Hampshire,* 152–153.

many teachers. In comparison with the War of 1812 and the Mexican War, the Civil War witnessed extreme repression of freedom both in the North and in the Confederacy. When compared, however, with the violations of freedom during the World War, Civil War repressions seem slight indeed. In both North and South large groups who had not wanted war criticized and opposed the Government at every turn. So strong was the opposition in the North to the war administration that it was questionable whether Lincoln would not be defeated for reëlection. With a people so divided, the rigid repression of World War days was impossible. Yet Copperheads were extremely unpopular, and, in the thousands of communities that whole-heartedly supported the Government, would not have been tolerated in the schools.

2. RECONSTRUCTION

In the South after the War, Northern military commanders attempted to prevent "disloyal" teachers from holding positions. This barred many Southern teachers from their own schools. The official test oath was required of teachers, where the army controlled and wished to enforce it. Some refused to take it and were replaced by Northerners. Then, too, insistence upon racial coëducation, where it was instituted, forced out many a Southern white who preferred to give up teaching rather than instruct a mixed school of Negroes and whites. Some teachers instructed for years without compensation rather than accept blacks as pupils.[6] Restrictions varied with the army officer in charge. On the whole the military officers were reasonable. Where they were not their control was onerous. Restrictions all disappeared as Northern force was withdrawn. While they lasted and were enforced, they left little official freedom to the ex-Confederate teacher. Popular opinion, however, was with the teacher and supported

[6] For example, the professors at the Louisiana State University. Walter L. Fleming, *Documentary History of Reconstruction,* II, 199–201.

much in the classroom that the army officer did not know or could not prevent. Even the most tyrannical Union commander found it impossible effectively to control, through military occupation, the thoughts and expression of a whole people.

Northern teachers flocked to the South after the War. Indeed, they followed the army during the War to conquer portion after portion of the Confederacy. In 1862, they were in New Orleans under General Butler's protection. Northern teachers and ideas were now even more disliked than before the War, for to earlier feelings was added the bitterness of defeat.

The attitudes of some of the Northern women who went into the South, expressed in their own testimony, make the South's feeling toward them understandable. They were earnest and devoted souls. But they did not understand the defeat-distraught nerves of the communities into which they went. Miss Armstrong, for example, complained with perhaps justifiable indignation that when the Southerners regained power in New Orleans they "left out" one hundred Northern teachers, including "every one who made any display of patriotism in school, or encouraged the children to love the Union or to sing national airs." Yet when Miss Armstrong's superintendent asked her not to sing songs obnoxious to the people and she submitted a list for approval there was not an item on it except Union and Northern war songs. "The Confederate cause," she testified, "was not permitted to be brought up on any occasion; but when I could bring up the Union cause I did so." Yet she asked why she lost her position. Marcia Taylor explained that they also sang "John Brown's body lies a mouldering in the ground." "It was pretty hard to get some of the girls to sing it. . . . I insisted on their singing anything that was determined to sing. . . . We sung all the Union songs and all the war songs."[7]

[7] *Ibid.*, II, 175.

3. Teaching of Negroes

Northern teachers in the South during Reconstruction were disliked particularly because of their views on the Negro problem. Southerners were trying to work out a *modus vivendi* with free Negroes that would avert the danger of economic breakdown during the transition from one labor system to another and would provide new social controls to replace the slave codes in the protection of whites. They were determined to "keep the Negro in his place." Industrial training had not yet become the fashion and cultural education seemed both useless and dangerous. Southerners wished to retain cheap and docile labor; education taught the Negro to demand better wages and labor conditions and to obey less implicitly. Poor whites dreaded the Negro's economic competition; education would make it impossible to hold him at menial tasks. Education might set the Negro to thinking and make him rebel against the rôle Southerners intended him to play. Southerners looked upon the Negro as inferior; the kind of education Northerners sought to give him implied human rights and equality. Northern treatment of the Negro as a fellow-man endangered the Southern caste system. Even Southerners who were interested in educating the Negro—there were some such—were alarmed lest Northerners put radical notions into his head. The result was vigorous determination in many communities to drive out teachers of negrophile views.[8]

In 1870 Colonel Edward Beecher, the superintendent of freedmen's education in Alabama, urged colored teachers in

[8] *History of the American Missionary Association* [1891 ed.], 23–24; Rev. M. E. Strieby, *The Nation Still in Danger . . . A Plea by the American Missionary Association*, 6; Virginius Dabney, *Liberalism in the South*, 166; Lyman Abbott, "The South and Education: a Record of Progress," *Outlook*, LXXXVI (July 27, 1907), 637; John Eaton, *Grant, Lincoln, and the Freedmen*, 192, 204; Charles S. Johnson, *The Negro in American Civilization*, 226–227; Benjamin G. Brawley, *A Social History of the American Negro*, 267–268; W. E. Burghardt Du Bois, *The Souls of Black Folk*, 32–33.

place of the whites. "The prejudices," he said, "which still exist, and I fear will continue for years to come, will, in many localities, prevent white teachers from being sustained. But colored teachers will not be at all molested, where whites would not be suffered to practice their vocation at all. They can find suitable boarding places when whites could not."[9] As late as 1881 Booker T. Washington reported many people in the community unfriendly to Tuskegee because "they questioned its value to the coloured people, and had a fear that it might result in bringing about trouble between the races."[10] In Louisiana the whites blocked efforts of the Freedmen's Bureau to get buildings for Negro schools.[11] In Texas whites would not sell land for schools or permit churches allotted to Negro congregations to be used for school purposes.[12] "The only schoolhouse which we could rent here," reported a teacher in Arkansas, "is a building consisting of a frame, covered with boards on the outside—I might almost say, at intervals, so large are the cracks between them. It has a fireplace, four doors and four windows, and the wind comes through every crevice, so that some days it is impossible for us to keep warm even with a large fire."[13] One Georgia teacher complained that the only place he could get in which to hold a school was a wretchedly built poultry-house.[14] In Memphis opposition was so intense that even under protection of the Union Army, teachers attempted nothing but "desultory private instruction under military auspices."[15] In 1870 a "political revulsion" in Tennessee forced most teachers of Negroes to abandon their

9 Edward Beecher, "Alabama," John W. Alvord, *Tenth Semi-Annual Report on Schools for Freedmen*, 28.

10 Booker T. Washington, *Up from Slavery*, 119.

11 U. S. Commissioner of Education, *Special Report on the Condition and Improvement of Public Schools in the District of Columbia, . . . 1870* (*House Executive Documents*, 41 Cong., 2 Sess., vol. XIII, ser. no. 1427, ex. doc. 315), 351.

12 L. W. Stevenson, "Texas," J. W. Alvord, *op. cit.*, 37.

13 *History of the American Missionary Association* [1891 ed.], 22.

14 *Loc. cit.*

15 John Eaton, *op. cit.*, 192–193.

schools.[16] In 1867 the *Norfolk Virginian* announced: "The Negro 'school-marms,' are either going, gone, or to go . . . our only fear is that their departure will not be eternal, and like other birds of prey they may return to us in season, and again take shelter, with their brood of black birds, under the protecting wings of that all gobbling and fowlest of all fowls, the well known buzzard—the Freedmen's Bureau."[17] In Charlottesville an editor refused to print graduation certificates for a teacher of Negroes because "the impression . . . is, that your instruction of the colored people who attend your school contemplates something more than the communication of the ordinary knowledge implied in teaching them to read, write, cypher, &c. The idea prevails that you instruct them in politics and sociology; that you come among us not merely as an ordinary school teacher, but as a political missionary; that you communicate to the colored people ideas of social equality with the whites."[18] Kentucky teachers of Negroes met great difficulty because Kentucky's decision not to secede made it impossible for the Freedmen's Bureau to operate there and protect them as it did in other states. Northern benevolent societies indeed were afraid to send their teachers into Kentucky.[19] Even in the national capital no lot for a Negro school could be purchased from a white man. Feeling was so tense that an order of condemnation was not deemed expedient. Where Negro schools did get a footing in Washington both pupils and teacher were subjected to insolence and abuse from white children.[20]

A universal difficulty of whites who taught Negroes was social ostracism, which not only made life unpleasant and isolated them from white companionship but prevented their

[16] J. W. Alvord, *Letters from the South Addressed to Major General O. O. Howard*, 28, 30.
[17] Edwin R. Embree, *Brown America*, 102–103.
[18] W. L. Fleming, *op. cit.*, II, 183–184.
[19] U. S. Commissioner of Education, *op. cit.*, 347–348.
[20] *Ibid.*, 275–276.

acquiring decent living quarters. For example, not a white person in Alexandria would give the Reverend N. K. Crow and his white teachers food or shelter in 1863. In 1865 Alexandria whites refused to board Caroline Moore, and, since Negroes were too poor to have suitable accommodation, she had to commute from Washington.[21] Just outside of Washington Frederick Lawton was similarly shunned by the white neighbors of his school. Miss Stanton was forced to walk so far to find food and lodging that she finally had to abandon teaching. One family told her, "If you are mean enough to teach niggers, you may eat and sleep with them."[22]

Southerners did not stop at social ostracism. In some parts of the South they resorted to violence to drive out the Yankee negrophiles. A Mount Holyoke graduate in Alabama was visited by the Ku Klux Klan, which fired a volley of beans and shot through her windows while she was teaching. She remained, and finally annoyance ceased.[23] An Alabama school taught by Congressman Benjamin S. Turner was destroyed by the Klan.[24] After 1870 teachers received warnings like the following:

Mr. Banks we thought we would give you a chance to save yourself one of the worst scourings that a man ever got. . . . You have set up a nigger school in the settlement which we will not allow you to teach if you was a full blooded negro we would have nothing to say but a white skin negro is a little more than we can stand you can dissmiss the school imediately or prepar yourself to travail we will give you a chance to save yourself and you had better move instanter.[25]

In Mississippi masqued members of the Klan called at midnight to drive a teacher out. Surprised to find her "a lady," they gave her twenty-four hours to leave town. She departed.

[21] *Ibid.*, 293.   [22] *Ibid.*, 273, 276.
[23] Augustus F. Beard, *A Crusade of Brotherhood*, 232–233.
[24] *Report of the U. S. Commissioner of Education*, 1902, I, 201.
[25] W. L. Fleming, *op. cit.*, II, 206.

Friends insisted a mob that would threaten a woman must have been "low down fellows," but she replied, "No; such men don't wear fine top-boots and have an address like theirs."[26] Cornelius McBride of Cincinnati was not so considerately treated in Chickasaw County. Klansmen dragged him out of bed, beat him unmercifully, and threatened to hang him. He finally escaped. In Noxubee County the county superintendent was ordered to resign and schools were burned. In Pontotoc County schoolmasters were warned to disband their schools and dared not disobey. In Lowndes County they were flogged and their schools closed. Governor Ridley C. Powers testified before a Congressional committee that for eight months not a Negro school or a white public school had been permitted in Winston County. All the schoolhouses but one had been burned.[27]

In New Orleans the military commanders at first refused to allow Negro schools. General Emory personally warned the Reverend Thomas Conway that it would be "very dangerous" to advocate them. Consequently, no public Negro school was established until October, 1863. In Thibodeaux the schoolhouse was broken open each night for months, "the furniture defaced, the books destroyed and the house made untenable by nuisance." Bricks and other missiles were repeatedly hurled through the windows. The Northern teacher of another school was driven to New Orleans in 1864, when Confederate soldiers defeated the protecting Union garrison. On a plantation near New Orleans a school was established by invitation of the manager. The Northern absentee owner, on his return, complained about the school, which soon afterward was attacked by a band of Confederates who put the Northern women teachers into a buggy and started to ride them out of the community. Northern troops intervened, rescued them, and established them in another school on a

---

[26] A. F. Beard, *op. cit.,* 232.

[27] Kate Brousseau, *L'Education des Nègres aux Etats-Unis,* 78–80.

confiscated plantation nearby. Soon that, too, was broken up.[28] In January, 1866, an outbreak against them temporarily closed most of the freedmen's schools in Louisiana and drove out the teachers. One teacher, a woman, was shot through the head in the process.[29]

Captain James McCleery, superintendent of education for the Freedmen's Bureau for northwestern Louisiana and Texas, encountered serious obstacles as late as 1870 in maintaining teachers at their posts. "The worst thing that could be said of a man was, 'He's going about starting Negro schools.'" Teachers were warned by numerous communities to keep away if they valued their lives. McCleery's agents had to travel in disguise and do business secretly. Abell, his clerk, was twice shot at from ambush. Another agent in the Sabine Valley was seized and stripped ready for one hundred lashes, which he escaped by promising, if released, to depart at once. Another time a mob seized him, took his horse, and burned his saddle. In the night a friendly Negro recovered his horse and helped him escape. He rode sixty miles through a wilderness before he reached safety. The superintendent himself had harrowing experiences. Once when attacked in Winn Parish he escaped only after hiding in a swamp all night, going thirty-six hours without food, and making a twenty-five-mile detour. It was hard to get teachers to come to his district. When he did, he could not get letters to them or from them. Often they were driven out. In the year 1869–1870 three of his schools were burned. Into one of the communities that threatened to kill him if he started Negro schools, McCleery sent a teacher who disappeared and was never again heard of. In Henderson County, Texas, one of his teachers was stripped, covered with tar and cotton, and given two minutes to get out of sight before a volley of

[28] [U. S. Army,] Department of the Gulf, Board of Education, *Report . . . 1864*, 4–5, 9–10.
[29] E. S. Philbrick to "W. C. G.," Jan. 12, 1866, *Letters from Port Royal Written at the Time of the Civil War*, Elizabeth W. Pearson, ed., 325.

musketry should follow him.[30] At Austin, Texas, a school was broken into by roughs, and the teacher was able to continue only because the post gave her a military guard to accompany her to and from school and stand watch all day.[31] L. W. Stevenson, superintendent in the second Texas district, received frequent threats but in 1870 reported only one case of actual violence.[32] In Lewisburg, Arkansas, W. J. Evans, the American Missionary Association teacher, left in haste when he was warned by the Klan to leave or be murdered.[33]

In the older South, too, violence was visited upon teachers of Negroes. In 1866 seven schools were burned in Georgia alone.[34] Charles H. Corey, head of Augusta Institute, now Morehouse College, was frequently threatened by the Klan. Occasionally the city authorities sent policemen to protect his school. In 1870 the new head, Siegfried, was attacked because in a Northern newspaper he had criticized the Southern treatment of Negroes. He had to leave, and the school was closed.[35] In 1869 an agent of the American Missionary Association wrote that in less than a week he had met: first, a male teacher who had fled from a neighboring community after the mayor had refused to be "answerable for the consequences" if he stayed beyond the day when the Klan had ordered him to leave; second, a teacher of a school on his brother's plantation in flight after being "dragged from his bed a few nights before, severely whipped, hanged by the neck till almost dead, and warned to leave in five days"; third, a Bureau officer who had just seen a Negro shot through the face for teaching school.[36] A Bureau teacher was driven from Greensboro in 1870, and the white man who had boarded him was dragged

---

[30] James McCleery, "Northwestern Louisiana and Northern Texas," J. W. Alvord, *Tenth Semi-Annual Report on Schools for Freedmen*, 33–35.

[31] A. F. Beard, *op. cit.*, 232.   [32] L. W. Stevenson, *op. cit.*, 37.

[33] J. W. Alvord, *Tenth Semi-Annual Report on Schools for Freedmen*, 40–41.

[34] U. S. Commissioner of Education, *op. cit.*, 340; K. Brousseau, *op. cit.*, 80.

[35] Benjamin Brawley, *History of Morehouse College*, 17, 20.

[36] Letter from a Secretary of the Association, *History of the American Missionary Association* [1891 ed.], 23–24.

from his home at night and "whipped unmercifully."[37] In
South Carolina the story was the same. A night school at
Orangeburg was fired into. A. M. Bigelow, the teacher at
Aiken, was driven from town with curses and threats against
his life. At Newberry, the contractor building a new school
was run out of town by armed men, who promised to kill
him if he remained. In Walhalla, since Southern chivalry
prevented such treatment of a woman, several white men
hired a drunken vagabond Negro to enter her school and
annoy her by accompanying her through the streets.[38]

Murfreesboro, Tennessee, hurled stones and other missiles
through the windows of the church where a Northern Negress
held classes in singing.[39] In North Carolina, too, schools were
broken up by organized bands. Some teachers were forcibly
expelled from town; others were scourged.[40] Miss Duncan's
school in Norfolk, Virginia, was burned. Captain Schaefer,
the founder of Christianburg Institute, was shot through the
hat. Fear of incendiaries led him to live in a stone house.
Eunice Dixon, who raised ten thousand dollars in England
for Hampton Institute, narrowly escaped death while a teacher
in Danville, Virginia.[41] In Hardinsburg, Kentucky, Marshall
Taylor, a Negro teacher who used a church for his schoolroom, was subjected to frequent annoyance. First the whites
tried to take the church from the Negroes on the ground that
it had been deeded solely for church purposes. When this
failed, they threw burning cotton filled with pepper into the

[37] J. W. Alvord to Major General O. O. Howard, Atlanta, Ga., Jan. 20,
1870, J. W. Alvord, *Letters from the South,* 22.

[38] Luther P. Jackson, "The Educational Efforts of the Freedmen's Bureau
and Freedmen's Aid Societies in South Carolina, 1862–1872," *Journal of Negro
History,* VIII (January, 1923), 30–31.

[39] Hallie Q. Brown, *Homespun Heroines and Other Women of Distinction,*
231.

[40] Doctor H. C. Vogell, "North Carolina," John W. Alvord, *Tenth Semi-
Annual Report on Schools for Freedmen,* 16.

[41] Letter from a missionary, *History of the American Missionary Society*
[1891 ed.], 23; William T. B. Williams, "The Yankee Schoolma'am in Negro
Education," *Southern Workman,* XLIV (February, 1915), 76.

schoolroom. They threatened Taylor with personal violence. In 1867 they blew up the building on the night of a Christmas "school exhibition."[42] In Washington molestation of Negro schools ceased when, after the burning of Nannie Waugh's school in 1862, the Federal Government provided protection.[43]

Of course, hundreds of teachers of Negroes performed their tasks in the South without molestation. The use of violence occasionally and the ever-present threat of violence did, however, exert a restraining influence over teachers or would-be teachers far more widespread than actual cases of violence.

The North, of course, would have objected strenuously during the Reconstruction era had Southerners moved in upon them and tried to educate their Negroes. Some Northern states had prohibited the migration of free Negroes across their borders. Others had objected to the teaching of Negroes, some even to the point of violence against schools that accepted Negroes.[44] Many Northerners still objected to having Negroes educated at public expense. Protests were still raised over coëducation of the races in *Northern* towns. In April, 1865, an Ohio mob, opposed to educating Negroes, burned Wilberforce University.[45] *Northern* troops broke into the schoolhouse of Miss Susan Walker near Washington and carried away her property and papers as a protest against her teaching Negroes.[46]

As the years passed, however, Northern unwillingness to educate the Negro died out and he was free to obtain whatever education his economic status permitted him. The public schools were soon opened to him, even where they had not been before the Civil War, and coëducation of Negroes and whites became a matter of course. The paucity of Negroes sufficiently educated to qualify as teachers and the absence of segregated Negro schools, in which they might have

---

[42] George W. Williams, *History of the Negro Race in America, 1800–1880,* II, 472.
[43] U. S. Commissioner of Education, *op. cit.,* 203.   [44] *Supra,* 126–132.
[45] U. S. Commissioner of Education, *op. cit.,* 373.   [46] *Ibid.,* 242.

taught, combined to prevent Negroes from teaching in the North. Whatever the views of abolitionists, it seems certain that a majority of Northerners would not have fought a war to free the slaves. Of the minority of Northerners who *were* sufficiently opposed to slavery to fight to free the Negro slave, many wanted no close contact with the Negro when freed. Even after laws preventing immigration of free Negroes were repealed and schools were opened to Negroes, many Northerners would not have wanted their children taught by Negro teachers had it been possible to find the Negroes capable of teaching them. It was only, therefore, after industrialism had brought a great influx of cheap Negro labor to create "black belts" in Northern cities that there was a place for Negro teachers in the North.

During the first decade of the twentieth century a number of Northern cities found themselves with Negro populations large enough to occupy whole school districts, sometimes many school districts. White unwillingness to live near Negroes led to a white exodus before the incoming Negroes that created extra-legal segregation. Negro children were not excluded from white schools, but, in Negro neighborhoods, there were now schools whose pupils were overwhelmingly if not entirely Negroes. At about this same time education began to produce qualified Negroes eager for positions as teachers. The result was that cities with Negro districts began to employ Negro teachers and found ways of appointing them to "Negro schools," all without any segregation before the law. Some cities like Pittsburgh, because of the absence of segregation, persisted in not employing Negro teachers at all. On the other hand, a few cities began to employ Negro teachers on merit and appointed them without discrimination in "white schools." Detroit, Michigan, and Salem, Massachusetts, each had a Negro teacher of whites soon after the Civil War. In 1889 Maria Baldwin, a Negress, became principal of the Agassiz School in Cambridge, Massachusetts, and for forty years taught in this school where practically all the pupils were white. In 1896 Suzan Frazier was appointed to teach whites in New York City. In 1910 Nellie Leftridge began teaching white pupils in the Enterprise School in Iowa. In 1915 in Chicago Louise Royal Cummings was appointed to a school in a white neighborhood where she remained for years. But, even after the World War, these cases have remained exceptions, not the rule, in the North. In the absence of segregated Negro schools or a white public opinion that will accept him to teach whites, the Negro teacher is rare.[47]

Southern opposition to teaching Negroes gradually decreased, and Southerners undertook the task themselves. In 1866, General Wager Swayne reported: "The presence of a school dispelled the prejudice against it, and the bitterness, at first so dangerous and obstructive, has been gradually converted to a positive approval."[48] In 1870 Colonel Edward Beecher reported in three Alabama counties a marked improvement in the feeling toward teachers of Negroes.[49] In the border states opposition always had been less intense. In Maryland, Superintendent Van Bokkelen reported in 1867: "Whatever prejudice may have existed in the minds of some of our citizens on this subject [of colored schools] is rapidly disappearing. . . . While there is not at present a willingness to educate colored children at the public expense, there is a readiness to grant them such facilities and encouragements as will not prove a burden upon the resources of the State."[50] The attitude of Northerners teaching Negroes changed, too. Atlanta University had been the subject of constant attack in its early days because of the ideas it taught Negro students.

[47] See H. K. Beale, *op. cit.*, 438–440, 503–509.
[48] W. L. Fleming, *op. cit.*, II, 180.
[49] One county superintendent wrote him, "The opposition to colored schools was deep and general; but the feelings of the people seem to have changed, to a great extent, on these subjects." Another reported, "Prejudices have now vanished, and whites willingly give their assistance to the education of the colored classes." E. Beecher, *op. cit.*, 26.
[50] U. S. Commissioner of Education, *op. cit.*, 355.

By 1878–1879 the State Board of Visitors could report: "The objectionable sectional books have disappeared from the library, and your committee are assured, not only that those Northern teachers do not try to alienate . . . [the pupils] from old masters and homes, and from their native State, but that every effort is used to counteract any tendency towards such alienation."[51]

After Reconstruction ended and they regained control of their own section, Southerners themselves slowly came to be more and more interested in providing certain forms of training for Negroes. Then white purposes in educating Negroes came to be an important factor in determining the degree of freedom possible in Negro education. Originally the chief supporters of schooling for Negroes had been Northerners. Their interest was likely to be a religious one. Negroes took readily to "getting religion," and the standards were often low, though courageous pioneer work was done by religious organizations. In the South, because of the nature of Southern religious denominations, religious control seems particularly apt to be narrowing and restrictive, and to this day the continuance of the religious tradition, particularly in private schools, places irksome restraints upon Negro teachers in conduct and ideas alike.[52]

In the early days those who helped Negro education sought to give the Negro the same schooling in content and method that prevailed in white schools, without any consideration of the needs of the Negro or his handicapped environment. Then about the time men began to establish special foundations to

[51] Charles E. Jones, *Education in Georgia*, 145–146.

[52] Concerning *Northern* religious organizations that aided Negro schooling, President Hope of Atlanta University testified, "On the whole, the attitude of the Northern home mission societies has been liberal; the restraints have been more a reflection of Southern attitudes (white and Negro) than of the Northern benefactors. The officers of the mission societies were men and women genuinely interested in education and not primarily interested in Negroes 'getting religion.' It is true, however, that the earliest teachers to undertake the work in Negro schools were very strict in their conduct and in their demands on the students." John Hope to H. K. B., March 28, 1935.

aid Negro schooling, there came a reaction to the other extreme. Disinterested persons saw that the early teaching had been faulty. Instead of adapting cultural training to the environmental difficulties of the Negro pupil, they decided that cultural education was a mistake and turned to programs of industrial schooling. To some extent this was part of a national movement for vocational training. In larger measure, though, it seems to have been the result of Southern white attitudes toward the Negro. Southern whites had opposed cultural education; many of them came gradually to believe that industrial training for the Negro would benefit the community as a whole. Then, too, the whole force of the man who for years was the greatest power in Negro education was turned toward vocationalism. A few Southern whites encouraged cultural education for Negroes, or helped an individual Negro to attain it.[53] Many, on the other hand, opposed any kind of Negro schooling. Still others favored industrial and opposed cultural training. Many Southern whites were interested in educating the Negro only if it would be economically profitable to the white man. Others honestly believed, as many Southern whites do today, that the Negro was incapable of cultural or intellectual attainment. Still others felt that he would always be excluded from places in society where cultural training would be of any use to him. Others felt that, if given cultural training, the Negro could never be "kept in his place." Others feared the social and economic implications of allowing him to be educated, thereby admitting that he was an intelligent being. Southerners instinctively sensed that permitting cultural courses for Negroes was a contradiction of the racial inferiority theory on which he is kept in an inferior position, socially, economically, and politically.

There is no reason to doubt that Booker Washington be-

[53] President Hope of Atlanta University tells, for instance, how "one of the most distinguished lawyers . . . of Augusta, an officer in the Confederate army, lent me his son's volume of *Plutarch's Lives,* telling me . . . that I needed to learn more." John Hope to H. K. B., Nov. 15, 1934.

lieved, as he so often said, that the best way for the Negro to win a place for himself was to make himself economically secure and necessary to the whites. Nevertheless, an equally important factor in determining his views was the fact that, with the temper of Southern whites what it was, there was no chance of gaining support for cultural education, whereas a strong appeal could be made to white men themselves, if the purpose of education was limited to creating skilled workmen and servants. It seems probable that once this much was accomplished he fully intended to go on to cultural subjects. He could never admit this publicly, however, and as the years passed he was forced by the opposition of new Negro leaders like W. E. Burghardt Du Bois into dogmatic support of industrial education only. Yet Negroes who knew him feel that he was dominated by his concern to win the support of Southern whites for Negro schooling rather than by his convictions about education itself. "Washington," says a leading Negro educator who was one of his friends, "was an opportunist. He was a prince of beggars. He was clever. He made friends with whites but he did not trust them. He was merely determined to get as much from them for his people as possible."[54] Negroes who studied under him at Tuskegee tell how, while white guests were being driven up from the station, the students would be hurried from the classroom into work clothes to be hard at labor in the workshop or field when the whites arrived.[55] Washington and other old-fashioned Negro educators varied their speeches as they traveled northward catering to public opinion and going as far as sentiment in any particular city would let them.[56] Washington struggled to give his own children a liberal college education.

But whatever his motive, Washington had tremendous power. His philosophy was expressed in his remarks at a meeting in 1915. "We should try," he said, "to keep the

[54] Interview in March, 1933.   [55] Interviews with Negro educators, 1933.
[56] Interview with Miss Mary White Ovington, New York City, December, 1932; M. W. O. to H. K. B., July 23, 1934.

young educated Negro from becoming bitter in his attitude toward people and things in general. Therefore, I believe in industrial education, which tends to make the Negro lose himself in his job. He does not then have so much opportunity to become bitter. . . . Our great problem now is to get ordinary white men to favor Negro education. If the vast numbers of Negroes are to be educated at all, it must be in the rural public schools. White men will vote funds for Negro education just in proportion to their belief in the value of that education. . . . We are trying to instil into the Negro mind that if education does not make the Negro humble, simple, and of service to the community, then it will not be encouraged."[57] Washington ridiculed college graduates; his apologists would say, a certain type of fatuous, boastful college graduates. His power was so great that for years only the most courageous dared oppose him.[58] "The man's power," says Miss Ovington, "was enormous. It is little exaggeration to say that there were not a half-dozen Negroes in the country in positions of educational or political importance that did not owe their jobs to Washington. The white man asked his advice on every conceivable subject, from appointing a minister to Haiti to putting bathtubs in a new colored Y. M. C. A."[59] Even during his life, a large group of Negro teachers was coming more and more to dislike and distrust his educational policies; since the World War, these policies have been largely repudiated even by Tuskegee and Hampton, which have become liberal arts colleges. While Washington lived, however, most Southern Negro teachers dared not voice disagreement.

The foundations on their part were motivated much as Washington was. There were sometimes Northern men among them who gave money to Negro education for economic motives of their own. In the 'nineties, for instance, Du Bois had a conversation about a position at Tuskegee with

---

[57] *Minutes of the University Commission on Southern Race Questions,* 29.
[58] Interview with John Hope, president of Atlanta University, March, 1933.
[59] Mary W. Ovington, *Portraits in Color,* 85.

W. H. Baldwin, president of the Long Island Railroad, who was slated for the presidency of the Pennsylvania Railroad. Baldwin, who helped solicit from his wealthy friends funds for Negro education, told Du Bois frankly that his purpose was to build up a rival class of skilled Negro workers to offset and compete with white labor and enable him as an employer to beat the unions. This, he said, was the way for Du Bois to get jobs for Negroes.[60] Not much freedom could be allowed in schools set up for this purpose.

Most of the men in charge of the work of educational foundations, whether the older ones like the Peabody Fund or those like the General Education Board and the Rosenwald Fund established in the twentieth century, were high-minded friends of the Negro. Yet they, too, favored industrial education—either through personal conviction or because they felt nothing else would be tolerated. Before the period of the World War, then, the foundations used their great power of giving or withholding money to encourage Negro teachers into industrial training. Their early lack of interest in liberal arts for Negroes tended to discourage those that believed in cultural education. The money they had to disperse they gave chiefly or solely to industrial schools. This was true of the Peabody Fund, the Jeanes-Slater Fund,[61] the Phelps-Stokes Fund, the Ogden Movement,[62] and the General Edu-

[60] Interview with W. E. Burghardt Du Bois, December, 1932. W. E. B. D. to H. K. B., July 17, 1934.

[61] The Slater Fund avowed a definite policy of contributing only to vocational schools. Dwight O. W. Holmes, *The Evolution of the Negro College*, 167.

[62] President Hope of Atlanta University points out that practically all the white people who visited Atlanta in the original Ogden party believed in industrial education, though not all of them definitely opposed college education for Negroes. The Southern Educational Association into which the Ogden movement crystallized did more for white than for Negro education. President Alderman of Tulane talked benevolently about educating the Negro but said the best way to serve Negro education was to give the money for white education to raise a generation of whites who would not be prejudiced against Negro education. Edward A. Alderman, "Education in the South," *Outlook*, LXVIII (Aug. 3, 1901), 780. There is reason to believe that Booker Washington inspired this Ogden device in the hope that it would mean better things for the Negro.

cation Board. No one can at this day prove whether the General Education Board withheld money from Atlanta University because Du Bois, the chief opponent of industrial education, was on its faculty producing sociological studies of a "radical" nature. President Hope of Atlanta and President Read of Spelman believe there were other reasons, namely, the various criteria the Board applied to all colleges. But the fact that Du Bois and President Ware at that time thought it was Du Bois's presence that deprived the University of support and the fact that Du Bois left for that reason had a profound effect upon attitudes of Negro teachers. Whether or not it was done as directly as through the *conscious* withholding of funds, the influence of the foundations was in the direction of industrial education for Negroes and in opposition to cultural studies. Not only Du Bois and Walter F. White, representing radical Negroes, but men like former President Adams of Atlanta University and President Holmes of Morgan College in Baltimore, who was formerly dean of the School of Education at Howard University, believe that the attitude of the foundations exerted a strong though subtle pressure upon friends of the liberal arts.[63]

The power that the foundations had over Washington himself is evidenced in a letter in which with obvious relief he thanked Curry for a check, said he was "very glad" Curry had liked his Chicago address, apologized for mentioning race

[63] Interviews with President John Hope, President Florence Read, Walter F. White, W. E. Burghardt Du Bois, and President Dwight O. W. Holmes; W. F. W. to H. K. B., July 19, 1934; W. E. B. D. to H. K. B., July 17, 1934; M. W. Adams to H. K. B., July 20, 1933, and July 30, 1934. President Adams says, "Du Bois has expressed it more bluntly and more positively than I would. . . . None the less . . . I confess that I have much sympathy with the feeling of Dr. Du Bois." But he adds, "I wish to testify to the uniformly courteous treatment which I myself received from the representatives of the foundations." This pressure of the foundations must not be exaggerated. Many Negroes believe and two leading Negro educators told the present author that a report made by Professor Hanus and others for the General Education Board on Hampton Institute in 1917 was suppressed because it was unfavorable to the vocational education carried on at Hampton. Professor Hanus, on the other hand, testifies that the report was actually favorable to vocational training, that while he did suggest improvements he *was* impressed with vocational education as

prejudice in it, pointed out in his defense that he had only done so a "very few times" in his life, and assured Curry that he still believed prejudice "must be *lived* down not *talked* down."[64]

What younger Negroes forget in condemning Washington and the attitudes of the foundations is that it was extremely difficult in the South of Washington's day to get even toleration for any kind of Negro education.[65] J. L. M. Curry of the Peabody Board, whom they criticize, apparently did not feel the Negro was capable of cultural education. "The hope of the race, in the South," he wrote, "is to be found, not so much in the high courses of University instruction, or in schools of Technology, as in handicraft instruction."[66] Yet Curry, powerful as he was, also feared Southern opinion and was held

---

he found it at Hampton, that the report was made for the staff of Hampton and not for publication, but that Abraham Flexner, then secretary of the General Education Board, suggested that he prepare for publication the parts of it that were of general interest and that he declined chiefly because he was too deeply involved in the endowment campaign of the Graduate School of Education at Harvard to give the time. Thus wrong impressions often gain wide credence. Paul H. Hanus to H. K. B., July 22, 1934. President Hope expressed great respect for the representatives of the foundations and testified that he himself had never been subjected to the slightest pressure from any of the foundations while president of Morehouse or Atlanta. Yet he recalled that, before his connection with it, Atlanta University did feel that it was under pressure from foundations with money to give it. He also pointed out, however, that the departure of Du Bois did not bring any money to Atlanta University from the General Education Board.

[64] Booker T. Washington, Tuskegee, Ala., to Doctor J. L. M. Curry, Oct. 24, 1898, J. L. M. Curry MSS., XII, 2796.

[65] J. C. Dixon, a liberal Georgian who as state supervisor of Negro schools was doing excellent service to the best type of Negro education, justified the foundations on the ground that it would have been impossible to put anything but an industrial supervisor into most Southern counties until the way had been prepared and people had become accustomed to any kind of education for the Negroes at all. C. A. Johnson, Negro supervisor of Negro schools in Columbia, South Carolina, believes that the foundations are motivated by the fact that training in the Hampton sort of institution fits men better to teach in the South than does the superior but irrelevant training one gets at a place like Columbia University from men who know nothing of the teaching problems Southern Negro teachers will have to meet. Interviews with J. C. Dixon and C. A. Johnson, March, 1933; C. A. J. to H. K. B., Aug. 2, 1934.

[66] J. L. M. Curry, *Difficulties, Complications and Limitations Connected with the Education of the Negro*, 19.

back by it. In a confidential letter in 1890 he wrote of the Negro:

> The discussion in the Senate mortified and depressed me. Civilization never encountered such a question. It is not to be solved by ignorance, partisanship, or sectionalism. It needs broad patriotism and statesmanship. To confine one's views to the political *status* of the Negro is to miss the gravamen of the problem. It is the *presence* of the Negro in such numbers in a limited area of the Union that creates the evil. If the Negro remain in such an undistributed map and the "solid" South is broken and parties cease to be divided on the color line, then miscegenation is inevitable, sooner or later, and we shall have the inert, degraded, mongrel population of Central America. If the "solid" South continue, with the present determination, at any cost, not to submit to be governed by the Negro, then we are to have the terrible demoralization of which I spoke to you under your own roof, near a year ago. In order to paralyze the Negro vote, expedients are devised which in the end will emasculate our people of *political* conscience. Parties and individuals justify themselves, under plausible pretexts, for doing what is not sanctioned by Divine or human law. That the white people should not consent to be governed by the Negro, I firmly, conscientiously believe. How to prevent that in the face of a hostile Administration and a compact, powerful, wealthy, unscrupulous party, is the rub. . . . These are things I could not publish, nor would I write except to eyes like yours.

Six months later he wrote:

> You and your colleagues would be surprised to know what censure I have, in some quarters, incurred by my courageous (excuse the word) advocacy of Negro education by State and local taxation. No one will ever know how potential has been [the] Peabody agency in informing and improving public opinion in this regard.[67]

Whatever their earlier policies, the foundations have in recent years supported cultural education. The Rosenwald Fund was not established until the tide had turned toward support of liberal arts education, too. The Slater Fund early stressed

[67] J. L. M. Curry, Richmond, Virginia, to Robert C. Winthrop, Feb. 1, 1890, J. L. M. Curry MSS., VII, 1735-1736; J. L. M. C., Asheville, N. C., to Robert C. Winthrop, Sept. 15, 1890, J. L. M. Curry MSS., VIII, 1872.

the need of training public school teachers and therefore made contributions to normal schools and colleges. As early as Theodore Roosevelt's administration, Wallace Buttrick of the General Education Board was apparently urging the need of colleges to train teachers, and universities to train the teachers of teachers. Back in 1914 Buttrick, in the report of the General Education Board, stressed the need of college education for Negroes. Florence Read and John Hope testify that in their presidencies of Spelman and Morehouse colleges they have met no opposition to liberal arts education but, on the contrary, have found the directors of the foundations with whom they have dealt distinctly friendly to it. Miss Read does not believe that Wallace Buttrick of the General Education Board or John D. Rockefeller, Junior, its generous supporter, ever intended to stop the training of Negroes at the industrial or vocational level.[68]

But the old tradition is strong. Many Negroes feel that the foundations still control the thinking of Negro teachers, that men trained under them cannot shake off the objectives set up, and that many teachers who do not believe in their aims force themselves to pretend to do so for the sake of getting financial support.

Yet the foundations have rendered great service. Without them Negro educational facilities would be more pitifully inadequate than they are. Many of the best present services are financed by Northern funds. The General Education Board has contributed millions of dollars for endowment and for current expenses of Negro liberal arts colleges and has aided college and university libraries. It has also made large gifts for professional training, especially in medicine. The white state supervisor of Negro education now established in every Southern state as a part of the state department of education is paid by the General Education Board. The county supervisors and

[68] John Hope to H. K. B., Nov. 15, 1934; Florence M. Read to H. K. B., Nov. 12, 1934; James H. Dillard, "The Negro Goes to College," *World's Work*, L (January, 1928), 337–340.

rural schools are financed partly by the Jeanes Fund. James H. Dillard, Trevor Arnett, Edwin R. Embree, and Jackson Davis have done inestimable service to Negro teachers. The Rosenwald Fund has helped build rural schools, supplied books, and contributed to salaries. Some of the best Negro teachers today have been trained on General Education Board scholarships. Furthermore, these foundations select able officials to carry on the work they support in the several states. Of great aid to freedom are the excellent men the General Education Board has put in charge of Negro schooling in each state. In at least one Southern state this supervisor has used his control of the Slater Fund to demand higher standards of the counties. County superintendents now sign a contract agreeing to use the fund in specific ways.[69] Whatever the past restrictions, little freedom would exist at all in the deep South were it not for the work of the foundations and the splendid men who represent them.

4. SECTIONALISM

After the Civil War, complaints were again raised about Northern textbooks. Benjamin F. Grady protested because "the writers of most of the cheap and attractive school histories . . . record the importation of African slaves into the Southern Colonies, while omitting their introduction into those of the North, and conceal altogether or misrepresent the essential facts on which alone can be founded a just judgment of the long controversy . . . which terminated in a war. . . ." *American History Stories,* an attractive volume published by the Education Publishing Company of Boston, expressed "sorrow that slaves in Virginia 'did all the work for their masters, and received no pay for it' "; it told that "the Georgians introduced slavery into their Colony because they 'were not a God-fearing people as were the Puritans and Quakers.' "[70] Such texts were

[69] Interview with the state supervisor, March, 1933, and letter to H. K. B., July 16, 1934.
[70] Benjamin F. Grady, *The Case of the South against the North,* 208–209.

barred after the old ruling white class regained control. Then Northern publishers quickly prepared books that catered to Southern sensibilities. As early as 1867 E. J. Hale & Son of New York began advertising "books prepared for Southern Schools, by Southern authors, and therefore free from matter offensive to Southern people."[71]

When Southerners provided their own texts or dictated what Northern texts should contain, they insisted upon pro-Southern prejudice as strong as the Northern bias of books they barred. The South entered upon a long period when texts and teachers were made to foster and preserve sectional prejudice and bitterness. Even arithmetics were carefully inspected for possible aspersions on the Confederacy. The War lost on the battlefields was now won over and over again in the schoolroom where "Northern sentiments" were routed. Daniel H. Hill, one of Lee's generals, wrote a series of "Southern" textbooks. In his mathematics text, written just before the War and used widely after it, appeared these problems: (1) "A milkman . . . in Boston . . . mixed a certain quantity of water with b quarts of milk .. .," etc.; (2) "A Yankee mixed a certain quantity of wooden nutmegs which cost him 1th/b part of a cent apiece, with real nutmegs . . .," etc.; (3) "At the Woman's Rights Convention, held at Syracuse, New York, . . . the old maids, childless-wives, and bedlamites were to each other as .. .," etc.; (4) "In the year 1692, the people of Massachusetts executed, imprisoned or privately persecuted 469 persons . . . for the alleged crime of witchcraft .. .," etc.; (5) "The year in which Decatur . . . [stated] that the traitors of New England burned blue lights on both points of the harbour to give notice to the British of his attempt to go to sea, is expressed by four digits .. .," etc.; (6) "The year in which the Governors of Massachusetts and Connecticut sent treasonable messages to their respective Legislatures, is expressed by four digits .. .," etc.; (7) ". . . the Hartford Convention . . . which . . . gave

[71] Robert L. Dabney, *A Defence of Virginia*, 358.

aid and comfort to the British during the progress of the war
. . .," etc.; (8) "A man in Cincinnati purchased 10,000 pounds
of bad pork, at 1 cent per pound, and paid so much per pound
to put it through a chemical process, . . . and then sold it at
an advanced price, clearing $450 by the fraud . . .," etc.; (9)
"The field of battle of Buena Vista is 6½ miles from Saltillo.
Two Indiana volunteers ran away from the field of battle at
the same time . . .," etc.[72]

Sectional feeling in the era between the Civil War and the
World War was particularly concerned over the control of
the history taught and the texts used in the schools. For a
generation after the Civil War little history was taught either
North or South that was not narrowly or even bitterly sectional. Each party to that war had to justify his position to his
children. Bitterness was too keen, the conflict too recent for
objectivity to be attained, or permitted in the schools even if
histories had attained it. Slowly the war generation died out.
At the same time a new scholarly method in historiography
created an ideal of objectivity among historians. Gradually
books and teachers appeared that, though frequently still
prejudiced, at least attempted to discard sectional apologies and
produce history.

The North grew out of its sectional emotionalism more
quickly than did the South. It inherited from ante-bellum days
better, freer, and more numerous training institutions. It had
more money to improve its educational facilities. It was too
busy developing its resources and growing prosperous, too
much occupied with creating a great future, long to concern itself with refighting past battles. At first the refighting of
them on the political rostrum served the purposes of the new
business giants by occupying the popular mind with sectional
hatreds, bloody shirts, the past "iniquities" of the "rebels."
Business men were thus left free to develop or exploit the

[72] Major Daniel H. Hill, *Elements of Algebra*, 121, 124, 129, 151, 316, 317,
321, 322.

nation's resources unhampered by popular interference or the necessity of facing really vital economic problems. By the end of the century, however, big business was well enough established and modern industrialism sufficiently accepted that protective campaigns of sectional hatred were no longer necessary. Furthermore, victory in war and subsequent prosperity made forgetting and forgiving easier for the North than for a defeated and impoverished South just emerging from long years of unhappiness under Reconstruction. Both sections were retarded in rewriting history by their regard for a host of aging war veterans whose feelings objective history might injure.

In the North reinterpretation began in the last years of the century. It precipitated a struggle between teachers of the newer history and those members of almost every community who felt it their duty to keep faith with the heroes of '61. Many a young teacher was forced to abandon his new history for the partisan bias of men who "knew because they had lived through it." In those days the G. A. R. was strong enough to make itself felt. A teacher's examination by an examiner who knew little history but had strong feelings consisted in a testing of the soundness of that teacher's views on the Civil War in order to keep Copperheadism out of the schools. Sectional loyalty required teachers to teach that slavery and the inherent wickedness of Southerners were the sole causes of the War and that there had been a great conspiracy of Southerners bent upon destroying the Union, which only the loyalty and courage of an almost unanimous North preserved. To have suggested that the Civil War was the result of many complex economic, social, and cultural conflicts or that Northerners were motivated by aught but high-minded devotion to country would have caused trouble. Teachers could not suggest that the Southern constitutional arguments had some validity or that the ante-bellum South faced serious and perplexing problems. They had to teach that the great battles were all really

Northern victories attained against great odds. Northern generals had to be great, however incompetent grim fact would have pictured them. It had to be forgotten that there was widespread opposition to the War in both sections and that the great Lincoln was almost turned out of office by members of his own party only a half year before the same men began capitalizing upon his martyrdom. All knowledge of corruption in public life and of political scandal in the party that won the War had to be kept discreetly concealed from the student. No teacher could suggest that many Northerners who went South during Reconstruction were scamps. Northern rule of the South had to be wise, just, and necessary because of a long continued "rebel" determination to destroy the Union if military rule were withdrawn. Any defense of Southerners or Copperheads or Andrew Johnson would have been dangerous. It was the business of history teachers to teach *Northern* history, not Southern. Most Northern teachers believed all this anyway. Those who did not found it wise in most communities to keep silent. By the time of the World War the passage of two generations and the gradual dying out of the G. A. R. led to lightening of sectional restrictions. The World War led to new emotional outlets, created a new national unity, and left in its wake new problems that have kept the censors busy suppressing more urgently objectionable doctrines than one's views on the Civil War. In the North, then, repression on sectional grounds growing out of the Civil War has become unimportant since the World War.

In the South, too, after the Civil War, sectional apologies were taught in the schools in place of history. Teachers had to teach that the South was both constitutionally and morally right in seceding, that the War resulted from a vindictive attack of an overbearing North bent upon stirring up servile insurrection, that the South was fighting a purely defensive war to protect her institutions, her property, and her homes from destruction. Teachers had to idealize the ante-bellum

South. Realistic treatment of its history would have been dangerous. The South was right on the Negro question; the meddling of Northern abolitionists destroyed an ideal and happy arrangement. The great generals, the heroism, the idealism of the War were all Southern. Though it lost the War, the South really won most of the battles. As in the North, the actuality of a divided public opinion had to be forgotten. Lincoln could not be mentioned—except in condemnation. It had to be forgotten that in 1861 many Southerners were boastfully eager for a war in which they fired the first shots. Teachers had to ignore the fact that war, which these Southerners desired, always brings destruction of property, looting, killing, in order to teach that all such acts done to Southerners were deliberate deeds of Yankee malevolence. Reconstruction was an act of vengeance Southerners had done nothing to deserve. All Southern Unionists, Northerners in the South, and Negroes in politics were dishonest, ignorant, and lacking in capacity for public office. The Southerner always had the Negro's best interest at heart and it was Northern laws and amendments and theories of equality that prevented the Negro's happy adjustment to the new environment.

In 1902 Professor Dodd testified that "public opinion positively demands that teachers of history . . . shall subscribe unreservedly to two trite oaths: (1) that the South was altogether right in seceding from the Union in 1861; and (2) that the war was not waged about the Negro. . . . Such a confession of faith is made a *sine qua non* of fitness for teaching."[73] In 1904 Dodd cried out:

In the South . . . public opinion is so thoroughly fixed that many subjects which come every day into the mind of the historian may not with safety even so much as be discussed. As already intimated, to suggest that the revolt from the union in 1860 was not justified, was not led by the most lofty minded of statesmen, is to invite not only criticism but an enforced resignation. . . . In matters further

[73] William E. Dodd, "The Status of History in Southern Education," *Nation*, LXXV (Aug. 7, 1902), 110–111.

removed from the field of politics, such as literature and art, it is exceedingly dangerous to give voice to adverse criticism of the South's attainments in the past or of her present status. . . . What is to be done under such circumstances? To speak out boldly means in many instances to destroy one's power of usefulness; to remain silent is out of the question for the strong and honest man; and to follow the smooth *via media* means failure to influence anybody or anything.[74]

Professor Trent was seriously criticized because in his *William Gilmore Simms* he said that the Civil War was fought over slavery, not state rights.[75] A professor at Roanoke College was very nearly discharged—and many friends and alumni of the college were alienated when he was not—because he used a text by Elson containing passages "detrimental to Southern ideals." The book admitted that Southern planters kept Negro mistresses in slave days, and it failed to give General Lee sufficient praise.[76] In 1911 Professor Banks was dismissed from the University of Florida because he used Elson's text and published in the *Independent* an article in which he compared the merits of Lincoln and Davis as statesmen and expressed the view that the South had made a mistake in fighting the Civil War instead of preparing for a gradual removal of slavery.[77] Southern sectionalism was particularly concerned to control the history texts used in the schools. In 1904 William E. Dodd, then professor of history at Randolph-Macon College, wrote, "And to make conditions worse our grand confederate camps fear what they call 'false history' may be smuggled in from the North and have history committees with

74 W. E. Dodd, "Some Difficulties of the History Teacher in the South," *South Atlantic Quarterly,* III (April, 1904), 119.

75 Carrol H. Quenzel, "Academic Freedom in Southern Colleges and Universities" (MS. dissertation, University of West Virginia), 100–102.

76 *Ibid.,* 102–103; "Educational Freedom," *Independent,* LXX (April 27, 1911), 913; *Crisis,* I (April, 1911), 10; *ibid.,* II (June, 1911), 50.

77 Howard C. Warren, "Academic Freedom," *Atlantic Monthly,* CXIV (November, 1914), 693; "Educational Freedom," *Independent,* LXX (April 27, 1911), 913; Newell L. Sims, "The Sociologist and Academic Freedom," *School and Society,* XXXVI (Sept. 17, 1932), 355.

representatives in every congressional district whose business is to keep watch and put out of the schools any and all books which do not come up to their standard of local patriotism . . . 'to report any book or books that fail to fasten in the minds of our children a becoming pride in the deeds of their fathers and that fail to give a truthful recital of the principles for which the confederate soldier fought.' That sounds very well and no historian could possibly take exception to it; but I have seen the very best books we have on American history ruled out of the South by these committees, for no board of education can live if it fail to heed the warning of the confederate veterans; and as a rule the very poorest books to be found anywhere are the favored ones on our *index expurgatorius.*"[78]

Since the World War sectional feeling has controlled teaching in the South less than formerly. An increasing number of Southerners are free from it. Yet the South as a whole is still supersensitive. It clings to its sectional prejudices with a certain pride. Sectionalism does still in many ways control Southern teaching and Southern teachers, either as restriction imposed from outside or as a subjective force from within.[79]

5. Science in the Schools

Science, like history, caused difficulties. Earlier in the century individual scientific discoveries had conflicted with generally accepted religious beliefs. New astronomical and geological concepts had caused concern. Nothing, however, had approached in momentous consequences the publishing in 1859 of Darwin's *Origin of Species*. As the spread of science through the colleges gave the theory of evolution currency, the importance of its implications became increasingly evident. It affected not only science but religion, philosophy, and educational theory itself. Hundreds of articles were written proving or disproving that religion and science are in conflict. That

[78] W. E. Dodd, "Some Difficulties of the History Teacher in the South," *South Atlantic Quarterly*, III (April, 1904), 120–121.
[79] See *infra*, 252–262.

question has not yet been settled. Much depends upon the kind of science and the kind of religion. But about the theology of most Americans in 1859 and the popular nineteenth-century conception of Darwinism there could be no doubt. Both could not stand. In the end—both were modified.

Violent controversies shook colleges and theological schools. Professors fought for their right to teach the new scientific hypotheses and to adjust theological dogma and religious concepts to them. Religious denominations sought to keep orthodox the teachings of colleges and universities they controlled. Acceptance of the hypothesis of evolution, they said, would destroy religion. The old democratic fear of too much learning had never died out. Bishop G. F. Pierce could still aver, "The best preachers I ever heard had never been to college at all—hardly to school. It is my opinion that every dollar invested in a theological school will be a damage to Methodism. Had I a million I would not give a dime for such an object."[80] This ancient distrust was fed anew by the acceptance of Darwinism in certain universities and theological schools. In 1878 the Tennessee Conference of the Southern Methodist Church resolved:

This is an age in which scientific atheism, having divested itself of the habiliments that most adorn and dignify humanity, walks abroad in shameless denudation. The arrogant and impertinent claims of this "science, falsely so-called," have been so boisterous and persistent, that the unthinking mass have been sadly deluded; but our university alone has had the courage to lay its young but vigorous hand upon the mane of untamed Speculation and say: "We will have no more of this."[81]

Even before the advent of evolution scientists found their freedom infringed upon, when their views conflicted with religious tenets. When the ruling religious orthodoxy attacked Thomas Cooper, Jefferson, the greatest contemporary expounder of freedom, could not sustain that professor at the university that Jefferson himself had founded. Fourteen years later Cooper

[80] V. Dabney, *op. cit.*, 192.   [81] *Ibid.*, 193.

was expelled from the presidency of South Carolina College.[82] Joseph Le Conte, his brother, and Henry Hammond aroused vigorous criticism at the University of Georgia by teachings akin to the later evolutionary hypothesis, but they were sustained.[83] Both Dana and Parker of the Harvard Board of Overseers opposed Charles W. Eliot's appointment as president in 1868 because scientific knowledge did not really constitute an education and because a man trained in chemistry could not maintain the standing of Harvard. Both men opposed John Fiske's lecturing at Harvard on the teachings of Darwin and Spencer.[84] In 1879 Crawford H. Toy was forced out of the Southern Baptist Theological Seminary at Louisville because he accepted the new scientific views. Teaching evolution caused Alexander Winchell's dismissal from his professorship of geology at Vanderbilt.[85] In 1883 the Presbyterian Theological Seminary at Columbia, South Carolina, ousted James Woodrow for the same offense.[86]

Freedom in teaching science had many defenders. One group argued that, since true religion and true science are not contradictory but complementary, both would benefit by unrestrained search for truth. Paul Carus, expositor of this view, wrote in 1900, "We must distinguish between faith and belief. . . . Belief, in the sense of accepting unverified and unverifiable statements, is not only not essential in religion, but is downright irreligious. What we need in life is not belief, but faith. Belief is a matter of intelligence, or rather, neglect of intelligence." Only "pre-scientific man" had looked upon "conviction" as "truth" and "naïvely accepted . . . the intensity of his conviction . . . as the measure of the reliability of truth."

[82] W. E. Dodd, "Democracy and the University," *Nation*, CI (Oct. 14, 1915), 464.
[83] E. M. Coulter, *op. cit.*, 254–255.
[84] Charles F. Adams, *Richard Henry Dana: a Biography*, II, 151–153.
[85] *Ibid.*, I, 313–316; John M. Mecklin, *The Survival Value of Christianity*, 180.
[86] A. D. White, *op. cit.*, I, 317–318; *History of the Presbyterian Church in South Carolina since 1850* (F. D. Jones, W. H. Mills, eds.), 169–170, 173–184, 186–187.

"Truths are discovered," Carus insisted; "they are not invented. . . . There are not two antagonistic truths, one religious, the other scientific. There is but one truth which is to be discovered by scientific methods, and applied to our religious life. . . . Religion is as indestructible as science, for science is the method of searching for the truth and religion is the enthusiasm and good will to live a life of truth."[87]

Another group defended freedom because attempts of religious leaders to suppress scientists would injure religion more than science. "The harm done to religion," Andrew D. White warned the churches, "in these attempts [to make teachers of science conform to religious dogma] is far greater than that done to science; for thereby suspicions are widely spread, especially among open-minded young men, that the accepted Christian system demands a concealment of truth, with the persecution of honest investigators, and therefore must be false. Well was it said in substance by President McCosh of Princeton, that no more sure way of making unbelievers in Christianity among young men could be devised than preaching to them that the doctrines arrived at by the great scientific thinkers of this period are opposed to religion."[88]

While this controversy of science *versus* religion rent the colleges and universities and led to dismissals in a few cases and to coerced silence in many more, the lower schools were left relatively unaffected by it. This did not mean that they were freer, but merely that they were preoccupied with their own physical development, improved teacher training, and new methodology. They were unaware of evolution. Evolution was still an academic question. One generation had to pass before so revolutionary a hypothesis could gain general acceptance in the higher institutions. It then took another generation to pass it on to the lower schools, and still a third to put it into the textbooks, where ordinary people of the older generation would

[87] Paul Carus, *The Point of View*, 58, 62, 196–198.

[88] A. D. White, *op. cit.*, I, 320. See also W. A. Lambert, "Liberty in Teaching," *Nation*, XCVII (July 3, 1913), 11.

discover it. It was only late in this period that modern biology found its way into the high schools at all. This was the era of old-fashioned physiology, which went peacefully on its way oblivious of evolution. Ordinary people, from whom school-teachers came, still held firmly to their old religious tenets. They knew that higher criticism had undermined the faith of certain theological schools. They began to be alarmed because "agnostic" professors were destroying the faith of increasing numbers of young men and women in a few large universities. But outside of the cities, where men had become indifferent to religion anyway, evolution did not touch the average man or the teacher of his children. Had a teacher introduced evolution into the average American school he would have found himself in difficulty, but teachers had no desire to do so. They would have been as quick as parents to decry the attacks of science upon religion. By the time biological science did find its way into the schools, the modern industrial age had secularized large portions of the population into indifference to older religious beliefs, or the World War had shaken the faith of men in much besides religion. In the rural regions of the country, particularly in the Middle West and the South, where men were little affected by industrialization and urbanization, religious faith continued vital and evolution was known only vaguely as a dangerous doctrine being taught in distant infidel centers. The hypotheses of modern science were finally to penetrate into the schools of these regions and provoke a new conflict more bitter and less dignified than the one that shook the universities in this era. The battle in the schools, however, did not come until after the World War.

One important by-product of this struggle of science and religion in the universities did affect the teacher indirectly. Ever since the Reformation, Protestant religion had been based upon the infallibility of the Bible. Now as science, history, and then critical studies of Biblical texts threatened belief in the verbal correctness of the Bible, theologians of the older school declared that Christianity itself must stand or fall upon the correctness of Biblical text. Yet the chronology of the Bible, details of its history, and its scientific teaching were indisputably overthrown. Toward the end of this era, recognition of this fact was forced upon men in the larger communities of the North. Thus for thousands of Americans the very foundation of belief—the authority of the Bible—was undermined. For some this meant loss of faith and indifference to religion. For some it led to a violent reaction against all that had been handed down by authority and experience. For others it led to a new searching for truth and to a desire for free discussion of others' opinions that one's own might be tested and, if found wanting, modified. Authoritarianism originating in religion had dominated the popular mind of America. The abandonment of authoritarianism in religion now began to affect men's thinking in other fields; it led men to appeal to reason and discussion instead of authority in many matters of which men once had been certain. If authoritarianism was not infallible in religion, perhaps it was a poor guide in economics, sociology, and government. This change in popular psychology came only gradually; it by no means reached all sections of the country or all people. But those affected no longer had confidence enough in authoritarian pronouncements of any sort to insist upon imposing them on teachers. Hence indirectly the conflict of Darwinism with authoritarian religion brought new freedom to many teachers of the social studies.

6. RELIGION AND MORALS IN THE SCHOOLS

A chief concern of the schools was virtue and morality. Toward the end of the period, as schools became more thoroughly secularized, courses in "good citizenship" and civics appeared in the curriculum. In the late nineteenth century, however, men still thought in terms of "virtue" and "morality" with social and civic as well as religious connotations. Most men agreed that a major purpose of teaching was to develop in children these homely qualities. Men did not agree on the best method of attaining this objective.

The traditional approach to character building was, of course, religion. But religious instruction raised increasing difficulties. Many teachers still regarded it as their duty to instil orthodox views into their pupils. In an age when in large sections of the country devout Presbyterians firmly believed that equally devout Campbellites could not possibly be saved, and when earnest Baptists were convinced that equally earnest Methodists would be damned because their form of baptism was not valid, it was difficult for teachers to give moral and religious guidance without treading upon dangerous sectarian ground. All sects agreed, however, in wishing to prevent sectarian teaching, since no one of them could hope to control the schools for its own doctrines. Therefore the process of desectarianizing teaching, begun as we have seen in the antebellum period, was now completed. New constitutions included prohibitions against sectarian instruction.[89] New laws forbidding the teaching or inculcation of sectarian or religious doctrine were added to earlier ones.[90] Numerous states enacted legislation barring all sectarian books, tracts, and catechisms not only from the classroom but from school libraries.[91] Protestant sects were agreed, too, in not wishing public money spent on religious schools. They themselves taught non-sectarian Protestant principles in the public schools, and the increasing influx of Catholic immigrants made them more de-

[89] Nevada's, for example, in 1864, South Carolina's in 1868, Nebraska's in 1875, Colorado's in 1876, California's in 1879, Idaho's, Washington's, Wyoming's in 1889.

[90] For example, in North Carolina (*Session Laws,* 1872–1873, 129), in Kansas (*Session Laws,* 1876, 266), in Arizona (*Session Laws,* 1879, 108), in Washington (*Session Laws,* 1883, 16), in Oklahoma (*Statutes,* 1890, chap. 79, art. I, sec. 6, p. 1119), in Idaho (*Session Laws,* 1893, 211), in South Dakota (*Session Laws,* 1901, 192).

[91] For instance, in North Carolina (*Session Laws,* 1872–1873, 129), in Colorado (*Session Laws,* 1883, 269), in Washington (*Session Laws,* 1883, 16), in Kentucky (*Session Laws,* 1891–1892–1893, 1415), in Idaho (*Session Laws,* 1893, 211; *ibid.,* 1907, 306).

termined than ever to prevent public aid to parochial schools. The ante-bellum prohibitions of state aid to church schools were now strengthened by constitutional provisions[92] and statutory enactment.[93] In a Des Moines speech in 1875 President Grant urged that education be kept free from "sectarian tenets."[94] In his message of December 7, 1875, he urged a constitutional amendment "forbidding the teaching . . . of religious . . . tenets, and prohibiting the granting of any school funds or school taxes, . . . either by legislative, municipal, or other authority, for the benefit or in aid, directly or indirectly, of any religious sect or denomination." A little later James G. Blaine proposed another amendment providing that "no money raised by taxation in any State for the support of public schools or derived from any public fund therefor, nor any public lands devoted thereto, shall ever be under the control of any religious sect, nor shall any money so raised or lands so devoted, be divided between religious sects or denominations."[95] By 1903 thirty-nine states had prohibitions against sectarianism in the public schools and against state aid to religious schools.[96]

Nevertheless, most nineteenth-century Americans still believed that virtue and morality were best taught through religion—the Bible, prayers, hymns, instruction in Christian prin-

[92] For example, in West Virginia in 1863, in Nevada in 1864, in Nebraska in 1867, in Arkansas, Mississippi, and South Carolina in 1868, in Illinois in 1870, in Pennsylvania in 1873, in Alabama and Missouri in 1875, in Colorado, North Carolina, and Texas in 1876, in Georgia in 1877, in Arizona and California in 1879, in Florida in 1885, in Idaho, Montana, North Dakota, South Dakota, Washington, and Wyoming in 1889, in Mississippi in 1890, in South Carolina and Utah in 1895, in Delaware in 1897, in Wisconsin in 1898, and in Oklahoma in 1907.

[93] For example, in Nevada in 1865 (*Compiled Laws,* 1900, sec. 1317, sec. 43, p. 312), in Texas in 1870 and 1884 (*Session Laws,* 1870, 116; *ibid.,* 1884, 40), in New York in 1871 (*Session Laws,* 1871, 1271), in Illinois in 1872 (*Session Laws,* 1871-1872, 735), in Arizona in 1879 (*Session Laws,* 1879, 108), in Montana in 1881 (*Revised Code* [1907], I, p. xlv), and in Louisiana in 1894 (*Session Laws,* 1894, 62).

[94] L. F. Parker, *op. cit.,* 105-106.

[95] Daniel C. Gilman, "A Century of American Education, 1776-1876," *North American Review,* CXXII (January, 1876), 191-192.

[96] Jesse K. Flanders, *Legislative Control of the Elementary Curriculum,* 149.

ciples. The prohibitions against sectarianism were therefore
not intended to exclude religion from the schools. Even laws
forbidding the teaching of "religious doctrine" were intended
to permit non-sectarian Protestantism. Whatever courts might
later read into them, the nineteenth-century men who framed
these measures fully intended Bible reading and other non-
sectarian religious exercises to be continued daily in class. In
fact, Kansas, Oklahoma, and both Dakotas took the precaution
of specifying that the prohibition of sectarianism should never
be interpreted to ban the reading of the Bible.[97] Mississippi in
1878 and Iowa in 1880 decreed that the Bible should "not be
excluded from the public schools."[98] Other states specifically
required that it be read.[99] The peak in such legislation, however, had apparently been passed by the turn of the century.
Ten states had laws prescribing Bible reading in 1903 and ten
(not all the same ten) in 1913. Only two states made it mandatory in 1913.[100]

Men were as eager to protect children against no religion
as against sectarian proselyting. Thus the Arkansas constitution of 1864 barred from public office any "person who denies
the being of God" and Washington in 1883 and Kentucky in
1893 forbade the teaching of "infidel" doctrine in the schools.[101]
Wisconsin's official annotation of her constitution in 1898 went
so far as to explain that her prohibition against sectarian teaching referred "exclusively to instruction . . . in religious doctrines which are believed by some religious sects and rejected
by others." "To teach the existence of a supreme being of
infinite wisdom, power and goodness and that it is the duty of

[97] *Kansas Session Laws,* 1876, 266; *The Statutes of Oklahoma,* 1890, chap.
79, art. I, sec. 6, p. 1119; *South Dakota Session Laws,* 1901, 192; *Compiled
Laws of North Dakota,* 1913, I, chap. XII, art. 17, sec. 1388, p. 333.

[98] *Mississippi Session Laws,* 1878, 106; *Iowa Session Laws,* 1880, 482.

[99] For example, Massachusetts (*Session Laws,* 1862, 41; *ibid.,* 1880, 126–
127), West Virginia (*Session Laws,* 1866, 62), Pennsylvania (*Session Laws,*
1913, 226), and Tennessee (*Session Laws,* 1915, 305).

[100] J. K. Flanders, *op. cit.,* 155–156.

[101] *Washington Session Laws,* 1883, 16; *Kentucky Session Laws,* 1891–
1892–1893, 1415.

all men to adore, obey and love him, is not sectarian because all religious . . . sects so believe and teach."[102] At Des Moines in his speech of 1875, President Grant urged the nation to free its schools from "pagan" and "atheistic" tenets;[103] in December he besought Congress to do it by constitutional amendment. Laws and amendments were, however, not necessary. The people chose teachers who would teach virtue and morality and Christian principles by example and precept. It was natural to bar "infidels," "pagans," "atheists," Hebrews, and Catholics from schools with this purpose. Their exclusion was accomplished by the local communities without the necessity of legislation. Constitutional provisions that no religious tests for public office should be imposed were no protection for these groups so long as this purpose in schooling remained.

The problem of freedom for teachers in the teaching of religion was a difficult one. About 1880 at Danville, Indiana, Charles Griggs punished whisperers by making them learn a chapter from the Bible after school. One Ella Morarity, a devout Catholic, refused to learn her chapter but recited "Maud Muller" for him instead. Day after day he kept her after school trying to force her to memorize her passage of Scripture. But she never did.[104] Here was a devout if bigoted person who believed it his solemn duty to punish his children into Protestant religion. Could he and a Catholic pupil ever both enjoy freedom for their respective consciences in the same school? The great majority of teachers wished to continue the current practice of reading the Bible, offering prayer, and singing hymns in school. But to ask Jews, Catholics, and agnostics to conduct Protestant religious exercises was denying them freedom of conscience. They had to violate their own religious convictions or stay out of the public schools. Protestant Christians who controlled the schools did not wish them to teach

[102] *Wisconsin Statutes,* 1898, annotated by A. L. Sanborn and J. R. Berryman, I, 120.
[103] L. F. Parker, *op. cit.,* 105–106.
[104] Reminiscence of Nellie K. Beale, a fellow-pupil.

under any circumstances, even if they could have satisfied their own consciences. Consequently, in most communities public opinion barred Jews, Catholics, and agnostics altogether.

Some states avoided the dilemma created by non-Protestant teachers by allowing the teacher to do as he pleased in regard to religious exercises. This solution, however, ignored the children. There were Jewish, Catholic, and agnostic children in many schools. To permit the Protestant teacher to read his Bible and offer his prayers ignored the right of these children to religious liberty. Furthermore, no community would have tolerated a Catholic or a Jew who had introduced his religious exercises into the schools under this rule. This solution was in reality merely freedom for the non-Protestant to decide to omit religion from the school. On the other hand, to forbid a Protestant teacher, as some places did, to read the Bible and offer prayers decidedly limited his freedom. To permit a small minority of Catholics to ban the Bible from the public schools, to which few of them sent their children in any case, while the vast majority of patrons of the schools looked upon it as an essential part of the curriculum, appeared unreasonable if not outrageous to the average devout Protestant of that day. He felt certain that, if the Catholics had controlled the schools, they would not have banned all Catholic religious exercises because a few Protestants objected.

The tendency at first was to uphold the right and duty of teachers to hold religious exercises and read the Protestant Bible. The famous Maine case of *Donahoe* v. *Richards*[105] in 1854 had emphatically decided against the validity of Catholic objection to the Protestant Bible in upholding the teacher's right to expel Bridget Donahoe for refusing to read from it. Interestingly enough the decision was based not upon the teacher's freedom but upon the state's right to decide, by majority vote, on a school curriculum and to subordinate all individual consciences thereto—a doctrine that, if only a majority

[105] 38 Maine 379. See also *supra,* 102–103.

so wished, could easily be turned against the Protestant teacher, whom the Court allowed to expel Bridget. In 1884 the Iowa Supreme Court upheld a statute forbidding the exclusion of the Bible from the schools.[106] In *Billard* v. *The Board of Education of the City of Topeka* in 1904, the Kansas Supreme Court decided unanimously that neither the constitution nor the statute prohibiting religious worship and the teaching of sectarian and religious doctrine in the schools had intended to exclude the Bible or the Lord's Prayer. In fact, the Court declared, "The noblest ideals of moral character are found in the Bible. . . . To emulate these is the supreme conception of citizenship."[107] The Kentucky Supreme Court in 1905 threw out a petition for an injunction against Bible reading and prayers in school, and pronounced the King James version nonsectarian.[108] In these Iowa, Kansas, and Kentucky cases, children were not required to be present during the Bible reading if their parents objected. In a Texas case, the children had to sit quietly through the exercises. Parents of two Catholics, two Jews, and an unbeliever took the matter to the courts. The Texas Supreme Court in 1908 decided unanimously that Bible reading, prayers, and hymns did not convert the schoolroom into a place of worship and were therefore not unconstitutional. Indeed, the Court proclaimed that the constitutional guarantee of religious liberty did not mean "that one or more individuals have the right to have the courts deny the people the privilege of having their children instructed in the moral truths of the Bible because such objectors do not desire that their own children shall be participants therein."[109] The Massachusettts Court upheld a teacher in excluding Ella Spiller for refusing to bow her head during a prayer. "One of the chief objects of education . . . 'the principles of piety and justice, and sacred regard for truth,' " the Court maintained, could be

[106] *Moore* v. *Monroe,* 64 Iowa 367.
[107] *Billard* v. *Board of Education of Topeka,* 69 Kansas 53.
[108] *Hackett* v. *Brooksville Graded School District, et al.,* 120 Kentucky 608.
[109] *Church et al.* v. *Bullock et al.,* 104 Texas 1.

carried out no more appropriately than by Bible reading and prayer.[110] The Connecticut Court also sustained the right of the teacher to read the Bible in class.[111] In four-fifths of the state and city normal schools of the country, daily chapel was required in 1903.[112] Colorado's constitution of 1876, Idaho's and Wyoming's of 1889, and Utah's of 1895 forbade teachers to require students to attend any religious service, but this did not ban Bible reading, prayers, and hymns.

Compromises were often reached whereby no child was required to attend these religious exercises. In 1895, after a thorough study, Cornelison decided that religion ought to stay in the schools, that no person conscientiously opposed ought to be required to participate, but that unbelievers ought not to be able to deprive the great majority of the religious training they desired.[113] President Schurman of Cornell proposed that the Protestant ministers be called in to work out a suitable program for school exercises for Protestant children, and that Catholics hold Catholic exercises for their own children.[114] In New York the State Board of Education ruled in 1866 and in 1870 that religious exercises must not be held during school hours.[115] This seemed about as happy a solution as any. It left the teacher free to hold religious exercises before school opened, and the child free to stay away if he had religious objection. But of course it subjected to the pressure of public opinion both child and teacher who did not conform.

Demands for the exclusion of the Bible continued. Catholics and Jews were joined by a so-called "liberal" movement in the 'seventies, which fanatically attacked all vestiges of religion in American life and tried to exclude from public places not only the Bible but all reference to deity. More important

---

[110] *Spiller* v. *Inhabitants of Woburn*, 12 Allen 127.

[111] Joseph H. Crooker, *Religious Freedom in American Education*, 73–74.

[112] *Ibid.*, 127–128.

[113] Isaac A. Cornelison, *The Relation of Religion to Civil Government in the United States*, 263–264.

[114] J. H. Crooker, *op. cit.*, 39–43.

[115] Charles N. Lischka, *Private Schools and State Laws, 1924*, 210.

was a group of ministers who had been shaken out of their dogmatism by the disproving of many tenets that the authoritarian religion of their youth had told them must be accepted without questioning. These men came to feel that nothing was to be gained by forcing religion upon teachers and pupils who wished none or preferred one of their own, and that required exercises did not best serve the interests of religion itself. They began defending the right of the Jew, the Catholic, and the agnostic to public schools free of religion.

The Catholics were torn between a desire to keep their own children in parochial schools and a concern to free their children and their teachers in the public schools from using the Protestant Bible. They never would admit that they wished religion or the Bible excluded from the schools, for the whole argument in favor of parochial schools was that religion formed a major part of education. In 1884 the General Council in Baltimore began a new drive for better parochial schools. This led to a renewed demand for public funds for them. Occasionally communities did support Catholic schools. The New York Legislature, for instance, in 1871 made an exception to its own laws by contributing funds to certain parochial schools in New York and Brooklyn.[116] For many years the mission of Goshenhoppen in Berks County, Pennsylvania, was owned by the Catholics, run by the Catholics as a Catholic school, yet taught by a principal teacher appointed by the County Superintendent with the approval of the priest, and paid by the public. The school was recognized as a part of the public school system.[117] In 1887 the Illinois Court upheld the action of a school board that allowed a public school to be held in the basement of a Catholic Church. The Court voiced no objection to the practice of hiring Catholic teachers, of holding mass for the children, of giving religious instruction for a half hour each morning before school, and of closing with a Catholic

[116] *New York Session Laws,* 1871, 1957.
[117] Louise G. and Matthew J. Walsh, *History and Organization of Education in Pennsylvania,* 67.

prayer—because these were all done voluntarily by a Catholic community.[118] In a Michigan school, where the land was owned by the Catholic bishop and the building by the state, and where the teacher was appointed by the school board but paid partly with church and partly with public funds, the Catholic religion was taught daily. Ultimately the school board dismissed the teacher, and the priest denied its right to do so. The Court, in its turn, held that the school was a public school in which the Catholic religion was taught, and it therefore sustained the dismissal.[119] In 1917 the Illinois Court reversed a contrary verdict of 1888 by upholding the payment of state funds to a Catholic school for girls in Chicago in place of maintaining a public institution.[120]

These were, however, exceptions. In most communities these situations would have been impossible. Since the Catholics could not get public funds for their own schools, and since they had no chance of teaching the Catholic faith or conducting Catholic ceremonies in the public schools, they fell back upon attacking the Protestant Bible in schools that they had to help support. A new stimulus was given to these attacks by the desire of Catholics to teach in the schools. In cities where Catholics had political power they were early successful in getting the Protestant Bible put out and Catholic teachers put into the public schools. But elsewhere their attacks upon religion in the schools, however justifiable from the Catholic point of view, contributed largely to the persistent prejudice that still handicaps Catholic teachers.

Probably Protestant opponents of coercion in religion and a general secularization of American life had more influence than Catholic protests, but the tendency, particularly at the

---

[118] *Millard* v. *Board of Education,* 121 Illinois 297. For a similar case in Wisconsin see 137 Wisconsin 147.

[119] *Richter* v. *Cordes,* 100 Michigan 278.

[120] *Dunn* v. *Chicago Industrial School for Girls,* 280 Illinois 613. For the 1888 decision see *County of Cook* v. *Chicago Industrial School for Girls,* 125 Illinois 540. See also H. K. Beale, *op. cit.,* 208–209, 213–215, 218–220.

end of this period, was toward dropping religion, Bible reading and all, from public-school exercises. In Cincinnati in 1872
the Board of Education forbade Bible reading. When a group
of taxpayers demanded that the order be rescinded, the Supreme Court upheld the Board's right to issue the order.[121] In
1890 the Wisconsin Supreme Court decided that reading the
King James Bible was sectarian instruction and an act of
worship and therefore unconstitutional.[122] A few years later,
however, when extremists tried to prevent the use of *Readings
from the Bible,* the Court held that in this form scripture was
literature and reading it was not an act of worship.[123] A similar
decision was handed down in Michigan in 1898.[124] In 1898,
too, the editors of an official compilation of Wisconsin law
incorporated this distinction into an annotation of the Wisconsin Constitution, explaining that it forbade the Bible but
permitted books of extracts upon which all could agree.[125] The
supreme courts of Nebraska, Illinois, and Louisiana in 1902,
1910, and 1915, pronounced Bible reading and hymn singing
to be sectarian instruction and acts of worship forbidden by
the state constitution.[126]

The changes, however, were not all in this direction. The
New York State Superintendent declared in favor of Bible
reading in 1903, and Cleveland added it to the school curriculum
in 1901.[127] The whole question was badly confused. Still, there
was much less Bible reading in 1900 than in 1880, and less in

[121] *Board of Education of the City of Cincinnati* v. *Minor et al.,* 23 Ohio
211.

[122] *State ex rel. Weiss et al.* v. *District Board of School District No. 8 of
the City of Edgerton,* 76 Wisconsin 177.

[123] J. H. Crooker, *op. cit.,* 70–71.

[124] *Pfeiffer* v. *Board of Education of Detroit,* 118 Michigan 560.

[125] *Wisconsin Statutes,* 1898, annotated by A. L. Sanborn and J. R. Berryman, I, 120.

[126] *State of Nebraska ex. rel. Freeman* v. *Scheve et al.,* 65 Nebraska 853;
People ex rel. Ring et al. v. *Board of Education of District 24,* 245 Illinois
334; *Herold et al.* v. *Parish Board of School Directors et al.,* 136 Louisiana
1034.

[127] J. H. Crooker, *op. cit.,* 57–58; "Religion in the Cleveland Schools," *Independent,* LIII (Oct. 10, 1901), 2431.

1910 than in 1900. Hundreds of articles were written proclaiming that removal of religion from the schools would lead to agnosticism and infidelity. For years the controversy raged. When one considers the deep earnestness of the thousands of men who still felt the chief purpose of education to be such creation of character as only religious training could give, one marvels that their opponents ever won a single victory. But growing secular interests and increasing indifference to religion were on the side of their opponents. These, and not defenders of liberty urging freedom of conscience or Catholics demanding their rights, were the determining factors.

The net result was that in many places teachers who believed religious training one of their most important functions were now denied freedom to instil religious attitudes into their pupils. Another result was that religion became, as it remains today even where Bible reading has returned, one of the strongest taboos of the school system. Many teachers, however, who for religious or pedagogical reasons objected to compulsory religious exercises were given new freedom, and one of the greatest barriers against Jews, Catholics, and non-religious teachers was let down. This problem is a difficult complex of conflicting freedoms and restraints. Fifty years ago in homogeneous Protestant communities prohibition of all religious exercises would have denied most teachers and pupils a generally desired privilege. At the end of this period, removal of the whole matter from the schools probably coerced fewer teachers and pupils into practices to which they objected than would any other solution.

7. Reform

About 1878 Mrs. Mary H. Hunt, formerly a professor of chemistry, became interested in "educating" children in regard to the evil effects of intemperance. She made investigations and coöperated with Miss Julia Coleman who had written a *Juvenile Temperance Manual*. They persuaded Hyde

Park, Massachusetts, and then a few other towns to add temperance to their curricula. Mrs. Hunt, however, wished to abandon the older sentimental brand of temperance and teach, instead, "scientific" temperance based upon biological knowledge. Individual work in gaining converts was slow. Therefore in 1879 Mrs. Hunt went to the Indianapolis meeting of the Woman's Christian Temperance Union and won that powerful organization to her plan of using the schools for temperance propaganda. The W. C. T. U. passed a resolution urging its members to bring pressure upon the school authorities. A committee was appointed of which Mrs. Hunt was chairman. To obtain better organization the W. C. T. U. created in 1880 a Department of Scientific Temperance Instruction. A great corps of workers was set up in almost military organization, with Mrs. Hunt in a position of centralized authority giving orders to lieutenants in each state.

Mrs. Hunt early became convinced of three needs. Lobbying must be done in state legislatures to win mandatory temperance instruction laws, since persuading individual teachers and school systems was too slow and too uncertain. Even after a teacher was won to the cause, his zeal might cool, or the next year he might again drop his temperance lessons. With a state law the W. C. T. U. would be able to whip all teachers into line and keep them there. Secondly, since propaganda is ineffective if too obvious, temperance instruction must be included as an integral part of books on biology and hygiene; separate temperance texts were not satisfactory. Finally, the aid of scientists, particularly medical men, must be obtained to give the cause professional authority. The task was made easier by the fact that a reaction had already set in against the excessive and ruinous drinking of a day when bad, unappetizing food, monotony of life, and quantities of hard liquor had combined to make drunkenness common. As men attained better standards of living, they wished to escape drinking habits of this earlier era. The saloon was a major social problem. Religion and morals, removal of the causes of the earlier drinking, desire for greater economic efficiency, new standards of respectability, and sheer common sense combined to encourage greater sobriety. Many men were therefore becoming temperance-minded. It was not hard to convert them. Other organizations besides the W. C. T. U. backed temperance instruction, the American Federation of Labor, for instance.[128] The American Medical Association in 1878, before it ever heard of Mrs. Hunt, had, out of its own experience, passed resolutions deploring the evils of "alcoholic liquors as a beverage," and warning that alcohol causes a "large amount of physical and mental disease" and that "it entails diseased appetites and enfeebled constitutions upon offspring, and . . . is the cause of a large percentage of crime and pauperism." It was not difficult, then, for Mrs. Hunt, who went to the Minneapolis meeting of the Association in 1882, to persuade the doctors to reënact their own resolution and to add to it a new one: "Resolved that the Association . . . urge that all State legislatures introduce hygiene as one of the branches to be taught in the schools."[129]

Armed with these resolutions Mrs. Hunt and her lobbyists called in the politicians and lobbied compulsory "scientific temperance" instruction through most legislatures. Some states already had laws of this nature. Massachusetts in 1789 had enjoined all "instructors of youth" to "exert their best endeavors to impress on the minds of children and youth . . . the principles of . . . sobriety, . . . moderation and temperance, and those other virtues which are the ornament of human society and the basis upon which a republican constitution is founded." During the 1880's most states and territories and the District of Columbia adopted laws requiring teachers to instruct children in "physiology and hygiene, with special reference to the effects of alcoholic beverages, stimulants, and narcotics

---

[128] See, for example, American Federation of Labor, *Proceedings,* XV (1895), 74.
[129] "Scientific Temperance Instruction in the Public Schools," *Report of the U. S. Commissioner of Education for 1889-1890,* II, 695-697.

upon the human system." Many states required the use of textbooks dealing with this subject. By 1903 Georgia was the only state that had no temperance legislation. Success led the W. C. T. U. to greater exertions. Where teachers were sympathetic they would gladly have included temperance lessons without legislation; the vast majority did favor some kind of temperance instruction. Yet some were indifferent; others actually opposed it and conformed only sufficiently to keep technically within the law. Therefore, the W. C. T. U. again visited the legislatures and got more stringent laws prescribing specified numbers of hours or a designated proportion of the total school time. More rigid penalties were enacted for teachers who did not live up to the full legal requirement. The W. C. T. U. set itself up as judge of methods and censor of texts. Many teachers who agreed with its general purpose objected to the W. C. T. U.'s interference in what they regarded as purely pedagogical problems.[130]

Diverse expedients were employed to force conformity. One required all prospective teachers to pass an examination on the nature and effects of alcohol and narcotics and on the "proper methods" of teaching the subject. Another entailed dismissal for every teacher who failed to teach the specified amount of temperance, and for principals or superintendents who failed to see that teachers complied.

With texts Mrs. Hunt encountered more difficulty. There were at first no satisfactory schoolbooks on temperance. The older physiologies that did teach it did not satisfy the "scientific" standards of the W. C. T. U. Mrs. Hunt set out to find people to write the kind of texts she wished. In the end she succeeded. She met, however, vigorous opposition from publishers and authors of the texts then in use. She tried to get them to modify these texts. That was expensive. At first pub-

130 *Ibid.*, I, 695–697; U. S. Bureau of Prohibition, *Alcohol, Hygiene, and the Public Schools;* W. O. Atwater, John S. Billings, H. P. Bowditch, R. H. Chittenden, and H. Welch, *Physiological Aspects of the Liquor Problem,* I, 1–136.

lishers were not convinced that this "scientific temperance" was more than a passing fad. When New York enacted a temperance law in 1884 publishers were convinced; thirty physiology texts were hastily issued. Many of these, however, were merely old books with temperance matter tacked on as an appendix, which Mrs. Hunt felt would never be read. That indefatigable woman set her pressures to work again, and in 1885 Pennsylvania and Massachusetts passed amended laws to exclude all texts with the temperance matter in the appendix. Still this was not enough. In 1886 Vermont passed the first of a series of state laws requiring that one-fourth of the space in physiology texts be devoted to temperance. In 1887 Mrs. Hunt sponsored a great petition to publishers, signed by many "leading citizens," urging conformity to the W. C. T. U. ideal of a physiology text.[131] Ultimately publishers, seeing a chance for a large trade in new temperance texts, modified their old books and issued specially prepared ones that the W. C. T. U. would sponsor in the schools.

This movement led to years of debate. The extremes of control to which the W. C. T. U. went led many teachers to revolt. In 1900 New Jersey replaced her earlier law with one less detailed and exacting.[132] Gradually, thenceforth, state laws were modified and less effective controls were substituted for the earlier rigid ones. Magazines printed attacks on the W. C. T. U. laws and answers in their defense. Once they were convinced that the movement would succeed, publishing houses, delighted at the W. C. T. U.'s devotion to the textbook method, aided the temperance movement and thereby their own book sales. Similarly liquor manufacturers, by the turn of the century a powerful business interest, abetted the opponents of W. C. T. U. temperance instruction. Mrs. Hunt, like so many sincere and earnest persons, cried out, against those who opposed her laws, that they were either interested

[131] *Report of the U. S. Commissioner of Education for 1889–1890*, II, 697–698.
[132] Cf. *New Jersey Session Laws*, 1900, 280, with earlier laws.

in the liquor traffic or devotees of bibulous, pleasure-loving, intemperate living. The business interests of both bookmen and brewers were heavily involved in the struggle. Yet it was also a battle between a group of devoted women with social consciences, who saw a chance to improve American life through utilization of the schools for moral reform, and equally disinterested opponents. Scientists objected to what they regarded as an abuse of science, and educators disliked both the pedagogical methods insisted upon by the W. C. T. U. and the use of schools for propaganda of any kind.

As an early example of organized propaganda in the schools this movement is instructive. In 1893 scientists set up a "Committee of Fifty" to study the "drink problem." Scientific investigations were undertaken by some of the most eminent physiologists and pathologists of the country. Ultimately a report on the *Physiological Aspects of the Liquor Problem* was drawn up by a sub-committee composed of Professor Atwater of Wesleyan University, Doctor Billings of the Astor Library in New York, formerly of the U. S. Army and Director of the Medical Museum and Library in Washington, Professor Bowditch of the Harvard Medical School, Professor Chittenden of the Sheffield Scientific School at Yale, and Doctor Welch of the Johns Hopkins Medical School. This committee, in objecting to "scientific temperance" instruction, pointed out several features of the movement that have characterized most later campaigns for reform propaganda in the schools.

In the first place, the committee agreed that the W. C. T. U.'s general purpose of temperance was excellent.

Secondly, it conceded that the backers of temperance laws were sincere persons of high moral purpose.

Thirdly, however, it objected that the reformers, while talking of "scientific" fact, perverted science to their own purpose. "Youth," it averred, "can hardly escape the conviction that an attempt is being deliberately made to deceive them, for a special, supposedly moral, purpose." The reformers did not teach hygiene and physiology as understood by the best scientific authorities in the colleges and universities. They set out to find men with scientific training who would subordinate science to their particular purpose. David Starr Jordan of Stanford University declared, "Such a treatise as the New York law contemplates cannot be written by a scientific man. . . . Indeed . . . [the W. C. T. U.] have the effrontery to demand of a scientific author in treating a certain scientific subject in the school courses that he shall introduce only so much of the subject as shall bear on a certain reform that they are advocating. Can even earnestness of purpose or the importance of the reform be a shadow of an excuse for such a course?"[133] The reformers insisted that no admission should be made in the schools that many medical men used alcohol and narcotics for medical purposes.

Fourthly, the committee found that the temperance reformers were carried away by their enthusiasm not only into suppressing unfavorable facts but also into exaggerated statements. "Failing to observe the distinction," it pointed out, "between diametrically opposite conceptions of 'use' and 'abuse,' some of its advocates have not hesitated to teach our children that the terrible results of a prolonged abuse of alcohol may be expected to follow any departure from the strict rules of total abstinence."

Fifthly, many educators and the committee objected to methods of teaching that defeated their own purposes. Memorizing passages from moralistic texts they felt was not the way to develop sobriety. Teachers objected that they were forced to teach notions completely out of adjustment with what was taught in colleges and universities. When their pupils later found, in college or in libraries, statements directly contradicting assertions their teachers had been forced to teach them as unquestionable fact, these pupils would throw over

---

[133] David Starr Jordan, "Scientific Temperance," *Appletons' Popular Science Monthly,* XLVIII (January, 1896), 351.

not only what they had "learned" about temperance but also what they had learned about all kinds of things that did have scientific support. They would even discount and disregard the laws of hygiene and facts of alcoholism, upon which medical science did agree with the reformers. "The text-books," the committee reported, "are written with a deliberate purpose to frighten the children, the younger the better, so thoroughly that they will avoid all contact with alcohol, an attempt fraught with danger on account of the natural re-action of healthy children, boys especially, to such exaggerated statements." Many teachers, then, who thoroughly believed in cultivating temperate habits in children objected to being coerced by the reformers into methods they felt were unsuited to this end.

Sixthly, the reformers, like so many recent propagandists, sugar-coated their propaganda by labeling it "science," when it was not as well as when it was, and by disguising it as physi-ology and hygiene. This did the double damage, opponents said, of making the propaganda more effective and insidious by disguising it, and of ruining necessary instruction in physiology and hygiene by distorting its balance and purpose.

Finally, afraid that persuasion would not work or impatient at the slowness of that method, the reformers abandoned argument and winning of individual teachers or school systems free to decide on curricular matters and resorted to emotional campaigns, politics, and force to dictate to teachers what they should teach and even how they should teach it. They coerced writers of texts as they coerced teachers. The author of an approved series of temperance physiologies testified to the committee: "I have studied physiology, and I do not wish you to suppose that I have fallen so low as to *believe* all the things I have put into those books." The committee commented, "That he had fallen low enough to put them in without believ-ing them did not seem to disturb his mind." In short, the reformers used outside power to coerce teachers into serving as propaganda agents regardless of the teachers' wishes and regardless of the effect on pedagogical methods and the balance of the curriculum as a whole. The committee concluded:

> There can be no doubt that the abuse of alcohol is a threat to our civilization. . . . That the originators of this educational scheme were honest in their intentions there is no reason to doubt, but . . . they have violated sound principles of pedagogy in forcing subjects upon the attention of children at an age when their minds cannot possibly be adapted to comprehend them, and have shown themselves absolutely indifferent to the demoralization of our educational system resulting from forcing teachers to give instruction in a way which their experience has shown them to be ill adapted to accomplish the ends in view, and from compelling children to memorize statements sure to be contradicted by experience of their later lives.

The power of the temperance reformers was great. Though the laws were eased up, they remained and still do. When in 1899 the Massachusetts Legislature considered a modification of the law, the W. C. T. U. measure was almost unanimously opposed by the medical and teaching professions. Yet such was the political strength of the reformers that it passed, and the milder bill approved by educators and doctors failed. In 1903 forty-seven states and territories and in 1913 forty-five required temperance instruction.[134] The W. C. T. U.'s activities did contribute largely, also, to the banishment of the saloon and, whether for good or ill, to the passage of the Eighteenth Amendment.

There were other reform groups who, on a smaller scale, sought to use the schools for propaganda purposes: anti-smokers, societies for the prevention of cruelty to animals, bird-lovers, conservationists, city-planning groups, safety-first organizations, and many others. None, however, had the power or met with the success of the temperance group.

[134] J. K. Flanders, *op. cit.*, 65–68.

8. INDUSTRIALIZATION

Between the end of the Civil War and the opening years of the new century, America had been transformed from a people primarily agricultural into a great industrial nation. Business was preoccupied with its own rapid growth. The rules of the game were chaotic. The country was still living under theories of agrarian individualism. Business found it profitable to encourage the application of this old-fashioned individualism to business practice. When the people did awaken to the fact that individual men could not compete on equal terms with great corporations, they found governmental machinery for the control of business difficult to create. Business could afford cleverer lawyers than could the Government and therefore found it easy to invent legal evasions of regulatory measures faster than the Government could enact new controls. Besides, the Civil War had left the country completely in the power of one party, and the certainty of continued possession of the Government, so long as the South was kept forcibly Republican, helped keep in control of that party corrupt politicians, whom business found it easy to buy. Furthermore, it took a great economic depression to awaken many men to the fact that reforms were needed in the business world.

In the 'eighties economics and sociology had developed into professions. In the 'nineties thoughtful men began to criticize the practices of American business. College professors, a few of them at least, began critical analyses of the economic order. Just as the struggle over freedom in science and religion was dying down, a new controversy burst forth over freedom in the realm of economic and social views. Successful business men, who had bought or ruthlessly crushed everything that had stood in their way, had no intention of brooking criticism from college professors whose very salaries they paid through taxes or money given out of their benevolence. Both business man and professor were surprised, the one that mere professors should have the temerity to question his business practices and economic theories, the other that freedom should be denied him in this realm just as he appeared to be winning it elsewhere. It had not occurred to most professors to question accepted theory and practice. But those who did voice criticism found themselves subjected to many subtle discomforts, in some cases even dismissal or threats of dismissal. Low tariffs, bimetallism, inflation of the currency, graduated income taxes, regulation of unfair business practices, friendship for labor, and socialism were all dangerous views to advocate. There was a general feeling that it was immoral for professors to criticize the way men had made the wealth that was now supporting their colleges. Furthermore, their criticisms were annoying, if not positively dangerous to business prosperity.

Gunton's Magazine expressed the common view of the proverbial average citizen of 1900 when it wrote:

On matters pertaining to the rights of life and liberty, of the safety of property and social institutions, which affect the welfare of the community, educational institutions are the intellectual bulwark. So far as they touch these matters at all, they are brought into existence to disseminate sound principles for influencing conduct conserving these institutions. Any sudden theory of disruption generally propagated would be a social and moral calamity to the community. It would disturb public faith in institutions, and consequently tend to destroy the efforts of economic and social development. Why should society be subjected to the risk of chaos by officially teaching this new unverified notion? . . . Now, in sociology the same law obtains. Economics and sociology deal with the questions not merely of individual relations but of the relation of society to property, home, and social and political institutions,—in short to everything that affects the personal right, protection of property and general security of individual effort in the community. All the wealth and institutional advantages of civilization are at stake. Here is a professor in a college who has arrived at the conclusion that private ownership of property is robbery; that justice demands the confiscation of existing wealth and its redistribution to the community. Are we to understand that on the theory of absolute liberty the university is to be used by this individual to advocate disruption of existing economic and social institutions, contrary to the consensus of the best current opinion both inside and out of the university? In other words, is it to lend its influence and wealth to the support of a person who propagates the idea of destruction of what it regards as the sacred institutions of civilized society?[135]

The majority of ordinary Americans would have felt this way had they thought at all on the question. When the President of Brown was given a choice between accepting the trustees' views on free silver and resigning, much of the public and the press sided with the trustees. "When a professor attempts to teach free-silverism in a gold-bug college," asked the *Minneapolis Times,* "why should he not be turned out if he lacks the grace voluntarily to resign?" The *Philadelphia Commonwealth* declared, "The trustees had indeed a right to expect him to shape his teachings in economics to meet their views." The *New York Mail and Express* announced, "This was not a blow at free speech, but a recognition of the absurdity of a free-silver champion drawing a salary from a sound-money corporation for teaching the students that which the supporters of the university condemned as pernicious and dangerous."[136] *Gunton's Magazine* expressed a general feeling when it said:

The limit line of individual innovation within established institutions is not the same in all subjects. In the domain of the physical sciences like astronomy, physics, chemistry, geology, botany, and of history and literature, there are practically no limits. . . . But in the domain of religion, morals and sociology the case is quite different. In the first case the new theories affect individual and societary action very slowly and with the greatest indirection, and consequently never can bring about any detrimental disturbances. In the latter case the innovation, if radical, may involve dangerous social eruption, undermine the moral basis of social order or the economic

135 "Liberty in Economic Teaching," *Gunton's Magazine,* XVIII (March, 1900), 231–232.
136 Quoted in Thomas E. Will, "Menace to Freedom: The College Trust," *Arena,* XXVI (September, 1901), 251.

security of property rights and interests, and thus destroy the safety of industrial action and arrest progress.[137]

In the South economic recovery from the Civil War and Reconstruction and economic adjustment to the free Negro brought the Negro into increasing competition with poor white men. The slow beginnings of improvement of the Negro race and the appearance of a few outstanding Negroes intensified the fear of the poor white. Southern white men added new reasons to old grounds for objection to having the race question discussed. On this there could be no freedom. Professor Dodd at Randolph-Macon College declared in 1904, "According to Southern opinion the whole race question is finally settled never to be opened again."[138] In 1907 he went further and averred that "many subjects which come every day into the mind of the historian may not with safety even so much as be discussed."[139]

The principle of academic freedom was yet to be established in America in fields where the public was directly concerned.

Besides, business was learning not only the danger of education if uncontrolled, but its value if properly regulated. In 1907 Professor Dodd pointed out that after a long struggle the old battle of freedom of speech in Southern colleges had been won. Religious views and even the race question could be freely discussed, he believed, in the better institutions. The newer industrial slavery, however, no one dared mention. "The beneficiaries of many concessions," he declared, "have wormed their way into the steering committees of the two great political parties, have found places on college boards of control, and now threaten both legislator and teacher who speak the truth about their doings."[140]

[137] "Liberty in Economic Teaching," *Gunton's Magazine*, XVIII (March, 1900), 229.
[138] W. E. Dodd, "Some Difficulties of the History Teacher in the South," *South Atlantic Quarterly*, III (April, 1904), 119.
[139] W. E. Dodd, "Freedom of Speech in the South," *Nation*, LXXXIV (April 25, 1907), 383.
[140] *Loc. cit.*

Many fears were expressed of dictatorship by the great educational foundations that wealthy men were establishing in the early years of the twentieth century. Edward Ingle, for instance, in 1907 wrote a pamphlet of alarm lest, through the Ogden Movement sponsored by the General Education Board, Northern men should subject Southern schools entirely to their will. Ingle was particularly worried over their attitude on the race question. He quoted the *New York Journal of Commerce* as sounding a warning and pointing out the danger of being obligated to large contributors who in schools, as in political parties, would insist upon dictating policies. He quoted the *Outlook* as boasting:

With this financial power in its control, the General Education Board is in position to do what no other body in this country can, at present, even attempt. It can determine largely what institutions shall grow, and, in some measure, what shall stand still or decay. . . . Its power will be enormous; it seems as if it might be able really to determine the character of American education. The funds it holds represent only a fraction of the amounts which it will really control; by giving a sum to an institution on condition that the institution raise an equal or a larger amount, it will be able to direct much larger amounts than it possesses.[141]

Bishop Candler published a pamphlet two years later sounding the same warning. "It is not safe," he wrote, "for the educational institutions of the country to be under the virtual dominion of fifteen men, however pure they may imagine their intentions to be. . . . Such a centralized educational system is perilous in the extreme. It is such a concentration of power in the matter of the highest interests of the nation as no fifteen men, however wise and virtuous, can be trusted to exercise without abusing it to the furtherance of their own views and interests and to the injury of those who do not agree with them in interest or opinion." He also cited the *New York World*, the *Journal of Commerce*, and the *Outlook* for evi-

[141] Edward Ingle, *The Ogden Movement*, 21–22.

dence of the danger. The *New Orleans Times-Democrat* he quoted as saying, "The fund which the General Education Board administers is largely provided by men whose interest in shaping public opinion upon certain matters of vital concern to society and to the State is very great. Whether their philanthropy serves as a cloak to attain the ends desired, or whether the plan is unselfishly conceived and the sinister influence unconsciously exerted, the effect is like to be the same in the end. The gifts are hedged about by restrictions and conditions." Even the *Manufacturers' Record* of Baltimore protested:

Control, through possession of the millions massed in the Educational Trust, of two or three or four times as many millions of dollars in education makes possible control of the machinery and the methods of education. It makes it possible for the central controlling body to determine the whole character of American education, the textbooks to be used, the aims to be emphasized. . . . It gives the financial controller power to impose upon its beneficiaries its own views, good or bad, and thereby to dominate public opinion in social, economic, and political matters. For, it would dominate the source of public opinion, the educational system of the country. Only a band of angels never subject to the weaknesses of human nature would be fit to exercise such power wisely.[142]

William E. Dodd, later ambassador to Germany, then professor at Randolph-Macon College in Virginia, wrote in 1907:

The General Educational Board of New York and the subsidiary Southern Education Board proclaim the greatest freedom of speech; but none of their members, with the notable exceptions of Albert Shaw and George F. Peabody, and none of their supporters in the South have ever found it possible to condemn publicly the methods of Mr. Rockefeller, their great benefactor. This is distinctly discouraging to those who have hoped still for better things, who even now wage a steady warfare against backwardness and deeply entrenched tradition. How can we ever bring our people to the high-

142 Bishop Warren A. Candler, *Dangerous Donations and Degrading Doles,* 48–49, 52–53.

est level of civilization, to real productivity in statesmanship, in letters and the arts, when a great field of activity is closed against investigation. . . . If one great theme is tabooed why not the others?[143]

The Carnegie Foundation was also feared for the control it might exercise over teaching. Even its pension fund was opposed for this reason. Bishop Candler warned that by withholding its funds from colleges with a religious affiliation it was forcing "disestablishment" upon some institutions and "death" upon those who refused "to deny the church parentage."[144]

The American Federation of Labor expressed concern. "A free people," says an executive council report, ". . . [is] greatly concerned whenever any undemocratic power or agent endeavors to get control over school management, over teachers or other instruction. . . . Perhaps the best planned, most dangerous efforts of this type are the great foundations that have been established by our captains of industry who have grown enormously wealthy and who subsidize foundations to be associated with the work of educational institutions. Since educational institutions are so closely associated with the lives of the people, . . . can we favor granting control over educational affairs to any agency that belongs or that is itself dependent upon the favor of a private individual or groups of individuals?"[145]

There were defenders of freedom of expression in the early days of industrialism. At a time when anarchism was the "radical menace" dreaded by sober and law-abiding citizens much as communism has been in the days since the World War, Ernest Freund wrote, "A proposition to forbid and punish the teaching or the propagation of the doctrine of anarchism . . . is inconsistent with the freedom of speech and

[143] W. E. Dodd, "Freedom of Speech in the South," *Nation*, LXXXIV (April 25, 1907), 383–384.
[144] Bishop W. A. Candler, *op. cit.*, 33–34.
[145] American Federation of Labor, *Proceedings*, XXXV (1915), 154.

press, unless carefully confined to cases of solicitation of crime.
. . . As the freedom of religion would have no meaning without the liberty of attacking all religion, so the freedom of political discussion is merely a phrase if it must stop short of questioning the fundamental ideas of politics, law and government. Otherwise every government is justified in drawing the line of free discussion at those principles or institutions which it deems essential to its preservation—a view to which the [czarist] Russian government would subscribe." But Freund was a professor, a theorist. The average American, whether rich or poor, would have agreed with *Gunton's Magazine* in its desire to make the schools a bulwark of the *status quo* against extremisms.

None the less with the new century came the age of the muckrakers. Greater freedom was gradually won in the more liberal colleges and universities, even on social and economic matters that vitally concerned the new industrialism. In the schools, this question, like the issue of evolution, did not arise —and for the same reasons. It took the newer economics and sociology a long time to trickle down to the schools. A new generation of teachers had to be trained first. The way was being prepared, however, in this as in evolution for a great struggle after the World War, when teachers began to awaken to the social and economic problems the new industrialism of this period had created.

Chapter VII

FREEDOM AMID THE COMPLEXITIES OF INDUS-TRIALIZED AMERICA, 1917–1939

1. The Post-War Environment

A combination of circumstances has given the problem of freedom in teaching extraordinary importance since the World War. By this time American schools had passed the rudimentary stage. Teacher training had improved until many teachers were capable of exercising a large degree of freedom. At the same time elaborate administrative organization had made effective control of teachers possible. History, civics, economics, and sociology had acquired new importance in the curriculum, and higher institutions were acquainting teachers with the results of modern scholarship in these fields. Through teachers trained elsewhere, the newer theories of science and modernist views of religion were reaching down into communities to which they appeared destructive of all that was good and holy. The War had speeded up the process of industrialization and intensified the resulting economic and social problems. Old conceptions of morality, long-established social controls, and ancient standards of conduct were destroyed by war-time experiences. The War left in its wake disillusionment that led many young teachers either to cynicism or to revolt against the old order and determination to improve it—attitudes certain to cause trouble in most American communities.

At the same time the War unleashed hatred, prejudice, and a whole swarm of passions usually kept under control in peacetime society. It accustomed men to making decisions and settling disputes by emotion and force instead of through reason and intelligence. It left behind it an excitable fear of criticism and "radicalism." It gave new life to a particularly blatant sort of "patriotism" and fathered a brood of patriotic societies organized to force chauvinism upon the people. War profits gave new power to big business, while war propaganda methods pointed the way to the creation of public opinion favorable to business control of the nation. Apparent prosperity and huge profits, which great masses of the people were making on paper, at least, in an orgy of speculation, rendered exceedingly unpopular the criticisms of the *status quo* and the warnings of disaster that were voiced by intellectual leaders who did keep their heads.

The increasingly obvious failure of education to prepare men to meet the great social and economic problems of modern society caused certain educators to question the effectiveness of the whole educational system. These educators then attempted to make the schools play a more vital rôle in American life. The result was a growing number of teachers interested in creating critical-minded students and in giving educational processes effectiveness in our complex modern society. This new interest of teachers coincided with a new-found determination of powerful business and propaganda groups to control the schools for their own purposes. Meanwhile the public, accustomed in war to coercive methods, was dominated by the emotionalism created by war. It wished to be left in peace to make money and was an easy prey to men ready to defend it against chimerical dangers. A small group of liberals stood ready to fight for freedom for teachers in the struggle that this social background made inevitable. Not one dominating question as in other periods, but a complexity of controversial problems now occupied the arena of educational conflict.

2. Freedom and Repression of Ideas[1]

The answers to the author's questionnaire reveal interesting differences in attitude toward teachers' expression of ideas on controversial subjects. In many communities merely believing in unpopular causes creates difficulty, if it is known. Other communities do not object to unconventional views unless they are extremely radical, provided the teacher does not talk about them publicly. In other places the teacher may go still farther and discuss unpopular ideas in class, provided he himself does not support them. He may maintain strict neutrality or he may oppose them, but he must not express approval. In some towns a teacher may not only discuss controversial subjects in class, but, in the course of that discussion, may express personal views on the unpopular side, provided he does not try to convert anybody to his own unorthodoxy. There are usually exceptions to this rule—certain extreme beliefs that it would be unsafe for a teacher to let his pupils know he favors. In a few places a teacher may openly propagandize in class for unpopular causes. He may usually propagandize if he supports the popular side of the controversy. In some communities he may even do so on the unpopular side. In theory he is freer to advocate unpopular causes outside class than inside, but in practice the advocacy of unpopular causes in the community gets him into trouble more quickly than doing so in school. There are exceptions to this rule. In many communities particular subjects arouse great feeling and must be entirely avoided. While usually a teacher is freer to believe in an unpopular cause than to discuss it even impartially, just the reverse is true in regard to certain extreme points of view. Many communities reported in 1933 that a teacher might dis-

[1] This is an attempt at summary and at weighing the relative forces of pressures described above. Much of this material comes from tabulation and analysis of the results of a questionnaire the author distributed to teachers and others connected with the schools. The questionnaire was compiled and these paragraphs were written in 1933. See *infra*, Appendix.

cuss communism, cancellation of war debts, recognition of
Russia, or the necessity of revolution by force to bring social
justice, but may not believe in any of these things himself.
On the other hand, birth control, the non-existence of God,
and evolution are not deemed fit subjects even for impartial
discussion in class in many places, where a teacher may believe in them himself. In the South certain points of view, such
as censure of Southern leaders for not accepting the results
of the Civil War, usually may not even be raised in class.

On all controversial subjects, teachers are much freer to express views on the conservative than on the unorthodox side.
Of all the various controversial issues, international affairs is
the one on which teachers are permitted the greatest amount
of freedom. There was, in 1933, least restriction on advocacy
of recognition of Russia, and only slightly more on urging
adherence to the League of Nations or the World Court.
About one in five teachers thought he must not openly favor
cancellation of war debts, oppose the doctrine of keeping out
of foreign entanglements, advocate a constitutional amendment depriving the Senate of its veto power over treaties, or
denounce our interventions in the Caribbean countries as
imperialistic.[2] One in four would not have dared openly favor
the abandonment of the Monroe Doctrine.

After international questions the various problems on which
sectional feeling once ran high seem to allow the greatest
freedom. Points of view in accord with sectional prejudice
may, of course, be freely voiced. For instance, in the North,
about four out of five teachers are at liberty to criticize the
secession leaders of the South and three out of four to censure
Southerners for their failure in Reconstruction to accept the
results of the Civil War. In the South and Border States, most
white teachers and about two out of three Negro teachers are
free to censure the activities of the abolitionists of ante-bellum
days and to censure Northern rule of the South after the

[2] Most teachers may *defend* our interventions.

Civil War. In most places even views in conflict with sectional feeling may now be expressed. For instance, about four out of five teachers in the North may criticize the activities of abolitionists and Northern rule of the South. The South is more sensitive. Only about two out of three Southern and Border State teachers dare criticize their secession leaders, and only a little over half of them may regret Southern failure to accept the results of the Civil War.[3]

The country as a whole is still somewhat sensitive about criticism of its own past actions. About one teacher in four is afraid to express the belief that the United States committed a wrong against Mexico in the Mexican War or to defend Germany's position in the World War or Britain's in the American Revolution. One in three is afraid to agree with modern historical research in its deflation of some of the heroes of American history.

On economic questions, popular or generally accepted points of view or opinions that please wealthy and powerful members of the community can be expressed without criticism.[4] There is also a class of economic questions on which teachers are fairly free to express even views on the unconventional side, namely, support of high income taxes, the belief that labor is pitifully underpaid, advocacy of low tariffs for revenue only, support of government ownership of public utilities, belief that "peaceful reform" of the capitalist system is necessary, and support of a capital levy.

But opinion on the unorthodox side of economic issues is usually more restricted than on international, sectional, or "patriotic" questions. One teacher in four is afraid to censure labor union leaders in sections where labor is well organized. A good deal of objection is raised to advocacy of confiscatory

[3] Of course, trouble rarely arises over this matter, because Southern teachers generally do not wish to express the interpretations that would be unpopular.

[4] There is, for instance, almost no objection to stating the traditional belief that in America "equality of opportunity" insures the success of the most capable.

inheritance taxes, belief that "all unemployed have a moral right to support from Federal relief," denunciation of the "profit system,"·and the charge that "our courts are corrupted by big business." Support of teacher membership in labor unions is frequently impossible. Dangerous, indeed, is disapproval of the practices of local business men like coal operators, utility owners, merchants, lawyers, or manufacturers.

Teachers are less free to take the peace side of the war issue than the unpopular side of economic questions. Most teachers may advocate a large navy or oppose an embargo on the shipment of arms to warring nations. Veterans' appropriations and military training in the schools are dangerous subjects whichever side one takes. Usually, however, it is opposition to war that teachers feel they are not free to express. Many are afraid to advocate total disarmament or to criticize the Supreme Court for its refusal to admit pacifists to citizenship. Still more dare not declare that our entry into the World War was a mistake or praise war-time "conscientious objectors." Most dangerous of all is swearing never to bear arms.

Criticism of the Government is dangerous. One teacher out of three was afraid even to criticize President Hoover for using the army to drive the bonus men out of Washington or to accuse state officials of corruption. It is more dangerous, however, to express censure of the President of the United States on other grounds, or of the local courts for unjust decisions, or of local officials for corruption.

Political questions are still more restricted unless one is on the orthodox side.[5] One in every three or four teachers thinks it unsafe to voice opposition to the "Buy American" movement or to denounce the Ku Klux Klan. Between a third and a half are afraid to censure the Federal Government or local police for prosecuting Communist hunger marchers for parading, or to criticize the activities of the D. A. R., the

---

[5] Only a small proportion of teachers felt it unsafe to denounce radicals as unpatriotic or to support the United States "whether right or wrong."

American Legion, or the Confederate Veterans. Some teachers object to a pledge of loyalty and an oath of allegiance because these imply a pledge to bear arms in any war whatsoever whether just or unjust; but nearly two-thirds of the teachers report it impossible to express this opposition.

Support of radicalism is still more dangerous, though most teachers are free to express opposition to radicalism.[6] One in three is afraid to approve socialism. A majority feel it unsafe to approve communism, criticize the breaking up of a meeting of "Reds" by local police, or suggest that revolution by force is necessary in order to establish justice.[7]

Ideas on social problems are dangerous to unorthodox teachers. In spite of the popular vote for repeal shortly thereafter, only six teachers in seven felt it safe in 1933 to favor rigid enforcement of the Eighteenth Amendment, while it was frequently unsafe to support repeal. In the South it is unwise to express approval of anything more than nominal political equality for Negroes, but in the North teachers are usually free to favor full equality. Approval of social equality for Negroes, however, is dangerous even in some Northern communities and is impossible in the South. Expression of belief in birth control or companionate marriage is impossible. In fact, in the great majority of schools neither subject can be discussed even impartially in its proper place in the curriculum.

Religion is the most restricted of all subjects. Here teachers generally are not free to express approval even of conservative tenets because there are certain to be liberals in the community who will object. Between a third and a half of the teachers are afraid to express acceptance of the theory of evolution, even if they make no effort to persuade their pupils. In the great ma-

[6] More than four out of five teachers were free to praise the anti-radical activities of the D. A. R., or the American Legion.

[7] Belief in the right of revolution was frequently voiced by Jefferson and other American Revolutionary leaders and was incorporated into the Declaration of Independence. See, for example, Merle E. Curti, "Our Revolutionary Tradition," *Social Frontier*, I (December, 1934), 10–13.

jority of schools favorable views must not be expressed on either the fundamentalist or the modernist interpretations of the Bible. It is unsafe to let the class know that one believes it dangerous to elect a Catholic to office. Almost nowhere can one admit to a class that he does not believe in the existence of God.

These comparisons are based on a teacher's freedom to express views upon a subject in the course of class discussion provided he does not try to convert students. There is much less freedom in advocating these same things outside of class and still less in propagandizing for them in class. While this picture portrays the relative degree of freedom in these various realms of ideas, it greatly underestimates for several reasons the extent of actual restrictions. In the first place, the South responded poorly and the freer parts of the country well, thus weighting the questionnaires in favor of freedom. It was harder, also, to get replies from small towns and rural schools than from large cities, where there is the greatest freedom. The teachers most interested in answering were those where there is a good deal of freedom but where teachers want more. An effort was made to reach those who had thought most about freedom and therefore could answer most adequately, and therefore the questionnaire was sent to a selected list of teachers. Still, even of this selected group, probably half reported that they had freedom merely because they had not thought enough about most of the questions to realize how little they really did have. In many cases, freedom seems to exist only because the subject under consideration is not an issue in the particular community. In such a situation, this apparent freedom could be replaced by rigid restriction if and when people became really interested in the subject discussed. Many teachers frankly reply that most of these controversial topics are unknown in their schools and that they do not know what the attitude is. In certain cases a well-organized group of Catholics, laborers, or business men will prevent or create restrictions on some subject that throw it entirely out of line with other attitudes in that community. Freedom to discuss military training depends largely upon whether it is offered in the school in question. The replies of teachers in the great number of schools that offer none over-balance the rigid restrictions against criticism of it in schools where it does exist. This makes freedom in the matter appear much greater than it actually is in schools where military training is an issue at all. Here, then, the restrictive forces are much more powerful than is revealed.

3. FREEDOM IN CONDUCT

Conduct outside the school gets more teachers into trouble than do ideas expressed in the classroom.[8] Teachers since the World War have been allowed to do many things that would once have caused instant dismissal. Theater-going and dancing are now usually permitted to teachers, though a surprising number of places still forbid dancing. Smoking by men teachers is widely permitted. In many places even women teachers smoke. In some larger cities drinking is at least not punished, even when not specifically permitted, though it is usually not publicly confessed. Divorce is no longer always fatal to the teacher, though it still is dangerous. Freedom is now permitted in dress, in conduct, in habits that would once have been considered "immoral" by a stricter pre-war generation. Church attendance and teaching a Sunday school class are still widely expected of a teacher, but much less generally so than formerly. For a time, continuing to teach after marriage was more extensively permitted than formerly. Now that is again rigidly restricted in communities that had come to accept it. The restriction is now based on economic grounds, however, not on moral scruples or views about the woman's place in the home.

[8] See H. K. Beale, *Are American Teachers Free?* 374–409.

Comparisons of detail make a teacher look much freer in 1939 than in 1900. Actually, it is questionable whether the teacher's position in relation to the rest of the community has changed much except in large cities. American standards of conduct have changed. Popular ideas of what is moral and respectable were revolutionized by the War. All sorts of inhibitions were broken down. The change in the position of women in American life has brought release to many a school teacher. The significant fact is not, however, that teachers in a given community can now dance whereas it was strictly forbidden them before 1920, or that women teachers here and there smoke whereas it would have meant instant dismissal in 1925. The significant fact is that the teacher is still subjected to all sorts of regulations and prohibitions that are not applied to members of the community in other callings. It is the community mores that have changed, not the relation of the teacher to the community. The teacher cannot indefinitely be denied some particular thing that the whole community does. The teacher, however, and the minister are about the last persons in the community to be allowed by public opinion to indulge in what was once considered improper. The teacher is still expected by the community to lead an exemplary life, to impress children with an ideal code of conduct that parents in theory adhere to but in private violate. Special codes are still imposed upon teachers.

What is more, the teacher is still required to participate in all sorts of community activities for which the public wants support. The teacher, even the civics teacher, is still not expected to take an active part in the determination of community policies on controversial matters. The teacher is still "only a teacher," not entitled to vigorous views on things that really matter in the community if his views differ from those generally accepted. As community interests change the particular implications of this attitude are altered. Many places no longer object to unorthodox religious practice. Yet where this is true it is not because the community attitude toward a teacher's enjoyment of active and independent citizenship has changed; it is simply because the popular interest in religion has waned. On social, economic, and political questions that really matter the teacher may no more be an active citizen than formerly unless there is community agreement on the question and the teacher conforms to the community desire. The teacher is still the "hired man" of the community that feels privileged to dictate what he shall and shall not do whenever his activity involves a question on which it cares what anybody does.

4. SOURCES OF PRESSURE UPON TEACHERS

Generalizations for the country as a whole are unsafe, because pressure upon the teacher varies with the type of school and type of community. In public schools, however, public opinion wins first place among pressures by a large margin except in cities of 100,000 or more. There the force of public opinion is not so great as a number of other influences. In private schools in smaller places, public opinion is an important restraint, but in those in large cities it counts even less than in public schools.

The other really great pressures come from parents, superintendents, principals, and school board members or trustees. So nearly equal are these pressures that no generalization is possible for the country as a whole. In private schools, since there is no superintendent, the principal exerts the greatest pressure and parents rank next. Private schools in large cities are usually so organized that the board of trustees, if there is one at all, does not count heavily in the teacher's life. In private schools in smaller places trustees usually exercise large control. In private schools run by individual owners all power is concentrated in this head of the school, except in so far as he in turn is subject to various pressures. In public schools the relative importance of these elements depends upon the size of the town. In cities of over 100,000 the principal ranks below public opinion but above the superintendent. Parents and school boards are weighted almost equally after the superintendent, school boards running a little ahead in cities of over 1,000,000 and parents a little ahead in cities of 100,000 to 1,000,000. In suburban communities parents outrank all the other pressures. School boards come next, then superintendents, and prinicpals last. In cities of 2500 to 100,000 the superintendent is, after public opinion, the most important restrictive force, with the school board next, and principals least important. In rural communities, the principal is still less important; the school board and superintendent outrank parents; but the school board instead of the superintendent becomes the great restrictive force. Next in importance among pressures on teachers come other teachers and students. Except in private schools in large cities and in public schools in rural communities the power of other teachers over a teacher is greater than that of students.

In this group of important restrictive pressures teachers also name business men, politicians, and religious groups. In private schools business men of the community and politicians have little power, but because of the religious connections or traditions of many of these schools, religious groups exert considerable influence. In public schools of great cities politicians outrank the other two, but both business and religious groups are important and exert almost equal pressure, largely because of the active Roman Catholic elements in the great cities. In rural communities, too, and in towns of 2500 to 25,000 the religious groups are much more powerful than business men or politicians. In the great number of American cities that have between 25,000 and 1,000,000 population, religious forces have much less power over teachers than do business men and politicians, and business is more influential than politicians. In suburbs of great cities religious groups and politicians are alike unimportant in comparison with business interests.

Lesser but important pressures are exerted by particular organizations and individuals. Generalization is even more difficult here because a group active in one town may not happen to be organized in another town of the same size and type. On the whole, however, the American Legion seems to be the most important. Next come benefactors of the school, the D. A. R., the Chamber of Commerce, and "other patriotic organizations," including in the South the United Daughters of the Confederacy. In private schools benefactors of the school have great influence and the other groups very little. The peace organizations and the Ku Klux Klan share honors for the place of next importance with bar associations not far behind. In private schools and in the Northeast, none of the three has great influence. In the Middle West the bar association is much less important than the Klan and peace organizations. A few teachers felt that other groups exert such an important pressure that they wrote them into the questionnaire —newspapers, the W. C. T. U., the principal's wife or secretary, and school supervisors.

Determination of the proportion of teachers whom the problem of freedom does not apparently concern, because they share the views of their community, is extraordinarily difficult. No teacher likes to admit that he merely reflects community attitudes. Besides, most of the teachers who in general do share them differ in some particular, perhaps in some petty matter, or have some grievance against the community, which makes them talk of freedom. The appalling fact is the pettiness of most of these matters in which such teachers disagree with community opinion. By and large, then, the majority of teachers in all essential matters agree with the community. These teachers are usually not aware of their own extreme conventionality. Furthermore, they have never done enough thinking or reading to know a "controversial subject" when they see one, for in their minds there can be no "controversy" or possibility of difference of opinion on any of them. These teachers naïvely answer with great regularity—thinking of some petty point of difference—that they do *not* agree with the community, but that they have "complete freedom."[9]

Those teachers who really do disagree with community attitudes, or would if they dared, are dominated by several forces in refraining from expressing that disagreement. The two most important of these are fear of dismissal and fear of public opinion. More teachers named fear of public opinion than did fear of dismissal, but those who named both rated fear of dismissal the more powerful dread. In large cities the dread of public opinion is relatively greater and the fear of dismissal less than in smaller places, partly because tenure in large cities is usually more secure than elsewhere. The public opinion, however, that is dreaded is not the old-fashioned sort that operates in small communities.[10] It is, instead, the views of one or more conflicting groups or individuals powerful enough to make themselves felt and to injure teachers they dislike in innumerable ways short of the dismissal that tenure laws and teacher organizations make difficult. Fear of disfavor that will prevent promotions, belief that a teacher should avoid controversial subjects, and fear of refusal of a good recommendation when applying for another position rival one another for the place of next importance. In great cities the fear of not getting promotions is the most powerful factor of all. In private schools the belief that teachers should avoid controversial subjects outranks all others. Other factors of great restrictive importance affecting all schools are a lack of interest in controversial subjects and fear of discipline other than dismissal. Lack of interest in controversial subjects ranks high in private schools and lack of knowledge of them in rural schools. Of only slightly less importance than these other factors is a general feeling, usually based on experience, that it is futile not to conform.

[9] See H. K. Beale, *op. cit.*, 665–673, 688–690.
[10] See *ibid.*, 664.

5. EFFECT OF THE SIZE OF THE COMMUNITY UPON FREEDOM

Freedom varies with the size of the community in which the school is located. In the great cities politicians and well organized business groups have great power. In spite of this, however, teachers in large cities on the whole have much greater freedom than elsewhere. There are several reasons for this. They are usually well organized into unions or other groups. They have obtained better tenure laws. A unified community opinion does not exist. Groups that in smaller places would control the schools are counterbalanced by opposing groups. The struggles of one group against another over the schools have left the teacher free from interference other than politics and favoritism. In the great city there is more teacher interest in controversial subjects than exists in the smaller places, and there are numerous "radicals" in the system. Yet the warring groups in the great city have learned from necessity to live and let live. City dwellers have become indifferent to much that seems important to the small town. Many other matters would still interest small-town folk removed to the large city, if there were still opportunity for interference. But the minute a teacher leaves the school building he is lost in the big city. Neighborly gossip is impossible, where one does not know his neighbors' names or faces. Parents of any two children under the same teacher seldom know each other. Finally, cosmopolitanism has created greater understanding and tolerance on many of the subjects that do vitally matter to city people.

The small town is more unified in sentiment. Church groups are more powerful. Teachers are known as teachers, wherever they go and whatever they do. Traditions, customs, and long-held ideas persist more tenaciously in the small town. Contacts with people of different ideas and different habits of life are infrequent. Communication with the outside world is difficult, particularly in the realm of ideas. New styles of dress arrive long before new ways of thinking. There are usually no tenure laws, and teachers' organizations with any power do not exist. The small community remains much more under the influence of Jacksonian democracy, the frontier, fundamentalism, and authoritarianism of all kinds. In short, the small American community is the heart of American conservatism. In small communities most of the social, economic, and international problems of modern America do not exist. Urbanization and industrialization, which have created the problems and conflicts that have liberalized urban thought, have not touched the small community. It is still rural and agrarian in ideas and thought processes, however many radios and automobiles it may own. It is significant that the ideas listed upon the author's questionnaire meant nothing at all to most small-town and rural teachers.

Between the great city and the small town, freedom varies with size and local conditions. Suburban communities fall into a class by themselves. In many respects they resemble the small towns. They lack many of the factors that give freedom to teachers in the great city, which they adjoin. People are more likely to know one another. There is possibility of close control over the schools. People and ideas are fairly homogeneous; a preponderance of self-satisfied, newly prosperous business and professional folk breeds conservatism and complacency. In many matters freedom is much more restricted than in the city.[11] Three factors, however, counterbalance the smallness of the place—the absence of powerful political and business groups, the proximity of the great city that dominates the thought and social life of the suburbanites, and the fact that the population is wealthy enough to demand and get modern, often "progressive" schools that lay great stress upon "free-

[11] The fashionable north-shore suburbs of Chicago, for instance, provide a happy hunting ground for Elizabeth Dilling of the *Red Network* and others of her ilk who perpetually seek to interfere in what would otherwise be unusually good schools.

dom" and educate the parents of the community to expect it in their schools.

6. Freedom in the Various Sections of the Country

Throughout this study sectional differences in freedom have been indicated. In general, teachers seem to have greatest freedom in the Northeast, except Pennsylvania. The Middle West and Far West have less, the Border States still less, and the South least of all.

The greater degree of freedom in the Northeast is explained by several factors. We have seen that large cities offer greater freedom than small places, and the Northeast is highly urbanized. Industrialization may or may not be an aid to freedom. In Southern mill regions and in the mining and industrial sections of the Border States and Pennsylvania, industrial communities live under a feudal system that usually crushes out freedom. Industrialized life in its more mature stages in the Northeast has been made somewhat more civilized in its industrial relations by the fact that labor is highly organized to protect itself. In these regions industrialization increases rather than restricts freedom. The Northeast, too, lives in the midst of a great diversity of ideas, creeds, manners, and cultures, and this very diversity leads to the necessity of tolerance of strange ideas and customs. The Northeast has long been used to a discussion of social and economic problems, of which other sections of the country have only recently become conscious. Large foreign populations have created a certain cosmopolitanism that other sections lack. Radicals are less rare and therefore less "dangerous." Furthermore, many of the better private schools of the Northeast allow, within limits, a great deal of freedom; wealthy men want for their own sons a free education that they are unwilling to grant to poorer men's sons in the public schools they dominate; and the practice of private schools in the matter influences other schools. Besides, the fact that many of the children of the "better class" go to private schools means that men of this class, who often interfere in the schools in other sections, know less about public schools than they would if their own children were in them. Progressive education, too, has established itself in many communities of the East, with its inevitable augmentation of a teacher's freedom of ideas. Then, too, the Northeast, though it has plenty of provincialisms of its own,[12] lives in more direct communication with the rest of the country and the rest of the world, and this tends to create greater freedom. Yet the small town in New England, especially if controlled by two or three mill-owning families, *can* restrict freedom as rigidly as similar small towns elsewhere.

The lack of freedom in the South can be explained by a number of factors peculiar to that region.[13] In the first place, illiteracy and general backwardness are greatest there. It is significant that support for both anti-evolution laws and lynchings come from people in states and communities where illiteracy is greatest. The inferiority of Southern schools, the poor training provided by Southern teachers' training institutions, and the ignorance of great masses of Southern people account in part for the lack of freedom for teachers. North Carolina, where there is a liberal state university and greater economic diversity, allows its teachers more freedom than states farther south. The South, moreover, is the center of fundamentalist, authoritarian religion. Besides, the South is essentially rural with all that that means in provincialism,

---

[12] There is, of course, no narrower provincialism in the nation than the provincialism of a Back Bay Bostonian aristocrat or upper middle-class New Yorker. But the provincialism of these classes is of a sort that does not impinge upon the problem of the schools, and, in general, the Northeast *is* less provincial in its outlook than other parts of the nation.

[13] There are, of course, notable exceptions in the South to all that is said here of the South in general, and the exceptions are growing in number. Individual Southerners there are who compare favorably in all these matters with the best in the nation. These Southerners are constantly laboring to change the South. Institutions there are like the University of North Carolina that contradict every generalization here made, but Southerners are the first to tell an outlander that "The University of North Carolina is not the South."

isolation from the world of ideas, and distrust of anything new. "Tennessee is a rural State," wrote Milton, in explanation of the anti-evolution law; "several of our counties haven't a railroad anywhere within their borders. Most of the members of our General Assemblies are from the country and the small towns, which means that they are reactionaries."[14]

The South seldom attempts self-criticism,[15] and, when it does in educational matters, it has so few good schools that it has no adequate standards of comparison. It hates to admit that anything in the North could be superior. When Southerners do essay self-criticism they usually compare themselves with themselves in an earlier period or with other Southerners in another state instead of with the higher standards of the North. "We are apt to be devoid of perspective and at times overrate our own men and our own institutions and our own selves," wrote one Southerner in 1905.[16] The President of the University of North Carolina declared in 1929:

We must concern ourselves less about comparisons with each other and more with our relationship in terms of achievement to the nation and the western world. It is a matter of secondary importance how Georgia and North Carolina compare with each other in education or in any other enterprise. The real question is how they both compare with the best national standards. It is dangerous and misleading to attempt to judge any area simply in terms of itself. As long as we think about southern education in terms of how it compares with yesterday, or of how its various parts compare

[14] George F. Milton, "Testing the 'Monkey Bill,'" *Independent*, CXIV (June 13, 1925), 661.

[15] There seems to be an increasing tendency to critical self-analysis on the part of some outstanding Southerners like Howard W. Odum and the University of North Carolina Institute for Research in Social Science, William T. Couch and the other authors of *Culture in the South*, and certain contemporary Southern novelists. But unfortunately for the cause of progress through self-criticism the Nashville group of agrarians who wrote *I'll Take My Stand* and who sponsor the *American Review*, have as much power as these others. And this Nashville group are laboring to accentuate the Southern tendency to run away from criticism; they bid fair, indeed, to carry on the tradition of "professional Southerners" of an earlier day.

[16] William P. Few, "Southern Public Opinion," *South Atlantic Quarterly*, IV (January, 1905), 4–5.

with each other, so long do we run the risk of a complacent self-satisfaction about things that, judged by more absolute terms, are really not good. We are all too familiar with the boosting type of persons and publications that magnify second-rate achievements beyond their real deserts because they are southern. The phrase "the best in the South" is one that I wish could be eliminated.[17]

Professor Knight says:

These social insanities [provincial prejudice and complacency] help to perpetuate educational backwardness in the South. Satisfaction with what we have done during the last three decades blinds us to the things we should do now. The South is in grave danger of ballyhooing itself into further backwardness. Educational inequalities are in some respects as glaring now as they were twenty-five years ago, but the professional southerner does not hesitate to describe as "conspicuous achievements" many educational improvements which would pass unnoticed in really advanced states. Exaggerated claims of progress by influential southern leaders are frequently taken in the South as actual defenses of its educational shortcomings.[18]

Public criticism of the South by a Southerner is unusual. An increasing number of Southerners will criticize deficiencies of the South in the privacy of a group of Southerners. Even these, however, are reluctant to do so with an outsider present or for publication. Criticism of the South by an outsider is resented.[19] "As a people," wrote Few, "we have been exceedingly conservative in our thinking and too sensitive to criticism, which . . . is apt to stimulate the minds of men and set them in the way to improvement."[20] Chapman believes that Southern "pride and an angry resentment to criticism" is

[17] Harry W. Chase, "Larger Contacts and a World Outlook," National Education Association, *Proceedings,* LXVII (1929), 489.

[18] Edgar W. Knight, "Education in the South," *Outlook and Independent,* CLIV (Jan. 8, 1930), 79.

[19] Southerners go North and frequently denounce loudly and often not too politely the way Northerners treat "niggers," but the Northerner who goes South is not free to criticize ever so gently Southerners' treatment of Negroes. If he did, he would quickly be made aware of his mistake.

[20] W. P. Few, *op. cit.,* 2.

caused by the "group isolation" from which Southern states suffer.[21] Professor Knight declares:

When any one, even a southerner, suggests that the southern states are not educationally advanced, that they appear to be somewhat afflicted with lassitude and complacency and with tendencies to boasting and sensitiveness to criticism, the professional southerner, a part of the press, and some schoolmen of that section stir themselves through protest and work themselves into a lather through bitter denunciations and denials and indulgence in personalities. Not all, of course, but many of them ridicule the criticism and then turn quickly to tear into the critic, who is generally described as "viciously impolite," "a sort of common scold engaged in telling us how remiss we are," and "given over entirely to vitriolic criticism and backbiting." He is likely to find himself out of love and charity with some of his neighbors and is lucky if he escapes with his hide. It is still fashionable in the South to brand as unpatriotic any question of its shortcomings or any inquiry into their causes. The South has not yet learned (if a Southerner may say so) that provincial prejudice is not patriotism and that acute sensitiveness to just criticism is not loyalty.[22]

The President of the University of North Carolina once said:

If the south is to take its proper place in the modern world, we must . . . learn to face our shortcomings, as well as our virtues with restraint, patience, and in a spirit of inquiry. We must build, not on a romantic picture of what we wish our states and communities to be like, but on what they are. . . . We need to be more critical of ourselves, and less inclined to assign the critic to unmentionable destinations.[23]

But some Southerners will not send their children to a University that tolerates a president and professor who make

[21] Maristan Chapman, "The Southern Mind," *Century,* CXVII (January, 1929), 372.

[22] E. W. Knight, *op. cit.,* 47; E. W. Knight, "Can the South Attain to National Standards in Education?" *South Atlantic Quarterly,* XXVIII (January, 1929), 12. A school superintendent in one Southern city who saw a portion of this manuscript in which appeared a statement that the South was less free than the North objected to the author's printing it because to say so was "not in good taste."

[23] H. W. Chase, *op. cit.,* 489–490.

comments like these and some towns will not hire its graduates as teachers.

Dabney in 1932 repeated the question asked by the Chancellor of the University of Georgia in 1900: "Have we freedom of opinion in the South? Must every man who thinks above a whisper do so at the peril of his reputation or his influence, or at the deadlier risk of having an injury inflicted upon the institution or the cause he represents?" Dabney continues, "Chancellor Hill sounded 'a word of warning against the worst evil in our intellectual, social, political, and religious life, the illiberality that is ready to inflict the urging of rebuke or ostracism as a penalty for difference in opinion.' "[24]

This illiberalism of the Southern public mind explains much of the lack of freedom of Southern teachers. Years of slavery, when they could impose their will on those about them, made members of the Southern aristocracy intolerant of opposition. The habits of slaveholding were strengthened by a romantic sort of imitation of chivalry characterized by frequent bursts of temper that settled arguments by violence in the name of "honor." Its defeat in the Civil War is important to an understanding of the South's dislike of new ideas. The experience of defeat and Reconstruction have combined to lead an unhappy and poverty-stricken people to romanticize the ante-bellum life of a few aristocrats into a symbol of what once was. The distant past has served as an escape from the inglorious present. No one must be allowed to shatter these ideals about the ante-bellum South.

Many descendants of former aristocrats cling to and idealize not only the manners but the ideas, thoughts, and prejudices of ante-bellum days. There are to be sure not many such descendants of great planters. Even in ante-bellum days, the majority of white Southerners did not own slaves. Many of the descendants of those who did are worn out and without influence. It is the grandchildren, not of planters, but of

[24] Virginius Dabney, *Liberalism in the South*, 338.

yeomen farmers, who dominate the South today. This present dominant group whose ancestors never owned a slave now aspire to social prestige. They attain recognition, not by the ostentatious spending of similarly ambitious people in the North, but by assuming and making much of what they believe were the thoughts, ideas, social practices, prejudices, and hatreds of ante-bellum aristocrats. Thus they have acquired an intolerance bred of slavery that they believe was characteristic of the ante-bellum aristocrat's "honor." The descendants of great planters are indeed more often liberal than newly arrived middle-class folk who are trying to climb socially by imitating what they think the "best people" of the old South were like.

It was easy for the victor to forget the Civil War; it has been difficult for the South, which, until the present younger generation, has been still bitter and unhappy over its defeat. The South cannot forget the sufferings and humiliations of Reconstruction. In fact it magnifies these in retrospection. This all makes it doubly determined to justify its position before, after, and during the Civil War. In so far as it suspects that it may have been wrong, it becomes the more determined to suppress such a belief. It suffered so much that it cannot afford to admit that the suffering was futile or unnecessary or caused partly by its own mistakes. This leads to sectional history and a suppression of other views than its own. The South was on the defensive for years under slavery. So it has been ever since, on secession, the Negro question, its poor schools, its economic and intellectual backwardness. Defense psychology is not conducive to freedom of opinion.

The Negro is another factor of importance. Wherever the Negro is concerned, the South is dominated by fear. Fear does not breed liberalism. Furthermore most liberals run into snags on the Negro question—because of inconsistencies in their own liberalism, if Southerners,[25] because of opposition to

[25] Sometimes when Northerners, too.

their views on the Negro, if Northerners in the South. The whole Southern attitude on the Negro is based on suppression, for the Negro must be held down. People who encourage him to unrest are dangerous. This psychology flows over into other fields and makes the Southerner distrust "freedom" in practice, however much he talks of it in theory. On account of the Negro danger Southerners have learned, when that issue arises, to lay aside all other differences, however heated, in order to put up a united front on the Negro problem. This tends to force conformity to general ideas in fields where there would be wide differences of opinion, if it were not for the presence of the Negro.

State pride is important. Most Southerners are proud of their state in the same way that Northerners are of their nation. In a South Carolina group of teachers, one history teacher kept telling the author that she supposed he would think she was "funny," but that she had all the freedom she wanted, she thought South Carolina was just about right, so did everybody else, and therefore there was no one to object to their teaching that it was.[26] The same factors that create nationalism, provincialism, resentment of criticism, ignorance of other nations, in the nation, tend to create all of these things in a Southern state in regard to the state. In South Carolina, for instance, efforts to hide subconsciously recognized inferiority and bolster an ancient pride make natives impervious to suggestion from without. In Iowa a suggestion that Minnesota's schools were better might cause unhappiness but it would provoke a determination to make Iowa's schools better than Minnesota's. In South Carolina a suggestion that North Carolina's schools were better than South Carolina's would merely bring a shrug of the shoulder. What could it matter what another state's schools do, since being a South Carolinian more than compensates for any superiority of another state?

[26] Interview with a group of teachers, Columbia, South Carolina, March, 1933.

In addition to state pride, there is in the South a highly developed local consciousness that applies to counties and communities as well as to states. A boy or girl who goes from the community to a college or university to prepare himself for teaching feels that he has an almost incontrovertible "right" to a teaching position in the community when he is graduated. The community feels it, too. This "right," acquired through nativity and residence, outweighs in his mind and in that of the community any qualifications a non-native or non-resident may possess that are based on mere training or experience or capacity as a teacher, even though the outsider is eminently better fitted for teaching. Even in colleges this feeling obtains. A young Southern professor with a doctor's degree from a first-rate university writes: "One of my colleagues is a person who formerly held the chairmanship of the department; he is now in his dotage and has not a doctor's degree. Last year he tried assiduously to get me ousted. His chief argument was that I was not a native of the State and he was; that he had devoted years of service to the State and that I was a newcomer. A teacher in this part of the country can 'get by' with the grossest inefficiency and 'backwardness' if he is a 'native' and if he keeps his political fences in good shape."[27] The result of all this is an unwholesome amount of inbreeding.

There is inbreeding of families and ideas alike. Not only residence but family is a matter of importance. South Carolinians claim to know from a man's name, even a Negro's name, what town he comes from, so static is the population. Everywhere except in the large cities the static nature of the population leads to a fixity of ideas and gives to the "best families," with their ideas that have not changed for generations, a practical dictatorship over the ideas of the community. One reason Columbia's schools are more liberal than others in South Carolina is that, besides the absence of mills, there are no "native Columbians." Columbia, being a mixture

[27] Letter to H. K. B., 1937.

of people from all parts of the state, is more cosmopolitan than other places.

Furthermore, the "one party" system of the South makes the discussion of national controversial issues futile since every one who counts will vote Democratic anyway. This increases the provincialism of the South and thereby affects teachers as well as the voting public.

Southern unawareness of most problems of the modern world prevents conflicts of ideas, which might ultimately create an atmosphere of freedom. "Problems of pacifists, radicals, etc., just do not arise," writes a teacher in one of the South's largest cities, "partly because most of the teachers share the views of the community, and have never had any training to make them think differently, partly because any teachers that did not share the social, economic, and general views of the community would hesitate to voice other views. It would at least give people like the Taxpayers League a handle against the schools generally, if not against them particularly. A few do belong to international interest groups, but these are so few and these groups are so unobtrusive that no one knows much about them."[28] "One reason the state waited so long before banning evolution," Jordan writes of Tennessee, "is that a large proportion of the inhabitants had never, until comparatively recent times, even heard of the theory. . . . I am thoroughly acquainted with the people in all sections of the state, and I am positive that not more than one-tenth of one per cent are even now any too well acquainted with the facts of organic evolution."[29] Some of the items on the author's questionnaire based on subjects of controversy in Northern cities were ideas the average Southern teacher has never heard mentioned.

"One explanation of the failure of Southern teachers to 'think' much on their backwardness and unhappiness," writes a teacher of the deep South, "is that they are so completely

[28] Letter to H. K. B., 1933.
[29] Royce Jordan, "Tennessee Goes Fundamentalist," *New Republic,* XLII (April 29, 1925), 258.

'swamped' with inescapable details of school and community affairs that little time is available for reflection. Eastern teachers cannot know the countless demands made upon their brothers in the South in the form of heavy teaching loads, sponsoring plays, banquets, and other projects, teaching Sunday School classes, raising money for school and community, engaging in 'drives' for every imaginable purpose, visiting the sick, burying the dead, and comforting the widows and orphans."[30]

Finally, the scarcity of "white collar" jobs in the South encourages resort to questionable tactics in seeking and holding teaching positions in both schools and colleges. Teaching offers one of the readiest releases from the humdrum and impecunious pursuit of farming in which many prospective teachers were brought up. In the North, boys and girls have a diversity of occupations and professions from which to choose; in the South, farming, teaching, law, and politics are the most common vocations now that preaching is out of fashion among "educated" youths. Farming is anathema to most college-trained people because of its unprofitableness and "boresomeness." Politics or the law offers greater inducements. School teaching affords a good opportunity to cultivate a community in which one may later pursue some other career or is, under the paucity of opportunities in the South, an inviting career in itself! Or at least it provides an escape from the farm into the life of a "gentleman" for farm boys who have been to college.

One thoughtful Southern teacher comments: "I believe that the unusual and relentless competition for positions is one of the most pertinent factors in the lack of freedom in teaching in Southern schools. I have often asked myself the question: Why will a college graduate go out to a rural community and teach year after year for sixty dollars a month, refrain from dancing, card playing, and other activities that he enjoys, forego

[30] Letter to H. K. B.

the saying of many things he believes, assent to many other things that he does not believe, contract to remain in the community three week-ends in the month, give high grades to nit-wittish and undeserving children of school trustees, instruct from Sabbath to Sabbath a Sunday School class forced upon him against his will in teachings utterly inharmonious with his own belief and way of living, refrain from 'dating' girls whom he likes because they do not 'rate' with the community 'fathers,' go with girls whose company he finds uninteresting because their families have influence, and submit to a hundred other infringements on his liberty? The inevitable answer is: Because he fears he will lose his position if he does not follow this unhappy course of action. The question naturally arises: Why doesn't he give up his position? The answers to this are several: First, he knows that many others can be found who would be glad to take his place; second, a position in another school would probably be no better; and, third, he would have difficulty getting other employment as remunerative as teaching that carried with it as much prestige in the eyes of his fellows. Faced with these alternatives, he shrugs his shoulders and continues to bear the yoke of bondage."[31] Ultimately he forgets that once he aspired to freedom.

7. Past and Present

Professor Knight believes that the dignity of the teacher's position has steadily increased, that he holds a much higher place in the public confidence than ever before.[32] John Dewey, too, thinks the situation has steadily improved through the past twenty-five years. He writes, "If the fight of to-day were between conservative reactionaries on one side and those of liberal faith on the other, I should be sceptical about the chances of the latter. . . . But the fight is not really at that point. It is between the reactionary and the method and spirit

[31] Letter to H. K. B.
[32] E. W. Knight, *Education in the United States*, 365–366.

of scientific method, the interest in the full play of the human mind. . . . Vested prejudices, class interests are deeply rooted, but not as deeply rooted in the nature of things as the joy of discovery and of communication."[33] That is a conclusion which must not be formed too hastily. Surely in particular matters the teacher is freer today than formerly. Teachers are rarely disciplined now for opposing human slavery. Yet it is questionable whether the teacher of 1939 is freer to criticize the capitalist system than the teacher of 1859 was to oppose slavery. In spite of New York's post-Lusk-Law change of heart, which, except for political interference and favoritism, permits more freedom than is possible in most cities, Superintendent O'Shea in January, 1934, issued a parting blast against the menace of radical teachers.[34] In 1934 a new loyalty oath for all teachers, those in private as well as those in public schools, was imposed by the Legislature[35] and is being brandished by red-baiters as a weapon against "radicals." Religious restrictions are far less general than formerly, but merely because of modern indifference to religion, not because of any greater love of freedom.

It must be remembered that restriction wears different garbs in different periods. A change of dress must not be confused with a change of heart. The principle of denial of freedom is the same whether one lives in the days of religious strife of the eighteenth century, the slavery controversy of the nineteenth, or the social and economic conflicts of the twentieth. The breakdown of authoritarianism in the past forty years has greatly increased the possibilities of freedom. But whether teachers are actually more free in matters that vitally interest the public than they have been in other days is doubtful.

[33] John Dewey, "The Liberal College and Its Enemies," *Independent*, CXII (May 24, 1924), 282.

[34] William J. O'Shea, "Radicals in the Schools," Board of Education of the City of New York, *Annual Report of the Superintendent of Schools, June 30, 1933*, 20–30; *New York Times*, Jan. 22, 1934.

[35] H. K. B., *op. cit.*, 244.

There seem to have been many more open violations of freedom in the past ten years than in all the rest of our history together. Intolerance has been as tense as in other periods. Still, on the other hand, many more teachers do hold unorthodox views today than ever before. Many of these are allowed freedom. The most encouraging symptom of the times, to those interested in freedom for teachers, is the great increase in teachers' resistance to repression. The past fifteen years have seen frequent, vigorous, and often successful protests against violations of freedom, never witnessed by any other two decades of our history.

8. Freedom in Prosperity and Depression

The last ten years of depression have nearly wrecked the schools in many parts of the country and have had serious effect upon the teacher's freedom. In matters of overcrowding, overwork for the teacher, and lack of materials, economies have put schools back where they were before the World War. Many of the improvements in educational method, gained through a long and slow process of educating the public to their need, have been destroyed at one blow. Salary scales, which in many places were at last coming to be adequate, have been slashed until thousands of teachers are reduced to poverty and financial stress that makes talk of freedom meaningless. Many of the best and most progressive modern features of school systems have been swept aside and abolished as "frills and foibles." School terms have been cut savagely. Some schools have been closed altogether. Taxpayers' leagues all over the country have attacked the schools and cut them to the bone instead of eliminating the graft, waste, and unsocial practices from which politicians and some of these wealthy and "respectable" citizens profit. So little public sense of the value of education had educators created that when depression came the schools were among the unessentials first sacrificed to economy. In one large city where an active Citizens' Committee had opposed state legislation that would have enabled the payment of teachers' back salaries, and had wanted to eliminate teachers' pensions, teacher leaders believed that every recent appointee to the board of education had been forced to promise that he would follow the dictates of the Citizens' Committtee.[36]

Behind these attacks on the schools are not only the usual greed and selfishness of business and large taxpayers but an underlying popular feeling that education is a non-essential, upon which altogether too much is being spent anyway. This is another sign of the revolt against intelligence. Economies could have been made with benefit to all concerned; but they were the economies of elimination of political corruption in the schools, and that still goes on. Chicago sat by and watched some of its teachers driven to poor relief and others, still employed, forced to the brink of starvation, all for the sake of "economy," while the spoilsmen still gorged themselves on school money, and Chicago did nothing, because in the minds of Chicagoans, in fact if not in theory, education and the integrity of the teaching profession had no really vital part in the "progress" that Chicago was celebrating on the lake front. Many another city can duplicate Chicago's story.[37]

The effect upon freedom of this starving of the schools is obvious. Teaching methods are no longer chosen because of their educational values. Teachers use whatever teaching methods they can under the depleted revenues. Furthermore, security is gone. "There has been a sense of security until

[36] A statistician who worked for the Citizens' Committee and met with it so testified to the head of the local teachers' association, who was his friend. Interview with the teachers' association head and with one of her lieutenants who has been an officer in the state Education Association and in the N. E. A.

[37] For the attacks of wealthy Atlanta real-estate owners and business men on Atlanta schools on the grounds of "economy," see Robert C. Mizell, President of the Tax Payers League of Atlanta, Georgia, *To the Teachers of the Atlanta Public Schools, Feb. 7, 1933* and *Bulletins of the Tax Payers League*. The League has attacked night schools, Negro schools, kindergartens, music, art, teachers' salaries.

alarming state legislation was passed this year," wrote a Des Moines teacher in 1933.[38] At Ann Arbor, Michigan, in 1933, a section was inserted into contracts providing that authorities were not bound by a salary clause if the money ran out.[39] Teachers have been dismissed in wholesale fashion. Contracts, tenure laws, teachers' unions are of little avail in the face of the necessity of "economy."[40] Most of these long-fought-for guarantees of security have been lost—perhaps permanently. The Tenure Committee of the National Education Association reported on July 6, 1934:

> During the past three years the seriousness of the financial problems of our public schools has tended to hide the invasion of politics into the schools of certain communities, the increase in the discharge of competent experienced teachers to make room for cheaper, unexperienced teachers, or for personal friends or relatives of board members, the elimination of important school subjects and activities, the overloading of classes, the injection of fear of unjust discharge into the consciousness of teachers. In many communities teaching morale is being destroyed; the building of a teaching profession has been halted.[41]

Married women have been dismissed from many of the school systems in which they had won places, and are being hired in almost no schools. Teacher after teacher wrote on the questionnaire, "Married women are not hired, but this is only since the depression." This means a reversion to the spoils ideal of teaching.[42] In the South, it is certain that, where economy is

[38] Letter to H. K. B., 1933.

[39] Interview in August, 1933, with Herbert S. Eiges, a Detroit teacher studying at the University of Michigan; copy of Ann Arbor teacher contract for 1933–1934.

[40] For the attitude of the courts toward dismissals for "economy," see I. Newton Edwards, "The Law Governing the Dismissal of Teachers," *Elementary School Journal*, XXXIII (January, 1933), 365.

[41] Donald DuShane, "Report of the Tenure Committee of the N. E. A.," 1934, 4.

[42] Chase G. Woodhouse, "May Married Women Teach?" *Journal of the American Association of University Women*, XXV (April, 1932), 140–141; Paul N. Garver, "Legal Status of Married Women Teachers," *School and Society*, XXXIV (Oct. 24, 1931), 572; "Married Teachers and Multiple Positions

necessary, the Negro schools suffered first and most.[43]   In Georgetown and Clarendon counties, South Carolina, for instance, Negro schools were closed entirely for a time in order that white schools might stay open.[44]

Much more devastating to freedom, however, than anything actually done to the schools has been the effect of uncertainty and fear that have seized teachers as they wait for further results of "economy." A teacher who lost his position in better days had some chance of getting another. Now being dropped means joining the unemployed. Furthermore, with all rules off and almost certain budgetary cuts ahead, teachers feel that those who do not conform, those who express their own opinions or argue with authorities, those who by word or deed win the slightest official displeasure will certainly be marked for dropping when the next "economy" comes. Insecurity and fear have cowed even courageous teachers and have gone far to destroy freedom. One New York teacher wrote in 1933, "The past three months have silenced any possibility of any kind of protest. Every one has the jitters due to Zangara's attempt on the President, the banks' closing, worry over salaries and unemployment. One knows enough to walk softly."[45] In these troubled times, moreover, public criticism of the politicians or of the bankers' and taxpayers' attacks on the schools is almost certainly fatal to teachers. Powerful teachers' unions have usually been able to fight to save the schools. They have done so in Atlanta, Chicago, and New York. In depression times, there

in the New York City Schools," *ibid.,* XXXIV (Nov. 7, 1931), 621; *ibid.,* XXXVI (Aug. 27, 1932), 276; *ibid.,* XXXVI (Oct. 1, 1932), 426–427; *ibid.,* XXXVI (Nov. 26, 1932), 697; "Reinstatement of Married School Teachers in New Jersey," *ibid.,* XXXVI (Dec. 24, 1932), 815.

[43] Interviews with J. B. Felton, superintendent of Negro Schools of South Carolina, Columbia, South Carolina, with J. C. Dixon, supervisor of Negro Schools in Georgia, at Atlanta, Georgia, and a meeting of Negro principals in Columbia, March, 1933; J. B. F. to H. K. B., July 17, 1934; J. C. D. to H. K. B., July 14, 1934.

[44] Interview with Negro principals of Columbia, South Carolina.

[45] Letters to H. K. B., 1933 and 1934.

have been vigorous attacks upon teachers' unions themselves.[46] Several teachers have pointed out that the only interest of the persons at present attacking the schools is saving themselves tax money, but that these people quickly grasp any unconventional idea of a teacher as an effective weapon in this tax campaign against the schools. They add that one reason the repression of freedom is not worse is that these men know and care too little about the schools to be aware of what is actually going on in them.

Out of the depression have also emerged two opposing tendencies that threaten freedom. Both grow out of disillusionment and despair over the inefficiencies or the inequities of present political and economic systems. Underlying both is an apparent trend toward collectivism. Many believe this, whether they like it or not, an inevitable fruit of industrialization. The one tendency is toward some form of socialized democratic state; the other, toward fascism. Both of these movements involve a greatly increased importance of the state and a minimization of the rights and the importance of the individual. Russia evidences what communism would do to freedom in teaching. Advocates of less extreme forms of socialism believe that, by placing restrictions on certain economic "liberties" of capitalist business, they would increase the freedom of the individual. American socialism has given many evidences of its devotion, at least while a minority group, to the cause of freedom for the teacher and other civil liberties. Yet there would be danger, both in the increased importance of the state and in the enthusiasm of its advocates for a new Utopia that might make it "necessary" to suppress freedom in the name of "the social good" to preserve the new social order against attack. What fascism would do to freedom of teachers and other liberties a glance at Italy or Germany reveals. Vigilante tactics in California in 1934 and the experiences of Louisiana under Huey Long suggest the form that American fascism might take.

[46] See, e.g., H. K. B., *op. cit.*, 592.

What the future holds only the future can tell. It is possible that a form of collectivist society will be evolved in America that can preserve freedom for teachers and other liberties. It is possible that the loss of civil liberty might be balanced under a collectivist society by compensating gains, but those who believe in freedom in teaching need take pause, lest they sacrifice it blindly without adequate social gain. In any case, no study of freedom in teaching can be concluded in 1939 without pointing out these tendencies, born of the depression, capable perhaps of rapid conquest of America, since current manifestations of them make it seem probable that they would destroy freedom of teaching and render impossible even the writing of this very book.

Offsetting these destructive effects of the depression, there is one factor of major importance to freedom in teaching. The depression has set thousands of people to thinking realistically about social and economic problems, who before 1929 did not know they existed. This has been true of the public. Citizens who in days of prosperity would have looked upon a teacher who pointed out evils in the social or economic system as guilty of disloyalty and would have demanded his dismissal, are themselves now demanding reforms. The depression has smashed many popular idols in the world of business. It has shown many an ordinary citizen who stood in awe of successful bankers and brokers how dishonest their pose of respectability and public spirit was. It has revealed what pitiful incompetents many of these "great figures of finance" are, when stripped of the opportunities that luck, the War, and America's vast resources and fortunate economic position in a prosperous world gave them. Furthermore, many ordinary citizens have cast aside the economic faiths and shibboleths imposed upon them through a half century by politicians and business men, who profited richly by popular acceptance of them. In short, depression and catastrophe have set thousands of Americans to thinking critically about problems that ten years ago it would have seemed heresy to American prosperity to mention. They remember now that scattered college professors sounded warnings which have proved astoundingly prophetic. In the days when Insull was Chicago's greatest citizen and was building up power and wealth by methods that helped bring on the depression and ruined thousands of people who thought him great, there was in Chicago an "impractical theorist" named Harold Ickes whose "fool ideas" were laughed at by the great and the wise and the respectable. These average citizens now remember that in those early years of prosperity this "theorist" pointed out about Samuel Insull just the things they have since learned, at the cost of ruin to themselves.

The experiences of depression have made many an American ready to listen to the ideas of theorists, reformers, and radicals, which they once would have denounced or ignored. This has had a profound effect upon freedom in the schools. One example will suffice. Harold Rugg of Teachers College, Columbia University, wrote for the schools a series of texts[47] that dealt with fundamental issues and expressed a radical point of view through the raising of countless questions and problems that once could not have been mentioned in a text. In the first volume he emphasized the scientific attitude and committed teachers and students to it. In the second he piled up illustrations of a trend away from unthinking one-man automatic control toward widespread democratic control. In the third he drove home the importance of assumed intelligence and consent in the theory of democracy and the absence of consent and intelligence in its actual functioning. In the fourth he described the trend toward socialized control. To be sure he presented his point of view through raising problems. Yet ten years earlier these books could not have been put in the schools. They would not even have been written. It is doubtful whether

---

[47] *An Introduction to American Civilization; Changing Civilizations in the Modern World; A History of American Civilization: Economic and Social; A History of American Government and Culture; An Introduction to Problems of American Culture;* and *Changing Government and Changing Cultures.*

Rugg's own publishers would have offered them to the public even as late as 1925–1926.[48] In 1935 they were widely used, in the Des Moines schools among others, and there were surprisingly few adverse reactions. They dealt with just the kind of problems people wanted treated, since the depression had aroused men to the existence of these problems.

Teachers, too, have been awakened by the depression. Alice Wood of Washington, suspended in 1919 for answering a question about Russia, believed by 1933 that "the attitude of the whole system" was "broader minded than in 1919."[49] At the meeting of the National Federation of Teachers held in June, 1933, at Milwaukee John A. Lapp pointed out that "the bankers are singularly unfitted to have a dominant voice in educational matters." "They have been tried," he said, "and found wanting." "The educational system," he continued, "has not done its job thoroughly and has failed to teach people to think or to desire to continue to learn. That is what ails most of our statesmen. They are trying to solve 1933 problems on the basis of what they learned forty or fifty years ago."[50]

In Chicago a few days later the conservative National Education Association, hitherto a great bulwark of the *status quo* and grateful friend of business in education, heard its own director of publications, Joy Elmer Morgan, declare: "For a generation, two opposing forces have been gaining headway in America. One of those forces, the ideal of democratic equality of opportunity, is best exemplified in the development of the common school. The other, the tendency toward a caste system with high concentration of wealth and control, is represented by the great financial czars, the gigantic mechanized industries and the privately owned utilities of America. . . . The selfish advantages of secrecy, inside management and mo-

48 Interview with Harold Rugg, professor of education, Teachers College, Columbia, New York, December, 1932; H. R. to H. K. B., Sept. 12, 1934.
49 Interview with Alice Wood, English teacher, Western High School, Washington, D. C., June, 1933; A. W. to H. K. B., July 28, 1934.
50 "Bankers Assailed by School Leaders," *New York Times,* June 29, 1933.

nopoly are so large that men of great ambition forget that industry should be the servant and not the master of life. It is not surprising that there should arise in America widespread propaganda to the effect that democracy is a failure. In my judgment the teaching profession should be the first to proclaim and prove the success of democracy."[51]

President Rosier of the N. E. A. threw defiance to the bankers. He told reporters: "When as a condition of making loans, the banking interests of Chicago, Boston, New York or any other community attempt to tell the educational authorities how to run the schools, they are stepping outside their sphere. The supreme issue is whether the best interests of the people of the country are to be curtailed to satisfy the desires of special economic groups or whether liberal and progressive influences shall dominate. Already in the Morgan and other investigations it has been shown that the social vision of the dominant group is limited. Bankers who were yesterday regarded as the lords of creation are on the defensive today."[52]

In Cleveland on February 26, 1934, Superintendent Campbell of New York told the National Education Association convention: "The gods of business and finance had a queer code of ethics and very little knowledge of economic laws or social problems. . . . Yet most of . . . [these business men] were the products of our system of education. This was our failure. If any one thing is clear it is that education has a more important part to play in the realizing of the new social order than has the government itself."[53]

The United States Office of Education has been another former center of reaction in social and economic ideas in education. Yet the N. E. A. heard F. J. Kelly from that Office tell them in 1933: "In a democracy education holds the key to social advance. State, county and city departments of education should encourage and ultimately require teachers now in

51 "Teachers Attack Banker Dictation," *New York Times*, July 1, 1933.
52 *Loc. cit.*   53 *New York Times*, Feb. 27, 1934.

service to manifest a broad understanding of social and economic issues."[54]

Charles H. Judd, dean of the School of Education of the University of Chicago, urged teachers not to be silent "while crude spoilsmen shut the schools," but to urge President Roosevelt "to do for American youth what he has done for American finance and American industry." "Let us appeal to him," Judd pleaded, "to provide for the creation and execution of plans which shall arouse adequate preparation . . . for life in a new era, so that the future shall not see a repetition of the mismanagement which has depressed a half-educated nation. . . . I advocate that the schools begin . . . to prepare lessons on taxation and present these in vigorous form to citizens of the next generation. I am in favor of such a reconstruction of the curriculum, worked out coöperatively by educators, that the American people will be compelled to talk at the dinner table with their children about taxes and legislators and tax reduction associations." He denounced bankers whose "definition of thrift is to save money and put it in banks." "The lawyers," he averred, "who are now getting themselves elected or appointed to school boards to enforce drastic retrenchments demanded by their clients, the business leaders, have for years carried on a campaign to compel the schools to teach the law of the land in classes separate from those in civics and history."[55] Superintendent Givens of Oakland, California, secretary of the conservative N. E. A., charged in 1933 that teachers are "criticized, brow-beaten, sued, and vilified," if they turn to politics. "Is there any reason," he asked, "why one million of our best educated people should be barred from real citizenship? With the American public school as a coördinating agency for all right-thinking groups, graft and corruption could be dethroned in business and politics."[56]

At the annual banquet of the Department of Classroom Teachers on July 6, 1933, the songs were parodies about lack

[54] *Ibid.*, July 1, 1933.   [55] *Ibid.*, July 5, 1933.   [56] *Loc. cit.*

of freedom.[57] A newly appointed classroom teachers' Committee on Academic Freedom with Karl W. Guenther as chairman made a preliminary report in 1933 and a fuller one in 1934 adopted by the Department. In 1934 the Department demanded and the N. E. A. actually voted $10,000 for the work of the Tenure Committee. The Classroom Teachers passed a resolution calling for teacher leadership in solving social and economic problems. Not only the Classroom Teachers but even the conservative N. E. A. itself passed vigorous resolutions demanding academic freedom for teachers.[58] "Never in the history of the summer session," Clyde Miller of Teachers College, Columbia, declared in 1933, "has there been such a response to the discussion of governmental, economic and social questions. By the hundreds, and with all the ardor of a football crowd, teachers are packing informal meetings on such themes. Last week at a discussion of the relation of 'progressive' education to our economic order they gathered in such numbers that the meeting overflowed the Horace Mann School auditorium and had to be transferred to the university gymnasium, where hundreds still were obliged to stand against the walls."[59] In August, 1933, both the Teachers Union and the conservative *New York Times* were urging an N. R. A. code for teachers. The Union demands included minimum salary scales, guarantees of secure tenure even in rural regions, and the right of teachers to participate in social and political movements and to organize into labor unions.[60]

There is no doubt that the teachers of the country are aroused to social and economic questions as they never have

[57] Banquet program entitled *A Century of Progress in Teacher Training,* Chicago, Illinois, July 6, 1933.

[58] Mimeographed and printed copies of the reports and resolutions; interview with Karl W. Guenther, August, 1933; K. W. Guenther to H. K. B., Aug. 31, 1933; personal attendance at the N. E. A. meeting in 1934.

[59] *New York Times,* July 30, 1933.

[60] *Ibid.,* Aug. 19 and 23, 1933.

been before. It is dangerous, however, to attach too much significance to this awakening. For example, the author interviewed one teacher reputed in her city to be a fearless "radical." A decade ago she got into trouble for venturing impartial discussion of a radical point of view that she did not share. In 1933 she told the author that she would not take nearly so conservative a stand now as she did then. Other teachers would not either. Yet she felt their more radical views now would not cause so much trouble as the more conservative ones did then. When, however, the author wrote to ask this teacher's permission to use her as authority for a description of this newer freedom she now feels, she replied that he must not use her name because her statement "might easily be misunderstood and lead to trouble." "You will think me pusillanimous. . . . I *am* pusillanimous, I admit. I'll play safe. I have to hold my job." Here is how free one "fearless" teacher is under the new freedom engendered by the depression. Nevertheless, in spite of the repressions of freedom created by the depression and the present fear and insecurity of teachers, this arousing of teachers and public alike to interest in vital problems of this industrial era may in the end be one of the great effects of the depression. For the moment the most repressive forces are great enough to counterbalance this awakened social conscience, but for the future the arousal of teachers to thought and questioning may have great results. Or will it disappear with renewed prosperity?

Many thoughtful people believe that democracy can be preserved only if the schools succeed in developing independent thinking in future citizens so that democracy may function intelligently. Only schools where teachers and pupils are alike free can develop this kind of citizen. If these hypotheses are sound, then much depends upon the outcome of this struggle between intensified repressive forces, on the one hand, and, on the other, a teaching profession newly aroused to independence of thought, a social conscience, and a professional attitude toward its function in society. Indeed, upon the outcome of this struggle may depend not only the preservation of American liberties but the very survival of democracy itself.

APPENDIX

A questionnaire presents serious problems. The author began with an intense dislike of all questionnaires and a distrust of the results of most of them. In the end he was forced to resort to one to obtain information otherwise unobtainable. His experience with his own questionnaire has left the author with an intensified dislike of questionnaires and an increased distrust of the "scientific" nature of any findings derived from them. Yet his own questionnaire gave him a picture that was invaluable. Besides, it would have been worth distributing had it contributed no more than the collection of specific instances of violations of freedom, individual experiences, and personal comments that teachers volunteered as supplements to their formal answers to the questionnaire.

The questionnaire was not constructed until the author had been at work on his subject for a year. Then the questions were framed not out of theory or abstractions but from the experiences of teachers whom the author had encountered in that year of study. It seemed important to have the questionnaire brief, but other considerations overpowered the author's desire for brevity. The subject of freedom and the information the author wished to acquire involved not specific, easily ascertainable facts but states of mind of teachers. This introduced a large element of individual judgment and interpretation that would have invalidated the results had the author been seeking "scientific" facts. Fortunately, it was a teacher's belief about situations that was important and not the actual fact of those situations. The author wished to know what teachers felt they dared do, say, and believe and not what it was actually safe to do, say, and believe. The fact that a teacher would not have been disciplined for teaching evolution was not so important as the fact that he refrained from teaching it because he believed, even if mistakenly, that he would have been disciplined if he had taught it. The fact that a woman teacher might have smoked without being dismissed was not so important to a comprehension of her state of freedom as the fact that she never did smoke because she thought, even if erroneously, that she would have been disciplined if she had smoked. After all, a teacher's freedom is measured by actions determined by his notion of what the facts are. Actual facts concerning what he might do, but does not, are unimportant in determining his freedom if they are contrary to what he believes them to be when he decides upon his actions. Many a teacher found it impossible to answer some questions with assurance because the problems involved in the question had never arisen in that community. The guess of a teacher who knew the community as to what would happen if and when the question did arise gave a good picture of the general atmosphere of freedom or lack of it in that community. It is, furthermore, upon his own guess that the teacher will act or refrain from acting when the question does some day arise. The results of the questionnaire were significant and valuable, then, so long as it was clearly understood by teachers and questioner alike that the answers were beliefs of teachers about situations and not "scientific" analysis of situations themselves.

It was highly important to eliminate as nearly as possible variations in interpretations of the questions. This made it imperative to ask not a few general questions about abstract concepts in the field of economic problems, social questions, issues of war and peace, and the like, but many questions of a concrete and detailed sort that would reduce variation of understanding to a minimum. Therefore, instead of asking if a teacher was free in her teaching of social questions, the author asked a series of questions as to whether the teacher was free to express this, that, or the other specific point of view on a specific issue. Similarly, the freedom to discuss political questions would have meant little; freedom to oppose payment of the soldiers' bonus is clear. Freedom to discuss economic questions would have been so variously understood that the answers would have evidenced nothing but the stupidity of asking the question; payment or cancellation of the war debts, a capital levy, and criticism of the practices of local coal operators are real problems in the lives of many teachers. "Are you free in your personal conduct?" again would not have been worth the asking. Teachers cannot misunderstand "smoking if a woman" or joining a teachers' union affiliated with labor. The author therefore transmuted his several general questions, which could have composed a delightfully brief but useless questionnaire, into many specific questions. In the questionnaire he mixed up the various groups so that the answer to one question on war and peace, for instance, would not be influenced by the answer just given to another in that group. In tabulating the results of the questionnaire these scattered questions were, of course, reassembled under the general heads of social, economic, political, and other problems to present their composite picture of the freedom that exists on those subjects.

Since this type of questionnaire was long and complicated to answer, it required careful distribution. It would have been useless to send it in great quantities to lists of teachers, principals, superintendents, haphazardly gathered together. It required careful answering. Filling it out took time and a certain degree of intelligence. It required interest in the problem of freedom or else friendship for the author. Furthermore, honest answering of the questionnaire required both confidence in the author and anonymity of the questionnaire. Hence, the method of distributing was important. If the questionnaire was worth sending out at all, it was worth the time, trouble, and expense necessary to put it into the hands of people who would answer it, would give it careful consideration, and would use intelligence in filling it out.

The author distributed it through several channels. Some of the questionnaires were sent to interested people like District Superintendent Tildsley of New York City, Superintendent Studebaker of Des Moines, or Professor Counts of Teachers College, Columbia University, to distribute. Professor Counts gave them out with full instructions to teachers in his classes whom he knew to be interested. Superintendent Studebaker sent them with a wisely composed letter to various principals with instructions to distribute them, with a further letter of instructions, to teachers selected for their interest in the subject and their variety of social, economic, and political points of view. Superintendent Tildsley, who was in charge of teaching in the New York City high schools, sent them to teachers whom he personally chose for their variety of outlook. A second method of distribution was through personal letters to a list of teachers supplied by educators like Clyde Miller of Teachers College or President Sills of Bowdoin College, who were willing to have their names used to vouch for the author and to urge coöperation of the teacher or superintendent. A third means of distribution was through teachers who attended meetings at which the author spoke and who there expressed interest in filling out the questionnaire. Finally, questionnaires were sent with a personal letter to every student now teaching who was in attendance at Grinnell or Bowdoin College while the author taught there.

Even with this care in distribution a large number of teachers did not respond. Inertia prevented some. Overwork and pressure of duties deterred others. Some fully intended to do so but kept putting it off. Others were appalled at the size of the task. Still others, and these a large number, protested that most of the subjects included in the questionnaire were so completely foreign to the subject taught or the small community where the teacher lived that they were outside the teacher's experience and meant nothing to him. This was the reply of many rural teachers all over the country, many Southern teachers even in larger places, and a whole class of teaching sisters to whom Father George Johnson at Catholic University gave the questionnaire. The questionnaire had to be composed to fit the large urban centers where social and economic conflicts arise and affect the schools. Adapting it to these communities made much of it entirely irrelevant to smaller places.

Furthermore, many teachers lacked the training, the intelligence, or the knowledge of social, economic, or political problems in the world about them necessary to understand the subject matter of the questions. One of the most appalling revelations of the questionnaire was the meagerness of reading of teachers and the ignorance of teachers concerning the world in which they live. The result of all this was that relatively few replies came from teachers in backward communities where there would be no freedom at all if controversial questions ever arose. The questionnaires were returned largely by teachers who have enough freedom that controversial questions really are issues but who, being somewhat free, want to attain greater freedom from restrictions they still feel. The questionnaires therefore indicated a much greater degree of freedom than is true of the country as a whole, because the teachers who answered them were these teachers from communities free enough for freedom to be an issue. A questionnaire of this sort will not reach the great masses of teachers in environments where controversial issues are completely suppressed or where the teachers and communities alike are so conventional-minded or so uninformed that they are unaware of controversial issues. It must be borne in mind that the worst restrictions on freedom are subjective or arise out of the teacher's own inadequacies. The author discovered in interviewing teachers that often a teacher's reply that he is free merely means that he has no desire to express unorthodox opinions and consequently is unaware that he would not be free to do so if he did so wish. Interviews with teachers indicated, too, that the reply that a teacher was free often indicated that he merely lacked a social philosophy or had done so little thinking that he had not realized how lacking in freedom he was. All of this means that the answers to the questionnaire paint a picture of much greater freedom than in reality exists.

The answers to the questions were carefully classified under general headings and compiled. Under each heading the answers were separated into public and private school categories and the private schools again into secular and religious institutions. Then within these general divisions the answers were further grouped by geographic regions. In the South and Border States, Negroes and whites were kept separate. The country was divided into: (1) Northern Atlantic states, including New England, New York, Pennsylvania, and New Jersey; (2) Border Southern states including Delaware, Maryland, West Virginia, Kentucky, Missouri, and Oklahoma; (3) Southern states including Virginia, North Carolina, South Carolina, Georgia, Florida, Alabama, Mississippi, Tennessee, Louisiana, Arkansas, and Texas; (4) Middle Western states including Ohio, Indiana, Illinois, Michigan, Wisconsin, Iowa, Minnesota, Kansas, Nebraska, South Dakota, and North Dakota; (5) Mountain states including Montana, Idaho, Wyoming, Colorado, Utah, Nevada, New Mexico, and Arizona; and (6) Pacific states including Washington, Oregon, and California. Under each heading and in each sectional group the answers were divided into subgroups based on the size of the community in which teachers taught. Rather arbitrarily the following groupings were chosen: (1) great cities with populations of over 1,000,000; (2) suburbs of great cities; (3) large cities with populations of 100,000 to 1,000,000; (4) cities of 25,000 to 100,000; (5) towns of 2500 to 25,000; and (6) rural communities with less than 2500 people. The final figures were computed so that they could be used to compare public and private schools, Negro and white schools, schools in the various sections of the country, and schools in communities of various sizes.

In using the figures, the author relied on the questionnaire only for general comparisons and conclusions. To say that a certain exact percentage of teachers is free would be preposterous. None the less, used carefully with awareness of its limitations and necessarily "unscientific" quality, the questionnaire did give valuable pictures of general situations. It gave useful comparisons of one region with another, of communities of one size with those of another, and of one type of school with another. It also indicated which subjects were more restricted than others and which pressures teachers felt more than others. Beyond generalizations of this sort the author has not attempted to use the findings of the questionnaire. The general picture was most illuminating.

Accompanying the questionnaires there came to the author a wealth of specific cases involving freedom and invaluable comments of teachers on the problem. These were sent in response to the author's request on the questionnaire for this type of supplementary material if the teacher saw fit to volunteer it.

The answers to this questionnaire are sought for use in a final chapter of *A History of Freedom in Teaching* preparation for the Commission on Social Studies in the Schools. The identity of the teacher or school system not sought and, if accidentally revealed, would be held in *strict confidence*. All of these questions will not fall within the personal experience of any given teacher or superintendent. Each person who answers the question-aire is earnestly besought, however, to answer them *all* on the basis (where they are not within one's personal experience) of what he believes would be the practice of his school or school system, if the issue did arise. Please mail the answers to Howard K. Beale, Study Room 52, Library of Congress, Washington, D. C.*

. General Information:

1. Title or rank of person filling out questionnaire _____

2. Kind of institution _____ 3. If a teacher, grade _____

4. If a teacher, subjects taught _____

5. If a superintendent, major subjects of study while in training _____

_____

6. Years of experience, as teacher _____ as superintendent _____

7. Salary _____ 8. Sex _____ 9. Age _____ 10. Race _____

11. Types of institution where training was received and number of years in each _____

_____

12. Degrees held _____ 13. Party affiliation _____

14. Religious affiliation _____ 15. Organizations

belonged to (e. g., College fraternity, American Federation of Teachers, Masons, Elks, D.A.R., Rotary,

League of Nations Association, etc.) _____

_____

16. State _____ 17. Approximate size of city or village _____

18. Leading business interests of community (e. g. cotton growing, shoe manufacturing, coal mining, etc.)

_____

Tenure:

Does a teacher have:	Yes	No
1. Permanent tenure after a probationary period	☐	☐
2. No protection save yearly contract	☐	☐
3. No protection at all against arbitrary dismissal	☐	☐
4. Guarantee of a hearing before dismissal	☐	☐
5. Appeal to courts if dismissed	☐	☐
6. Other comments on tenure		

It is assumed that any of the attitudes included in this questionnaire would have to be expressed in terms appro-priate to the school grade involved. The author submits, however, that future attitudes of children toward most of these subjects are formed before they are mature enough to *understand* the subject, and are influenced by attitudes of teachers of subjects as innocuous as Reading or Geography.

III. Ideas:

In *each* of the 5 columns place:
(1) A check for "Yes" or "No" on the basis of the practice of your school or school system, *and*
(2) "X" (check) where you agree with and "O" (zero) where you disagree with this practice

A teacher may:

	believe in if he does not say so publicly			discuss impartially in class if he expresses no opinion			express favorable views on in class if he does not attempt to convert students			propagandize for in class			advocate outside of class		
	Yes	No	Agree or Disagree	Yes	No	Agree or Disagree	Yes	No	Agree or Disagree	Yes	No	Agree or Disagree	Yes	No	Agree or Disagree
1. American adherence to the League of Nations															
2. Socialism															
3. High income taxes															
4. The theory of evolution															
5. Censure of the Supreme Court for its refusal to admit pacifists to citizenship															
6. Repeal of the Eighteenth Amendment															
7. A big navy															
8. Political equality for negroes															
9. Communism															
10. Opposition to the placement of an embargo on the shipment of arms to a warring nation															
11. Censure of labor union leaders															
12. Defense of Germany's position in the World War															
13. A capital levy															
14. The doctrine that in America "equality of opportunity" insures the success of the most capable															
15. Censure of the activities of the D.A.R. or American Legion or Confederate Veterans															
16. Birth control															
17. Mr. Hoover's proposal of 33-1/3% all-around reduction of armaments															
18. Recognition of Russia															
19. Government ownership of utilities															
20. Social equality for negroes															
21. Censure of President Hoover for using the Army to drive the bonus men out of Washington															
22. Fundamentalist interpretation of the Bible															
23. Censure of the secession leaders of the South															
24. Objection to military training in schools															

	believe in if he does not say so publicly			discuss impartially in class if he expresses no opinion			express favorable views on in class if he does not attempt to convert students			propagandize for in class			advocate outside of class		
	Yes	No	Agree or Disagree	Yes	No	Agree or Disagree	Yes	No	Agree or Disagree	Yes	No	Agree or Disagree	Yes	No	Agree or Disagree
26. Necessity for revolution by force to bring justice															
27. Denunciation of the "profit system"															
28. Non-existence of God															
29. Defense of our interventions in Cuba, Haiti, Nicaragua, as altruistic and unselfish															
30. Rigid enforcement of the Eighteenth Amendment															
31. Denunciation of local officials for corruption															
32. Advocacy of military training in schools															
33. Denunciation of local courts for unjust decisions															
34. Censure of Northern rule of South after Civil War															
35. Companionate marriage															
36. Censure of radicals as unpatriotic or dangerous															
37. Curtailment of the power of the Supreme Court to declare laws unconstitutional															
38. Objection to putting the "homeless boys" into military camps															
39. Praise of "conscientious objectors" to World War															
40. Censure of the President of the United States															
41. The doctrine that our entry into the World War was a mistake															
42. Confiscatory inheritance taxes															
43. American adherence to the World Court															
44. Denunciation of state officials for corruption															
45. The charge that our courts are corrupted by big business															
46. Opposition to reduction of the Veterans' Bureau appropriation															
47. Censure of the activities of advocates of abolition of slavery in antebellum days															
48. Censure of pacifists as unpatriotic or dangerous															
49. Low tariffs for revenue only															
50. Censure of the Federal Government or local police for preventing Communist hunger marchers from parading															
51. Abandonment of the "Monroe Doctrine"															
52. Censure of the practices of local business men such as coal operators, utility owners, merchants, lawyers, factory owners, as unjust															

A teacher may: (Continued)

Column headings:
- believe in if he does not say so publicly — Yes / No / Agree or Disagree
- discuss impartially in class if he expresses no opinion — Yes / No / Agree or Disagree
- express favorable views on in class if he does not attempt to convert students — Yes / No / Agree or Disagree
- propagandize for in class — Yes / No / Agree or Disagree
- advocate outside of class — Yes / No / Agree or Disagree

53. Censure of Southern "failure to accept the results" of the Civil War
54. Opposition to the breaking up of a meeting of "Reds" by local police
55. The doctrine that it is dangerous to elect Catholics to office
56. Praise of the D.A.R. or American Legion anti-Radical activities
57. Defense of Britain's position in the American Revolution
58. Modernist interpretation of the Bible
59. Teacher membership in labor unions
60. Necessity of peaceful reform of capitalist system
61. Swearing never to bear arms
62. The doctrine that the United States committed a wrong against Mexico in the Mexican War
63. Total disarmament
64. The doctrine that labor is pitifully underpaid
65. Deflation of heroes of American history based on modern research
66. Refusal to take a pledge of loyalty or an oath of allegiance
67. Payment of the soldiers' bonus
68. Denunciation of our intervention in the Caribbean as imperialistic
69. The doctrine that one must hope the United States will be right, but support it whether right or wrong
70. Necessity of maintaining American institutions just as they are for sake of happiness and liberty
71. Opposition to the "Buy American" movement
72. Denunciation of the Ku Klux Klan
73. A constitutional amendment to deprive the Senate of its veto power over treaties
74. Denunciation of the doctrine of keeping out of European entanglements

IV. Race, Creed, Origin, Sex, Party:

Which of the following would in your school or school system be disqualified or seriously handicapped: (Please check each one "Yes" or "No")

	in getting a position Yes	No	in keeping this position after the fact becomes known (where no previous misrepresentation is involved) Yes	No
1. Jews	☐	☐	☐	☐
2. Negroes in white schools	☐	☐	☐	☐
3. Unnaturalized foreigners	☐	☐	☐	☐
4. Persons with foreign names	☐	☐		
5. Naturalized citizens	☐	☐	☐	☐
6. Residents of other towns	☐	☐	☐	☐
7. Residents of other states	☐	☐	☐	☐
8. Northerners	☐	☐	☐	☐
9. Southerners	☐	☐	☐	☐
10. Easterners	☐	☐	☐	☐
11. Westerners	☐	☐	☐	☐
12. Men	☐	☐		
13. Women	☐	☐		
14. Divorced persons	☐	☐	☐	☐
15. Feminists	☐	☐	☐	☐
16. Married women	☐	☐	☐	☐
17. Democrats	☐	☐	☐	☐
18. Republicans	☐	☐	☐	☐
19. Socialists	☐	☐	☐	☐
20. Communists	☐	☐	☐	☐
21. Anarchists	☐	☐	☐	☐
22. Pacifists	☐	☐	☐	☐
23. Military men	☐	☐	☐	☐
24. Conscientious objectors to war	☐	☐	☐	☐
25. Fundamentalists	☐	☐	☐	☐
26. Religious liberals	☐	☐	☐	☐
27. Unitarians	☐	☐	☐	☐
28. Agnostics	☐	☐	☐	☐
29. Atheists	☐	☐	☐	☐
30. Catholics	☐	☐	☐	☐
31. Protestants	☐	☐	☐	☐
32. Mormons	☐	☐	☐	☐
33. Gentiles (non-Mormon or non-Jew)	☐	☐	☐	☐

V. Personal Conduct:

Can a teacher in your school or school system be known to do the following and hold his position (check either "yes" or "no"):

	Yes	No
1. Attend the theater	☐	☐
2. Smoke in school if a man	☐	☐
3. Smoke in school if a woman	☐	☐
4. Smoke away from school if a man	☐	☐
5. Smoke away from school if a woman	☐	☐
6. Drink in school if a man	☐	☐
7. Drink in school if a woman	☐	☐
8. Drink away from school if a man	☐	☐
9. Drink away from school if a woman	☐	☐
10. Dance	☐	☐
11. Swear	☐	☐
12. Play cards	☐	☐
13. Gamble	☐	☐
14. Commit fornication or adultery	☐	☐
15. Practice homosexuality away from school	☐	☐
16. Become the subject of unproved charges of immorality	☐	☐
17. Visit speakeasies	☐	☐

	Yes	No
18. Decline to participate in the social activities of the community	☐	☐
19. Mix socially with negroes	☐	☐
20. Picket in a local strike	☐	☐
21. Join a labor union	☐	☐
22. Join the Ku Klux Klan	☐	☐
23. Wear a religious garb	☐	☐
24. Run for office	☐	☐
25. Campaign for a political party	☐	☐
26. Bring unfavorable publicity to the school	☐	☐
27. Exhibit "lack of judgment"	☐	☐
28. Make himself unpopular though a good teacher	☐	☐
29. Bring in pacifists or radicals to talk to students	☐	☐
30. Bring in military men or members of D.A.R. or American Legion to talk to students	☐	☐

VI. Criticism of Local School or Community:

Is the teacher free openly to criticize (Please check "Yes" or "No"):

	Yes	No
1. School board policies	☐	☐
2. The school superintendent	☐	☐
3. Required teaching methods	☐	☐
4. The principal	☐	☐
5. The business practices of a benefactor of the school	☐	☐
6. Textbooks used	☐	☐
7. The business practices of a school trustee or board member	☐	☐
8. Teaching of "evils of alcohol" and advocacy of "temperance"	☐	☐
9. "Patriotic exercises," flag salutes, etc., as chauvinistic	☐	☐
10. Good-will days, world peace days, etc., as undermining "patriotism"	☐	☐
11. Local social leaders and their activities	☐	☐
12. Local ministers or churches as breeders of radicalism	☐	☐
13. Local ministers or churches for their failure to attack social or economic abuses	☐	☐
14. The doctrines and practices of the local D.A.R. or American Legion	☐	☐

VII. Source of Pressure:

In the first column, check *each* of the following groups that puts upon teachers direct or indirect pressure which hampers their freedom of conduct or expression. In the second column, number those you check, so far as you can, in the order in which you rate the power of the pressure each exerts, marking the most powerful pressure no. 1, etc.

1. Other teachers	☐	☐
2. Students	☐	☐
3. The principal	☐	☐
4. The superintendent	☐	☐
5. School board members or trustees	☐	☐
6. Parents	☐	☐
7. Public opinion of the community	☐	☐
8. Business men	☐	☐
9. Benefactors of the school	☐	☐
10. The American Legion	☐	☐
11. Peace organizations	☐	☐
12. The Ku Klux Klan	☐	☐
13. The D.A.R.	☐	☐
14. Other "Patriotic" organizations	☐	☐
15. The Bar Association	☐	☐
16. The Chamber of Commerce	☐	☐
17. Politicians	☐	☐
18. Religious groups	☐	☐
19. Other sources (Specify)	☐	☐

VIII. Reasons for Avoiding Controversial Subjects:

(A) If teachers refrain (in class or out) from discussion of controversial subjects is it because of (check in the first column as many as apply):

1. Fear of dismissal _____ ☐ ☐
2. Fear of other discipline _____ ☐ ☐
3. Fear of disfavor that will prevent promotions_____ ☐ ☐
4. Fear of refusal of a good recommendation when applying for a new position _____ ☐ ☐
5. Fear of public opinion _____ ☐ ☐
6. Feeling of futility of not conforming _____ ☐ ☐
7. Belief that teacher should avoid controversial subjects _____ ☐ ☐
8. Lack of interest in controversial subjects _____ ☐ ☐
9. Agreement with the community view on controversial subjects _____ ☐ ☐
10. Other reasons (State them) _____ ☐ ☐

(B) In the second column above, number, as far as you can, those you have checked in order of their importance:

(C) Would you like to see freer expression of views on controversial subjects, if the community attitude would permit it? _____

(D) Have adult forums on controversial subjects been held in your community? _____
If so, what has been their effect upon the amount of freedom the teacher can be allowed in these matters?
_____

Were these forums sponsored by the school?_____If not, who
did sponsor them? _____

IX. School Rules:

If your school or school system has ever drawn up rules or a statement of policy concerning a teacher's conduct or his freedom in expressing views on controversial subjects, please send them in as they will be very helpful.

X. Specific Cases:

Please give on a separate sheet, *details* of any cases within your knowledge where a teacher has been dismissed or disciplined, and any cases where a teacher has been sustained under pressure. Give facts concerning charges, dates, names of parties, real causes of difficulty, sources of complaint, and factors that led to dismissal or retention. If you are willing to be quoted on these cases (this will make them historically much more valuable) or to permit the author to correspond with you further about them, please give your name and address with the cases and send them in separate from the questionnaire. If you wish to sign your name to these specific cases but do not wish to have it divulged in connection with them, it will be held as confidential. If you prefer, just send these particular facts with the questionnaire without your name.

N.B. Qualifications or amplifications of "yes" and "no" answers or further comment on any of the questions is invited.

BIBLIOGRAPHY

Material on freedom in teaching, particularly that dealing with its history, is buried away in small items in works on many subjects. No effort will be made to list the great mass of material which it was necessary to use in order to find here or there a detail upon freedom.

THE QUESTIONNAIRE[1]

On the present period, the author's questionnaire yielded valuable information both in direct answers to it and in comments sent in with it.

INTERVIEWS

Much of the best material came from interviews with individual superintendents, principals, classroom teachers, and others actually in touch with the problems of the book. Many of these people—especially the teachers—have asked not to have their names mentioned. In order not to cause trouble inadvertently for any of these teachers whose confidence and helpfulness have made this work possible, the author will list none of them. A list follows of those not actually teaching in the schools who supplied valuable material and points of view in interviews with the author: Will Alexander, then director of the Interracial Commission, Atlanta, Georgia; Brent D. Allinson, formerly director of the Social Studies in the public schools, Cleveland, Ohio; Clarence A. Bacote, assistant professor of American history, Atlanta University; William C. Bagley, professor of education, Teachers College, Columbia University; Roger Baldwin, secretary of the American Civil Liberties Union, New York City; Frank W. Ballou, superintendent of schools, Washington, D. C.; Alice Barrows, U. S. Office of Education, Department of the Interior, Washington, D. C.; Charles A. Beard, historian and textbook writer; Anna E. Boardman, formerly principal of a private school at Lakewood, New Jersey, and before that a teacher at the Bennett School at Millbrook; Ivan Booker, assistant director of Research, National Education Association, Washington, D. C.; Selma Borchardt, legislative secretary of the American Federation of Teachers, Washington, D. C.; Aaron J. Brum-

---

[1] See *supra,* Appendix.

baugh, professor of education, School of Education, University of Chicago; Sallie Caldwell, Bureau of Educational Service, Teachers College, Columbia University, formerly principal of an elementary school and supervisor in Alabama schools; J. McKeen Cattell, editor of *School and Society,* New York City; Oscar L. Chapman, assistant secretary of the Interior, Washington, D. C.; Mrs. A. R. Childs, principal of the Logan Elementary School, Columbia, South Carolina; Walter R. Chivers, professor of sociology at Morehouse College, Atlanta, Georgia, formerly in the Birmingham schools; M. E. Coleman, supervisor of attendance, Board of Education, Atlanta, Georgia; Flora Cooke, principal of the Francis Parker School, Chicago, Illinois; George S. Counts, professor at Teachers College, Columbia University; E. R. Crow, principal of the Columbia High School, Columbia, South Carolina; Myrtle Hooper Dahl, president of the National Education Association Department of Classroom Teachers, Minneapolis, Minnesota; J. C. Dixon, state supervisor of Negro Education, State Department of Education, Atlanta, Georgia; Barbara Donner, professor of history, Oshkosh State Teachers College, Oshkosh, Wisconsin; W. E. Burghardt Du Bois, editor of the *Crisis,* New York City, formerly (1896–1910) professor of economics at Atlanta University; Donald DuShane, superintendent of schools, Columbus, Indiana, and chairman of the Tenure Committee of the N. E. A.; Marie Duggan, assistant director of the Bureau of Educational Service, Teachers College, Columbia University; Harold Easterby, professor of history at the College of Charleston; I. Newton Edwards, professor of the history of education, School of Education, University of Chicago; Robert B. Eleazer, director of Educational Work, Interracial Commission, Atlanta, Georgia; Charles Ellwood, professor of sociology, Duke University; Mercer Evans, then professor of economics, Emory University, and Mrs. Evans, formerly a teacher in the Atlanta schools; Edward S. Evenden, professor of education, Teachers College, Columbia University; Elizabeth L. Fackt, assistant director of the Foundation for the Advancement of the Social Sciences at the University of Denver; William L. Felter, former principal of the Girls' High School, Brooklyn, New York; J. B. Felton, state supervisor of Negro Education, State Department of Education, Columbia, South Carolina; G. H. Ferguson, assistant director of the Division of Negro Education, State Department of Public Instruction, Raleigh, North Carolina; A. Cline Flora, superintendent of schools, Columbia, South Carolina; H. S. Floyd, superintendent of schools, Struthers, Ohio; Ben W. Frazier, assistant in the Publications Division, Office of Education, Department of the Interior, Washington, D. C.; William C. French, professor of education, George Washington University, formerly assistant superintendent of schools at Tulsa, Oklahoma; Harry O. Gillet, principal of the University of Chicago Elementary School, Chicago, Illinois; George D. Grice, principal of an elementary school, Charleston, South Carolina; Karl W. Guenther, chairman of the Committee on Academic Freedom of the Classroom Teachers' Department of the N. E. A., formerly on the faculty of the Michigan State Normal College, Ypsilanti, Michigan; Florence Hale, former president of the N. E. A. and head of N. E. A. radio broadcasting; Margaret Haley, head of the Chicago Teachers' Federation, Chicago, Illinois; Miss M. S. Hanckel, supervisor of schools, Charleston, South Carolina; Frances E. Harden, former leader in the Chicago Teachers' Federation and in the Classroom Teachers' Department of the N. E. A.; Heber R. Harper, professor of International Relations at Teachers College, Columbia University, formerly chancellor of the University of Denver; Kemper Harreld, professor of music at Spelman and Morehouse colleges, Atlanta, Georgia; Mrs. Claudia White Harreld, member of the Interracial Committee, Atlanta, Georgia; Abram Harris, professor of economics, Howard University; Carlton J. H. Hayes, professor of history, Columbia University, and textbook writer; Mrs. W. S. Hefferan, member of the Board of Education, Chicago, Illinois; Nelson B. Henry, associate professor of education, School of Education, University of Chicago, and financial expert for the Chicago Board of Education; Lillian Herstein, teacher in the Crane Junior College (later closed by economy), Chicago, Illinois; Howard C. Hill, textbook author and head of the Social Science Department, University High School, Chicago, Illinois; Dwight O. W. Holmes, dean of the School of Education, Howard University; John Hope, president of Atlanta University; Virginia Hoge, seminar student of Professor Harold Easterby, College of Charleston; H. Reid Hunter, assistant superintendent of schools, Atlanta, Georgia; Walter C. Jackson, dean of the school of Public Administration, University of North Carolina; C. A. Johnson, supervisor of Negro Schools, Columbia, South Carolina; Father George Johnson, Educational Division of the National Catholic Welfare Conference, Washington, D. C., and professor of education, Catholic University of America; William H. Kilpatrick, professor of educational philosophy, Teachers College, Columbia University; W. G. Kimmel, secretary of the Commission on Social Studies in the Schools, and managing editor of the *Social Studies,* New York

City; Arnold K. King, professor of education, University of North Carolina; Edgar W. Knight, professor of education, University of North Carolina; Leonard V. Koos, director of the National Survey of Public Education, and professor of education, University of Chicago; Abraham Lefkowitz, then vice-president of the American Federation of Teachers, New York City; Henry R. Linville, then president of the American Federation of Teachers, New York City; Rayford W. Logan, *Journal of Negro History,* Washington, D. C.; Allie B. Mann, head of the Teachers' Union, Atlanta, Georgia; T. D. Martin, chairman of the Membership Committee of the N. E. A., Washington, D. C.; H. H. McCarley, county superintendent of schools, Charleston County, South Carolina; Mrs. C. P. McGowan, member of the Interracial Committee, Charleston, South Carolina; Jean Mackay, president of the Classroom Teachers Association of Highland Park, Michigan, and president of the Southeastern Michigan Associated Teachers Clubs; Clyde R. Miller, director of the Bureau of Educational Service, Teachers College, Columbia University; Robert C. Moore, secretary of the Illinois Education Association, Carlinville, Illinois; Joy Elmer Morgan, editor of the N. E. A. *Journal* and chairman of the National Committee on the Radio in Education; Josiah Morse, professor of psychological philosophy, University of South Carolina; David S. Muzzey, professor of history and textbook writer, Columbia University; N. C. Newbold, assistant superintendent of Education in charge of the Division of Negro Education, State Department of Public Instruction, Raleigh, North Carolina; Jesse H. Newlon, director of the Lincoln School, New York City; Howard W. Odum, director of the School of Social Research, and professor of sociology, University of North Carolina; Mary White Ovington, a founder of the National Association for the Advancement of Colored People, New York City; William Pickens, secretary of the National Association for the Advancement of Colored People, New York City; Bessie L. Pierce, professor of history, University of Chicago; George A. Plimpton, official of Ginn and Company, New York City; F. Blanche Preble, president of the Illinois Education Association, Chicago, Illinois; R. B. Raup, professor of education, Teachers College, Columbia University; Florence Read, president of Spelman College; A. B. Rhett, superintendent of schools, Charleston, South Carolina; W. A. Robinson, principal of the Laboratory School at Atlanta University, formerly state supervisor of Negro Schools in North Carolina, and principal of a high school in Knoxville, Tennessee; George R. Rogers, acting superintendent of schools, 1933–1934, Charleston, South Carolina; Harold Rugg, professor of education, Teachers College, Columbia University; Mrs. Bachman Smith, president of the Parent-Teachers Association, Charleston, South Carolina; Tucker P. Smith, secretary of the Committee on Militarism in Education, New York City; George D. Strayer, director of the Institute of Educational Research, Division of Field Studies, Teachers College, Columbia University; John W. Studebaker, superintendent of schools, Des Moines, Iowa (now U. S. Commissioner of Education, Washington, D. C.); Willis A. Sutton, superintendent of schools, Atlanta, Georgia; Emily A. Tarbell, eastern regional director of the N. E. A. Department of Classroom Teachers, Syracuse, New York; Claude E. Teague, director of the Extension Division, Woman's College, Greensboro, North Carolina, formerly superintendent of schools in Garford and Asheboro, North Carolina; Charles H. Thompson, professor of education, Howard University; R. J. Tighe, Federal Land Bank, Columbia, South Carolina, formerly superintendent of schools at Muskogee, Oklahoma; John L. Tildsley, district superintendent of high schools, New York City; H. L. Trigg, supervisor in the Division of Negro Education, State Department of Public Instruction, Raleigh, North Carolina; Rolla M. Tryon, professor of the teaching of history, School of Education, University of Chicago; W. Walmsley, supervisor of Negro schools, Charleston, South Carolina, formerly principal of a white elementary school; Harry Ward, professor at Union Theological Seminary, and member of the board of the American Civil Liberties Union, New York City; Goodwin B. Watson, professor of education, Teachers College, Columbia University; Leroy J. Weed, member of the firm of Ginn and Company, New York City; Edith B. Wertz, principal of the North Shore School, Huntington, Long Island, formerly teacher at the Bennett School at Millbrook; Walter F. White, executive secretary of the National Association for the Advancement of Colored People, New York City; Garnet C. Wilkinson, a first assistant superintendent of schools, Washington, D. C.; Chase G. Woodhouse, vocational director and head of the Appointment Bureau, Woman's College, Greensboro, North Carolina; Edward J. Woodhouse, professor of political science, University of North Carolina; George F. Zook, then U. S. Commissioner of Education, Washington, D. C.

CORRESPONDENCE

During two years and a half the author corresponded with a great number of teachers and others who had been suggested to him because they had had experiences in the realm of freedom or because they were particularly interested in the problem. Letters from these people have yielded rich material, but they are too many to list and again many of them have asked the author to withhold their names—often even those of their towns.

MANUSCRIPTS

Limited time did not permit extensive use of manuscript collections, but a few proved exceedingly valuable. The American Civil Liberties Union Manuscripts, except the most recent ones, are deposited in the New York Public Library. Those of the last two or three years are available in the files of the Union itself. These contain many volumes of in- and out-letters and the Union's newspaper clipping books. For the last twenty years this collection provides a rich source of material, as "academic freedom" has been one of the major interests of the Union. The J. L. M. Curry Papers and the last three or four volumes of the William Jennings Bryan Papers in the Library of Congress contain interesting material, the former on Negro education in the post-Reconstruction South, the latter on evolution in the schools in 1924–1925.

The manuscript records of the hearings of the Federal Trade Commission on electric power and gas utilities in the offices of the Commission in Washington provided a vast amount of material on the control of teachers, texts, and schools by this branch of business. The collection consists of the record of the hearings and exhibits composed of the correspondence of the various "education" committees with each other, with teachers, and with publishers, material printed by the utilities for use in the schools, and even the cancelled checks with which educators were paid for their "services" to the utilities. The printed report makes about forty volumes, but, since this does not cover all of the material and is unindexed, the author used the manuscript material, deposited with the Commission, which has compiled a card index to the exhibits themselves.

PERIODICALS

Newspapers contain valuable material, but the time limit again made any extensive use of them impossible. Some old issues of the *Pennsylvania Gazette* in the Rare Book Room of the Library of Congress provided material on Colonial teachers. The *Chicago Tribune,* the *New York Herald-Tribune,* and the *New York*

World were used for several important controversies during the last twenty years. The *New York Times* for the last twenty years with the aid of its *Index* was used. The files of the American Civil Liberties Union were rich in newspaper clippings from all over the country, and several individuals have contributed their clipping collections for particular events.

The author used *De Bow's Review* for the pre-Civil War period, the *American Legion Weekly* and *Monthly* for the Legion's activities in the schools, the American Federation of Labor's *Proceedings*, 1881–1933, for labor's educational program, the *Crisis*, 1910–1933, for the Negro teacher's problem. These he went through thoroughly as they are all rich in material. The most fruitful single periodical is *School and Society,* which has followed problems of freedom in all its implications from its organization in 1915 to the present. The *American Teacher,* organ of the American Federation of Teachers, also prints much on this subject. The author used the National Education Association *Journal* for the last fifty years but found it peculiarly unfruitful. For what other periodicals might offer, *Poole's Index* and the *Reader's Guide* were carefully searched, since much of the best material is found not in books but in scattered articles.

GOVERNMENT DOCUMENTS

Laws and court decisions have been extremely important in this study, but the non-existence of topical indices for either laws or decisions makes the use of them difficult. From the time he began the study the author has been collecting laws and decisions that appeared to bear on freedom in teaching. The list grew to enormous proportions. Eventually the laws and decisions on this list were looked up. For the period since the World War, the Legislative Reference Division of the Library of Congress has compiled a subject index to the state session laws. A portion of this has been printed; the rest of it is available in card files in the Library of Congress. It proved an invaluable aid. For the Colonial Period, the author had gone over all the collections of laws for a study of tolerance and had covered the educational laws as well, in the original, up to 1789. For a period from 1789 to 1917, gathering the laws has been a matter of chance. The various compilations of Colonial laws repaid careful reading; they are usually arranged topically.

Miscellaneous

Journals and travelers' accounts were disappointing, since travelers and diarists were strangely uninterested in freedom in teaching or even in schools. The *Journal and Letters* of Philip V. Fithian and Alexis de Tocqueville's *Democracy in America* proved happy exceptions.

Like travelers, general historians and even historians of education were disappointing. Because it was so difficult to find records from which the story of freedom in teaching could be built up, the author ran through literally hundreds of histories: general, state, local, and educational histories. State histories and histories of particular schools were characteristically barren. With few exceptions, histories of education were about as fruitless. Records were scant. Communities were too busy getting schools at all to bother about freedom in them, much less to leave records. Educators who have written histories have all told of the same famous cases, but beyond that they have been distinctly uninterested in the freedom of teachers. Social historians have done little better. Therefore, one detail had to be gleaned here, another there. Professor Edgar W. Knight in his several writings has shown more interest than others in the various elements of educational history that determine freedom.

Much of the material of the book came from use of widely scattered materials on special topics related to the general subject, material discovered by use of the Library of Congress card catalogue, the periodical guides, and other bibliographical materials. Much of the best material was dug out of periodicals. Some of it came from old pamphlets in the Rare Book Room of the Library of Congress. The coöperation of many individuals put át the author's disposal pamphlet materials and newspaper clippings otherwise unavailable. Bessie L. Pierce's generosity, for instance, gave the author access to the collections of pamphlets and broadsides she has gathered in her various studies of pressure groups. Much of all the above described material proved fruitless. But the list of books, pamphlets, and articles actually of value for this study—a list which has been carefully compiled—would necessitate an additional hundred pages and cannot be reproduced here. Some of them have been cited in footnotes throughout this volume.

INDEX

Abell, Mr., shot for teaching Negroes, 180
Ability and appointments, 105
Ability to support oneself. *See* economic competence, vocational training
Abolition literature, burned by mob, 147; exclusion from mail demanded, 147; fear of, 119, 134, 135, 136; imprisonment for possessing, 149; suppressed, 145-146; whipping for possession of, 145-146, 150. *See also* anti-slavery literature
Abolition Society of Wilmington, Ga., teaches Negroes, 115
Abolitionism, compared to communism and socialism, ix-x; death threatened for, 149-152; definition of, 149; dismissal for, 146, 149-150, 151, 153; fear of, in teaching of Negroes, 118-119; imprisonment for, 150, 152; mobbing for, 151-153; murder for, 152; opposed, 114, 118-119, 141, 143-156, 159-160, 166; permitted in North, 155-156; permitted in South, 143-144, 151; suppressed, 143-156, 157; teaching of opposed, x, 118-119, 166; unpopularity in North, 151. *See also* anti-slavery views
Abolitionists, called names, 166; cause suppression of freedom in South, 117, 118; censure of and freedom, 238, 239; denounced, 147, 200; law against, 157; meetings broken up, 151-152, 153; slavery a moral issue to, 111; slavery attacked by, 111, 200; suppressed to preserve business prosperity, 154; teachers rare among, 155; threatened with death, 147; unable to get insurance, 151-152; unpopularity of, 151-154
Academies, and freedom, 166; cause of, 53-55, 94; freedom restricted in, 53; religion in, 53; secularization of teaching in, 53, 94. *See also* female seminaries, private schools, religious schools
Active citizenship, demanded for teachers, 274; denied to teachers, 244-245; restricted, x-xi
Adams, James T., appraises New England schools, 3
Adams, Rev. Jasper, writes *Elements of Moral Philosophy*, 158
Adams, John, and freedom, 50
Adams, Mrs. F. C., urges teaching of Negroes, 120
Adams, Myron W., president of Atlanta University, believes foundations prevented freedom, 191; praises foundations, 191
Administration, improvement in, xi, 169-170, 235
Administrators, restrict freedom, xi, 169-170; training of advocated, 89
Advertising and purpose of education, 84

Affability and purpose of education, 20
African Colonization Society opposes Negro education, 127
African Free School, New York City, established, 115
Agassiz School, Cambridge, Mass., has Negro principal, 184-185
Agnosticism, and purpose of education, 218; professor attacked for, 206
Agnostics, freedom denied to, 213; freedom for, 218
Agrarianism and freedom, 227. *See also* rural ideas
Agrarians. *See* Southern agrarians
Agricultural products, Northern, opposed, 136
Agricultural schools, establishment of, 109
Agriculture, aid to and purpose of education, 109; state of and freedom, 134; treatment in geographies, 159
Aiken, S. C., teacher of Negroes, driven out, 182
Alabama, free Negroes, teaching of, permitted, 120; Negro teachers of Negroes urged, 175-176; Negroes, opposition to teaching of decreases, 185; Negroes, teaching of forbidden, 120, 127; Northeners opposed, 139, 178; sectarianism forbidden, 95; state aid to parochial schools forbidden, 209; violence against teacher, 178; white teachers of Negroes opposed, 175-176, 178. *See also* Mobile, Mobile County
Alcohol, examination of teachers on evils of, 221; teaching evils of required, 220-221; teaching on restricted, 218-222, 224, 226; warning against excessive use of, 220, 226
Alderman, Edward A., president of Tulane University, urges white education as best aid to Negro, 190
Alexander, Nathaniel, governor of North Carolina, urges free schools, 73
Alexandria, Va., Negro schools closed, 125; teaching of Negroes forbidden, 121, 125; teaching of Negroes permitted, 121, 125, 178; teachers of Negroes ostracized, 178
Alton Seminary, charter refused, 94
American Anti-Slavery Society, dissolved at Lane Theological Seminary, 152
American Colonization Society, dissolved at Lane Theological Seminary, 152
American Federation of Labor, business control of schools feared by, 233; foundations' control of schools, feared by, 233; temperance teaching in schools urged by, 220. *See also* labor
American Federation of Teachers, N. R. A. code for teachers urged by, 274. *See also* teachers' unions